D1080654

Amarillo Slim
in a World Full
of Fat People

AMARILLO SLIM PRESTON

WITH GREG DINKIN

YELLOW JERSEY PRESS

LONDON

AMARILLO SLIM

in a World Full of Fat People

THE MEMOIRS OF THE GREATEST GAMBLER
★ **WHO EVER LIVED** ★

Published by Yellow Jersey Press 2004

2 4 6 8 10 9 7 5 3

First published in Great Britain in 2003 by
Yellow Jersey Press
Random House, 20 Vauxhall Bridge Road,
London SW1V 2SA

Random House Australia (Pty) Limited
20 Alfred Street, Milsons Point, Sydney,
New South Wales 2061, Australia

Random House New Zealand Limited
18 Poland Road, Glenfield,
Auckland 10, New Zealand

Random House (Pty) Limited
Endulini, 5A Jubilee Road, Parktown 2193, South Africa

The Random House Group Limited Reg. No. 954009
www.randomhouse.co.uk

A CIP catalogue record for this book
is available from the British Library

ISBN 0-224-07102-5

Papers used by Random House are natural, recyclable products made
from wood grown in sustainable forests; the manufacturing processes
conform to the environmental regulations of the country of origin

Printed and bound in Great Britain by
Cox & Wyman Limited, Reading, Berkshire

This book is dedicated to my seven grandbabies: Heather Rebecca, Hayley Elizabeth, Hannah Lea, Austin Ackerly, Molly Allison, Caroline Abby, and Jack Andrew

He said, "Son, I've made a life out of readin' people's faces,
And knowin' what their cards were by the way they held their eyes."

—KENNY ROGERS, "The Gambler"

Contents

Amarillo Slim
in a World Full
of Fat People

Here I am with my oldest granddaughter, Heather, on a horse named Rabbit. This was taken in the lobby of the Sahara Tahoe before I backed Rabbit up and told the casino manager that I'd show him how that craps table got its name. *(Courtesy of the author)*

Introduction

If there's anything worth arguing about, I'll either bet on it or shut up. And since it's not very becoming for a cowboy to be arguing, I've made a few wagers in my day. But, in my humble opinion, I'm no ordinary hustler. You see, neighbor, I never go looking for a sucker; I look for a champion and make a sucker out of him.

I knew that I wasn't going to get an amateur to play me in Ping-Pong for money, but Bobby Riggs, the 1939 Wimbledon champion—now, that was a man who might be interested in making a wager. Shoot, if a man doesn't think he's hustling you, then you got no shot of him making you a bet.

Not only was Bobby one of the best tennis players going, but he was also a personality, a celebrity who was recognized the world over. He was so famous that he had been asked by Uncle Sam to give tennis exhibitions for the troops during World War II and used it as an opportunity to hustle. At Pearl Harbor in 1944, some unfortunate stranger, who had no idea Bobby was a champion, challenged him to a high-stakes tennis match. Without hardly breaking a sweat, Bobby walked away with all the man's money, his car, and his quaint little bungalow in Honolulu. As the story goes, Bobby felt bad for the cat, blew his own cover, and gave everything back—except $500 that he said was for "advice." Now, that's pretty expensive advice, but I reckon it could have been a lot worse for Bobby's unsuspecting victim.

Bobby was also known for his tennis proposition bets. To entice suckers who wanted a shot at him but knew they couldn't beat him even up, he'd come up with the craziest of things. He'd play with a poodle leashed to each leg, or he'd play in a raincoat and galoshes while carrying an open umbrella in his left hand. I'm telling you, this boy had some imagination, and he didn't slow down one bit as he got older.

In May 1973, at age fifty-five, Bobby took on the world's number-one women's player, Margaret Court, in a challenge match at the San Diego Country Estates that was billed as "The Battle of the Sexes." Somehow that old hustler came up with enough tricks to beat her. Well, Billie Jean King, the number-two player in the world, whom Bobby had called the "real sex leader of the revolutionary pack," didn't like Bobby running his mouth about the superiority of the male race and came up with a challenge of her own. In front of more than thirty thousand spectators at the Astrodome in Houston, in September 1973, the twenty-nine-year-old woman beat the fifty-five-year-old man in straight sets. And it made news all over the world.

Because it was an event where the outcome was in doubt—in *Texas* no less—you can be sure that I was there, and it's likely I made a little wager as well. I had met Bobby briefly the year before in Las Vegas at the World Series of Poker, and when I talked to him after the tennis match, Bobby told me I was welcome anytime at the Bel Air Country Club in his hometown of Los Angeles.

The poker was good in southern California back then—still is today—and on my next trip out there, I paid old Bobby a visit at his fancy country club. It didn't take long for him to try to hustle me, and since I wasn't a tennis player, he tried to set me up to play Ping-Pong. We both knew he was the much better player, but after that incident in Pearl Harbor, Bobby had wised up and learned never to give anything away. In other words, he wasn't looking to make no five hundred dollars for advice; he was looking to bust my skinny country ass.

Like you'd think two gamblers would do, we went back and forth trying to find a fair bet, but Bobby kept refusing to give me a spot. So finally I told him that I'd play him straight up with one stipulation: that I got to choose the paddles.

"We both use the same paddle?" Bobby asked.

"Yessir."

"So when you show up with two of the *same* paddles, can I get my choice of which one of them?"

"Yessir, so long as I can bring the paddles."

Bobby thought I was pulling a schoolboy's scam—that it was a weight thing or that one of the paddles was hollow or something. But once I told him that he could choose whichever of the two paddles he wanted to use, he couldn't post his money fast enough.

We bet $10,000 and agreed to play at two o'clock the next day. Before I left, just to avoid any misunderstanding, I confirmed the bet: We were to play a game of Ping-Pong to twenty-one, each using the paddles of *my* choosing.

I showed up the next day at the Bel Air Country Club ready to wage battle. When Bobby asked to see the paddles, I reached into my satchel and handed him two skillets, the exact same weight and size, and told him he could use either one. Now, Bobby was about as coordinated an athlete that ever lived, but he was swinging that skillet like a fry cook on speed. It wasn't until I had him buried that he started to get the hang of that skillet, but it wasn't soon enough. I won the game 21–8, and it could have been much worse.

Once again I proved that you can make a living beating a *champion* just by using your head instead of your ass. The easiest person in the world to hustle is a hustler, and Bobby had taken the bait like a country hog after town slop. You see, I had been practicing with that skillet since I saw him in Houston, and after I collected the money, I shook Bobby's hand and we both had a good laugh.

Naturally, word spread like wildfire about old Slim fleecing Bobby Riggs, and seven or eight months after it happened, I was in Knoxville, Tennessee, at an American Legion club, to play some poker. There were quite a few wise guys there, including a man named Lefty, who said to me, "Slim, that was a pretty good thing you did, playing Ping-Pong with Riggs."

So we bantered back and forth about it, and finally Lefty said to me, "I've got a buddy that can beat you at Ping-Pong."

"You haven't got a buddy who can beat me *if I choose the paddles,*" I said.

Now, this guy knew how I beat Bobby. The whole *world* knew how I beat Bobby. And I knew *he* knew it, so I couldn't just set up a match to play with skillets, now, could I?

So I told Lefty, "Well, I'm busy here playing poker, and then I have to go back to Amarillo." But in the back of my mind, I knew I had to find a way to relieve old Lefty of his money. I left for Amarillo the next day, wondering how in the hell I was going to find a way to beat Lefty's pal at Ping-Pong. About a month later, I was doing a promotion for a charity in Amarillo with my old buddy Wendell Cain at the television station where he worked, and we started playing Ping-Pong between takes.

Since I don't drink alcohol, I usually drink coffee when I want something hot and Coca-Cola when I want something cold. That day I was drinking a Coca-Cola from one of them six-ounce glass bottles while we were playing, and just as I finished it, I reached down with the bottle and hit the Ping-Pong ball and it went plumb over the net.

"*Holy cow*, Slim!" Wendell said, "Do that again."

I started trying, but I couldn't. You see, there's an area of only about a sixteenth of an inch on a bottle that will make the ball go over the net. So I practiced and practiced until I could hit the ball over the net every time, and right then I knew that Coke bottle was going to make me a boatload of money.

My only problem was that I couldn't just show up in Tennessee looking for Lefty—that would have awoken the dead—so I had to find me a reason to go back to Tennessee. I waited a few months for the next big poker game up there, and when I showed up, Lefty didn't waste any time approaching me. "I guess you've been practicing your Ping-Pong back in Amarillo," he said.

"You said it, Lefty. I've been playing Ping-Pong *all* day, every day, for thirty hours a day."

"That right? My friend will be here in two days."

"Well, I'm gonna do a little bit of fishing as soon as I bust these poker players. If he wants to play me some, let me choose the paddles and he's got him a game."

"What if he's a good player?"

"I don't give a damn if he's a good player or an aviator. If I get to choose the paddles, we'll play."

"Oh, I'll guarantee you he'll play."

So I went fishing for a couple of days, and when I came back, boy, they didn't disappoint me with their ringer. Wouldn't you know it, but they had gotten themselves the world-champion table-tennis player from Taiwan, and he was there waiting for me, licking his chops like a dog at a luau.

"Let's get it on," Lefty said.

"No," I said, savoring the moment. "Let's post our money and play thirty days from now. I need to practice a little, now that I see you got yourself a real-life Ping-Pong champion."

While I can play a fair game of Ping-Pong with a skillet, I'm not interested in speculating, nor am I interested in making a small score. You see, friend, when I make a wager, the bet has already been won. And if I'm gonna win, I sure as hell want to break somebody doing it.

Even though Lefty and the rest of them wise guys had suitcases full of money, I knew that if I stalled, word would spread that old Slim was going to receive his comeuppance—and Lefty would have the rest of his rich buddies there to get a piece of me, too. So we agreed to hold the match in thirty days—and then we'd play for *real* money. Not only did I want to give Lefty an opportunity to tell all his associates, but I also wanted to give that champion even more time to practice with his skillet.

Before I left town, just like I had done with Bobby, I made sure that we were clear on the bet: We were to play a game of Ping-Pong to twenty-one, each using the paddles of *my* choosing.

About a month later, just a day before the match, I got a call from one of my associates saying that the champ was practicing with the biggest frying pan this side of Texas. That wasn't news to me—I knew that was their intention all along—but I suppose they underestimated this here country cowboy.

The next day I arrived in Tennessee, and it looked like the marines had landed—there were eleven private planes that hit that tarmac. Every rounder and hustler in America was down there to bet on this guy playing me in Ping-Pong. Knowing that this champion was gonna fleece me, those gamblers brought enough hundred-dollar bills to burn up thirty wet mules.

I bet with everybody who wanted to bet against me at even money, and when I couldn't get any more action, I bet everything else I had laying 6 to 5, which meant that if I lost, I'd pay them suckers $6 for every $5 they bet me. Now it was time to play, and everyone was standing around waiting for me to pull out those skillets. They figured I was just stalling when I went over to a vending machine, put in a dime, and bought a bottle of Coca-Cola. Then I put in another dime and bought another one. I opened both bottles and walked over to a wastebasket and dumped the Coke right out.

Lefty and the rest of the crowd were getting impatient, but I didn't say a word. I simply walked over to the Ping-Pong table with the Coke bottles and I said to that champion, "It's your choice of paddles, son. Which one will it be?"

"Paddles?" he asked.

"Yeah, these here Coke bottles are our paddles. Have your pick."

Well, that boy looked like he couldn't swallow boiled okra!

Once he grabbed one of the bottles, I said, "I'll even give you the choice—do you want to serve or return serve first?"

This champion glanced over at Lefty, who didn't look so good himself. "Well, goddamn," Lefty said, "take the serve."

"Okay," I said, "let's go."

On his first round of serves, he never even hit the ball over the net. Not one shot. So it was love–5 when he threw me the ball. When I served it over—I'll give that boy some credit, he did hit it every time, but it would go either straight up in the air or right into the net. He never did return one of my serves.

I'd rather not say how much I had on the match, because it caused a severe audit when word got around. But suffice it to say that no one—not even a world champion—ever challenged me to a game of Ping-Pong again.

♠ ♣ ♦ ♥

I like to bet on anything—as long as the odds are in my favor. In past years I've bet big money that I could pick any thirty people at random and two of them would have the same birthday, that a stray cat could carry an empty Coke bottle across the room, and that I could hold on to a horse's tail for a quarter of a mile. I even wagered $37,500 that a fly would land on a particular sugar cube. At the fanciest casino in Marrakech, Morocco, I bet that I could ride a camel right through the middle of it. I won every one of those bets, and, if you pay attention, I'll let you know how.

The more I won, the more people wanted to beat me, and, let me tell you, partner, the bigger they come, the harder their money falls. I beat Willie Nelson for $300,000 playing dominoes right on Fremont Street in downtown Las Vegas. I took Minnesota Fats for big money playing pool—with a broom. And I won too many wagers to remember from Evel Knievel, but the one everyone likes to talk about is the time I beat that old daredevil in golf when I played with a carpenter's hammer.

I once made a well-publicized bet with Jimmy "the Greek" Snyder that I could go down the "River of No Return," a twenty-nine-mile stretch of rapids in northern Idaho—in the middle of winter no less. I had Jacques Cousteau make me a special wet suit to keep me from freezing to death, but even that wasn't enough to convince Lloyds of London to insure me—and they insure *anything*.

Kenny Rogers came to me in 1978 with his hit song "The Gambler," and we sat down right in the poker room at the Golden Nugget in Las Vegas to practice. Country singer John Lutz Ritter wrote a song about me—"Do You Dare Make a Bet with Amarillo Slim?"—and when Robert Altman made *California Split* in 1974, that great gambling movie with Elliott Gould and George Segal, he cast me in a role that suited me just fine: Amarillo Slim.

A reporter named Ted Thackrey from the *Los Angeles Times* caught my exact feelings when he wrote in a story about me, "He plays constantly, devotedly, joyously, wholeheartedly, and with passion—as certain consecrated artists practice their art." He might have added that poker is my nourishment, since my six-foot-four, 170-pound frame doesn't require much grub to keep it going. I'm so damn skinny that a friend of mine once told me that I look like the advance man for a famine.

I've played poker with presidents—Lyndon Johnson and Richard Nixon—and George Bush Sr. considers me a friend. And while I've never taken a drug in my life, I have rubbed elbows, for better or worse, with Texas drug king Jimmy Chagra and Colombian drug lord Pablo Escobar (who almost killed me). And the mayor of Las Vegas, Oscar Goodman, has a picture of me in city hall. Me—a gambler!

As you probably can figure out from my name—and if you can't, I reckon you're welcome to play poker with me whenever you'd like—I settled in Amarillo, Texas, where at age seventy-four I still live with my beautiful wife. I raise cattle and horses on a 3,000-acre ranch and still stay active riding horses, roping calves, or digging postholes. Amarillo's a good town, where the population has been 173,000 for the past fifty years, never varies—every time some woman gets pregnant, some man leaves town.

I do most of my globetrotting during the winter months and I spend summers with my family. Our home in Amarillo has a swimming pool in the backyard and a flock of young ones (three children and seven grandbabies) who love to go swimming. When I'm in Amarillo, I lead an ordinary man's life. I've even coached Little League baseball (no, I didn't take action on the games). My lovely wife of fifty-three years, Helen Elizabeth, has never played a game of chance in her life. She still thinks a king is the ruler of a country and a queen is his bedmate.

Now, ordinarily, I'd rather see early frost on my peach trees than write some book giving away my secrets to success, but, as I said, I've got seven grandbabies—six fillies and one baby boy—and it's about time they learned my life story.

So grab yourself a cup of coffee and hold on to your britches. I'm fixing to tell you a few things that I've been keeping to myself for a lot of years. If you're not careful, you just might learn how to get rich without ever having a job.

All dressed up at the Paramount Recreation Club at Sixth and Polk in Amarillo; heck, I wasn't but sixteen years old back in 1945. *(Courtesy of the author)*

1

From Arkansas to Texas—the Making of Amarillo Slim

On December 31, 1928, I was born Thomas Austin Preston Jr. in Johnson, Arkansas, a town of about two hundred between Fayetteville and Springdale in the foothills of the Ozark Mountains. Johnson's one distinction is a limekiln, which turns out a product that's put in a urinal to kill the smell.

It didn't take long for my folks to see the error of their ways, and when I was just nine months old, we moved to Turkey, Texas. They must have had a thing for small towns, because Turkey, a little farming and ranching community about 130 miles southeast of Amarillo, had fewer than a thousand people when we showed up. My folks were ordinary, churchgoing, hardworking people.

We moved around Texas quite a bit while I was young, and when I was in sixth grade at a junior high school in Mineral Wells, Texas, I set junior-high track records in the fifty- and hundred-yard dash and as the anchor for the four-by-one-hundred relay. I was tall and skinny, and I could run like the wind—a skill that would come in handy when I was old enough to bet.

I never did have any siblings, so I had to learn the fine art of competition on my own. My folks divorced when I was about eleven, and I spent part of the time with one and the rest of the time with the other. The situation wasn't the greatest, but it taught me a lot about being independent, becoming my own person, and learning how to look out for myself.

When my folks split, Mama went back to Arkansas and Daddy moved to Amarillo to run some restaurants and later a car lot. And it's a good thing he did, because Amarillo Slim sounds a heckuva lot better than Turkey Tom or Arkansas Austin. Having spent just about all my seventy-four years in the Lone Star State, I'm a bona fide, dyed-in-the-wool Texan—and I sure as hell like it that way.

Sometimes people wonder if I come from a long line of professional gamblers—frontiersmen from the Old West who would just as soon shoot a man dead for looking at him the wrong way. But I was down in Auckland, New Zealand, not too long ago, researching my family name, and I found out that the Prestons were silversmiths from England. I was hoping they were stagecoach robbers or something, but, like my daddy, they were straight shooters. My old man didn't gamble—no, not T. A. Preston Sr.—and my mama, Pearl Caldwell, didn't either. Heck, she was squarer than an apple box, which suited her well when she became an elementary-school teacher.

I guess you could say I had a knack for arithmetic as a kid—as most professional gamblers do. If you're going to make your living putting the odds in your favor, you damn well better know how to calculate them. The late, great Stuey Ungar, one of the best damn card players I ever saw, was a mathematical genius. Chip Reese, who at age forty was the youngest player ever inducted into the Poker Hall of Fame, got a degree in economics from Dartmouth. And not long after he dropped out of Cal Tech, Huck Seed won the World Series of Poker in 1996. Part of the hustle may be pretending *not* to be smart, but behind every gambler is a razor-sharp mind.

I did the third and fourth grades in one year, but it wasn't until I was in junior high school that anyone suggested I had some kind of gift besides running footraces. By that time my mama was living in Johnson, Arkansas, again—in the same house where both she and I were born. Figuring I was some kind of math whiz, my mama wanted to give me every advantage to get ahead in this world, so she arranged for me to attend Peabody Academy starting in the ninth grade. Peabody was a preparatory school on the campus of the University of Arkansas in Fayetteville, where students from the university would ply their trade on gifted kids as they learned how to be educators.

It turned out that Mama was right about Peabody helping to advance my career. The school offered the one tool that would be the most influential element in my education: a snooker table in the student-services building. I never could tell her that I spent most of my spare time (and some of my class time) playing snooker, a game similar to pool except that it's played on a bigger table with smaller pockets and smaller balls. I always said that I learned more about life from poolrooms and casinos than I ever did in the classroom. To this day I have *never* in my life had occasion to diagram a sentence, but I sure as hell had plenty of occasions to hustle pool. I suppose, however, that I learned a little something about politics while I was at Peabody, because I was elected president of the sophomore class.

W. C. Fields said, "Too great a proficiency at pool bespeaks a misspent youth," but that timeless nugget didn't apply to me. I wasn't all that mischievous growing up, and I didn't start playing snooker or pool until I arrived at Peabody. Once I started, though, I couldn't stop, and it seems like I've been making up for lost time ever since.

Even though I was tall, I never weighed more than 155 pounds in high school and was too skinny to play football. When I was a kid, I had to get out of the bathtub before they pulled the plug. But I played a decent game of basketball, and I still win money shooting free throws to this day. As a high-school student, I continued to run track and have won quite a few footraces for money, including the time I outran a horse—but more on that later.

Two years back in Arkansas was enough to remind me how thankful I was my parents had left in the first place, and after my sophomore year at Peabody, I moved back to Amarillo to live with my daddy. It didn't take me long to find the pool halls, which didn't please Senior too much. In fact, when he'd find me at my favorite place, the Paramount Recreation Club on Sixth and Polk, not only would he kick my butt out of there, but while he was doing it, he'd tell the owners he was going to get them shut down if they kept letting an underage boy play.

Even against my daddy's wishes, I found a way to play pool, and I learned the first rule of hustling before I was old enough to drive: Find a game where you can win. Back then, and still today to an extent, Amarillo is somewhat segregated, and since I knew that my daddy never made it to the Mexican side of town, that's where I made most of my scores. And while I know it didn't suit my daddy, shooting stick with the old-timers is where I learned to be a man.

People constantly ask me why I've stayed in Amarillo all these years, but for this country cowboy it's always been home. Back when I was playing poker throughout Texas, Amarillo was a good home base, and now I like the fact that it's less than a two-hour drive from the borders of New Mexico, Colorado, and Oklahoma—good states for three of my favorite pastimes: hunting, fishing, and riding horses.

Anyone who's ever driven through Texas knows Amarillo for the Big Texan Steak Ranch & Opry, a place that will give you a steak for free—provided you can eat all seventy-two ounces of it in less than an hour. But that's just for tourists—and certainly not for a man named Slim. What most people don't know about Amarillo is that it's the largest city in Texas on Route 66; it is home to Palo Duro Canyon, which at nearly a thousand feet deep is one of the nation's largest canyons; and it is the site of the state's largest livestock auctions. And even though Oprah was here under some trying circumstances in 1998—when she was sued by a few wealthy Amarillo cattlemen over comments she had made about mad cow disease—she stayed for five weeks and taped her show at night at the Amarillo Little Theater. When I had lunch with her one day at the

Plaza One bank building, Oprah was as friendly and as classy as she seems on TV.

Amarillo means "yellow" in Spanish, and while some of them historians here tell me that it was chosen because of the color of the soil in Amarillo Creek, my theory is that it was chosen to describe the disposition of the gamblers in town—at least until I arrived. Located in the northwestern part of the state, it sits on the high plains at an elevation of 3,676 feet above sea level. The only thing between Amarillo and the North Pole is a barbed-wire fence—which is broken down most of the time. This probably explains why it's even windier than Chicago.

When most people think of Texas, they think heat, but what I like best about Amarillo is the cold winters (the average minimum temperature in January is 20 degrees). I also like the fact that I can make it by car to Dallas in six hours, Houston in nine, El Paso in eight, Midland in four, to my ranch in Clarendon in less than an hour, and to my other ranch in Elida, New Mexico, in two hours and twenty minutes. I know that most of you folks probably think of South Fork from that TV show *Dallas* when you envision a Texas ranch, but my ranches are for working and hunting, not living. My ranch in Amarillo is twenty-three miles from my home, which is on Virginia Street in west Amarillo, the poor folks' part of town.

A HUSTLER IS BORN: MY FIRST ROAD TRIP

During my junior year at Amarillo High, I used to cut sixth-period study hall with my friend Jack Seale, who went on to become the mayor of Amarillo. We'd hop on Jack's motor scooter and go down to what we called Mexicantown, which was just about a mile east of our school, and I'd bust all them Mexicans playing pool every day. That kept Jack and me in plenty of spending money—what was in our pockets didn't jingle, it folded. For a couple of young kids from Amarillo, having that kind of money made us strut when we walked, and that confidence did me a lot of good.

It wasn't very long until word spread about my pool playing, and one of the local gamblers got ahold of me one day and said, "Kid, do you wanna make some serious money?"

Naturally, I told him that I did, and I wasn't but sixteen when John Kuykendall and Elmer Huneke, the two boss gamblers in town, took me on my first pool-hustling trip. You'll hear me use the term "boss gamblers" or "bosses" a lot, and that's just my way of describing the people who call most of the gambling shots in a town. John and Elmer booked sports and ran three craps games in Amarillo, and they really gave me an education on what it was like to be a gambler.

Our first stop was in Prairietown, Texas, to play a kid named Bobby Turner from a rich ranching family up there. Bobby was about twenty-three at the time and the best player in the northern part of Texas. No one up there thought he could lose, and when a sixteen-year-old kid showed up, that certainly didn't change anyone's mind. I think the whole community bet on Bobby, and John and Elmer were more than happy to take their action.

If you asked me if I thought I could win, I was liable to say something like, "You're goddamn right I can, just as fast as he can draw it back." Was I cocky back then? Lord, you ain't got no idea. Smart-ass, popping-off skinny sonofabitch is how I would have described myself. But it was that attitude—that brashness and fearlessness—that allowed me to become a professional gambler. Sure, as I got older and more mature, I was able to mix charm and wit with that arrogance, and I learned that self-assurance mixed with a touch of modesty endeared me to a lot of people.

My deal with John and Elmer was that they would put up the money and I would get a third of the winnings. I didn't know if they were skimming, but it didn't make any difference, because when I left Prairietown, I had the first hundred-dollar bill of my life. In fact, I left with $800—which was more money than I'd ever seen.

It was a good thing I had told my dad that I was gonna be hunting with Jack all weekend, because from there we were thinking about cutting across to Tucumcari, New Mexico. There was an older Mexican gentleman over there who played real good snooker. So John, who called me "Junior," said, "Junior, you haven't been playing a lot of snooker these days, have you?"

"I haven't played too much since I came back from Arkansas. Why?"

"There's a good snooker player in Tucumcari."

"I'll thrash him," I said. "I just hope he's got plenty of money."

"Sounds like you're not lacking for confidence."

"Let's go get 'em."

So we went to Tucumcari, and there was this skinny Mexican guy, about fifty years old or so, and the first thing he said was, "You're that kid from Amarillo."

"That's me."

"Do you play snooker?"

"I haven't played much recently. Pool's my game. But let me tell you something: I can beat everybody in New Mexico playing snooker."

"Pardon me, young man," he said.

So I looked him right in the eye and told him the same thing and he said, "You need to taxi up to the table, son. I'm fixing to teach you an expensive lesson."

Then John pulled me aside and asked, "How much should I bet?"

"Bet as much as you got," I said.

"Goddamn, Junior," John said, "you're mouthing off to this here guy who can play. You sure about that?"

"As sure as fat meat's greasy," I said, and that convinced him to bet pretty high. True to my word, I thrashed the guy. Heck, while I should have been studying poetry at Peabody Academy, I was writing my own poetry on their snooker table.

After Tucumcari we went to Clovis, New Mexico, about ninety miles southwest, to play a railroader named Tom Christensen. Christensen was one of the best players in New Mexico, and when we got into town, another gentleman by the name of "Mexican" Tom, said to me, "Say, son, you're kinda setting the woods on fire."

It's a small world, and Mexican Tom—who owned the local poolroom there—had already heard about my two other scores. "I can't imagine you beating that boy in Tucumcari playing snooker," Mexican Tom said. "Listen, if you can beat Christensen playing snooker, you're liable to win enough to buy the whole state of New Mexico."

"Can you get him on the phone?" I asked. And when he said he could, I said, "Then get him down here. I believe he's got himself a game."

"Don't you wanna play some of the weaker players first?" Mexican Tom asked me.

"What?" I screamed, acting like he'd just stepped on my toe.

Of course, I was cocky as hell and probably shouldn't have been so quick to challenge their best player, but I guess that's where my whole philosophy of looking for a champion and making a sucker out of him came from. You know, if you play a champion, folks are gonna be willing to make a bet that's got some whiskers on it.

Mexican Tom got in touch with Christensen, and everyone in town came out to see this young gun from Amarillo get whupped by the best snooker player in New Mexico. We played for eleven hours straight, and after maybe thirty games or so, Christensen was ahead of me by one game. He really was a heckuva player, a worthy champ.

I didn't want to stop, and I suppose John wanted me to keep playing too, because he said, "Can you miss school tomorrow?"

"You ain't even kiddin'," I said. But then came the hard part—calling Daddy. I had told him that lie about going hunting, and since I knew I couldn't keep that up, I just picked up the phone and explained what had happened.

When I told him where I was, he didn't say nothing at first, and then he said, "Are you doing any good, son?"

"Daddy," I said, "I've got over a thousand dollars cash in my pocket."

"Whose is it?"

I told him it was mine, and when I said that I'd need him to write me a good excuse to miss school the next day, old Senior, who had been kicking me out of every pool hall in town not a month earlier, said, "I sure will." I guess that was a lesson in showing what money can do to people, because his reaction surprised the hell out of me.

Sigmund Freud did research on gamblers and found that a true gambler is a loser. People who enjoy speculating—deep down—*want* to lose. I can't explain it as good as old Siggy, but he had it right about certain people not feeling worthy of having any money. And that's why most gamblers deserve the bad reputation that they get. But what most people don't realize is that a *professional* gambler—or an even better word for it might be "competitor"—isn't the same thing as an ordinary gambler.

Ted Thackrey, my old buddy from the *Los Angeles Times*, wrote, "The stereotype image of the gambler as a compulsive loser who tempts the gods of chance from subconscious motives of suicide is as remote from Slim's character as his home is from the mountains of the moon." I play to win, neighbor, and, just as most people can't stand being around a broke gambler, they love being around a winner. Even though Daddy didn't say it at the time, I knew that winning a grand changed his perception of me in a hurry.

I wanted to keep playing because I knew that the only reason Christensen had stayed with me so long was his home-court advantage, which in pool is even stronger than in golf. Without knowing the speed of a table and all the subtleties that come with regularly playing on it, it takes a while to get warmed up.

I explained all this to John, and he said, "I'm not ready to back out. What do you think we should do?"

"After we play about three more games," I said, "let's shoot up the stakes and get this over with."

So we played a few more games, and Christensen was one more game up on me. "Say, Christensen," I said, "this is a tough-ass game, and we've been playing a long time and never have raised it. Let's shoot this sonofabitch up a little."

"Well, why don't we just double up?" he said. And why shouldn't he have said that? He was already ahead two games on me and was considered to be the best player in the state.

I looked at John and Elmer, and they both nodded their heads, and we doubled the stakes. I truly don't remember the amount—I was just playing while John and Elmer were handling the finances. So we doubled up, and after we did, it lit a fire under me. I must have beaten him about eleven out of the next fifteen games. It was incredible. This awesome feeling of invincibility came over me that was like nothing I'd ever experienced before. That feeling, combined with the money I knew I could make gambling, got me hooked forever. I was so fired up that I wanted to play Christensen until I keeled over and died.

Then Christensen finally said, "Junior, I hate to quit you, but I've got to go to work. You know I'm not just a pool hustler; I also work for the railroad."

I was a bit disappointed that he wanted to stop, because like they say about athletes, I was truly in the *zone*. I had no choice but to settle for a $2,000 score.

We drove back to Amarillo, and after cutting Daddy in on the profits, I bought my first automobile—a new Chrysler Windsor. Here was a kid who had money for something besides a hamburger and a milk shake, and who wasn't shy about telling everybody about it. I thought I had just about died and gone to heaven.

The next weekend, I went back to Clovis with John and Elmer, and I started out playing Christensen for $300 a game. After I won the first two, he called it quits. He knew that he couldn't beat me—not since I had gotten the hang of that pool table. Coming home, I remember saying to John, "Look at the difference. We're ten times off. Last week I had more than two thousand, and this week I got two hundred." Even back then I had one of the most important traits of any hustler: greed. I never did want to just beat somebody; I always wanted to break a sonofabitch.

That was my first pool-hustling trip, and, depending on how you view my life, it was either the worst thing that ever happened to me or the best thing that ever happened to me, because from that point on all I ever wanted to do was gamble. And, boy, was I lucky to have John and Elmer as teachers. On those two road trips, and then for the next year when I was a stickman at their craps games, I heard them talking about all sorts of schemes and laughing at all the suckers.

They taught me that all the stock in trade that a gambler has is his word, so you better be good for it. In the world today, nobody does any business without signing contracts, except professional gamblers. I got cigar boxes full of bad checks from Square John Businessmen, but not one from a gambler. You do a deal with a Square John Businessman, you get a note notarized by four or five people. Did you ever see anybody sign a note in a card room?

In the frontier days, a man's word was good enough for deals involving thousands of dollars, and it's still that way in our circle. That's why I think one of the biggest reasons for my later success in poker was that I learned to like and to know people. I can go back anywhere I've ever played, because I always kept my promises. A gambler's word is his bond. If one of them boys tells you a goose'll pull a plow a hundred yards, then hook him up, neighbor, 'cause he'll damn sure move it out.

John and Elmer also taught me that it never hurts for potential opponents to think you're more than a little stupid and that you can hardly count all the money in your hip pocket, much less hold on to it. Back then, and still to this day, it's the reason I wear a big Stetson, cowboy boots, and western duds and play the role of the country bumpkin who thinks he can shoot pool against the local champs. My best line, and one I still use if I go someplace I'm not recognized, is, "I'm about the fourth-best player in Tulia, Texas." Now, what self-respecting city slicker is gonna turn down that challenge?

I also learned that there are people who love action and others who love money. The first group is called suckers, and the second is called professional gamblers, and it was a cinch which one I wanted to be. I made up my mind almost sixty years ago that I was never gonna be one of those punters that John and Elmer were laughing about. I was going to be the one doing all the laughing—all the way to the bank, that is.

MINNESOTA FATS AND HOT SPRINGS, ARKANSAS

Fresh off my big win, I went down to Mexicantown, and all the guys down there would say, "C'mon, let's play some two-dollar nine ball."

"No," I said, "let's play some two-*hundred*-dollar nine ball." Boy, was I a smart-ass little sonofabitch.

Between my ability and my mouth, before long, I got labeled as something worse than I would ever have wished for: the best player in my town. I was extinct as a pool hustler in Amarillo before I'd even graduated high school, so whenever I could get away, I traveled around "undercover," looking to fleece the big shots in any town.

The biggest shot of them all was a pool hustler from New York named Rudolph Walter Wanderone Jr.—a man you probably know as Minnesota

Fats. Born in the Washington Heights section of New York in 1913, he was called Roodly by his parents, who had immigrated from Switzerland. By age ten he weighed 150 pounds and used to cut class at P.S. 132 to go shoot pool. When he turned thirteen he headed down to Broadway to become a full-time hustler. Fats always used to say, "I got my postgraduate training on Broadway. Broadway was like going to Harvard *and* Yale."

New York in the late twenties was a golden age for gamblers. Fats met up with sharpies like Titanic Thompson, Nick the Greek, Hubert Cokes, and Arnold Rothstein at poolrooms around the city, including Louis Kreuter's, which was next to the Forrest Hotel, where Damon Runyon of *Guys and Dolls* fame lived. At famous eateries like Lindy's and Hector's Cafeteria, Fats rubbed shoulders with Runyon, Ed Sullivan, and Walter Winchell.

When I met Fats in Hot Springs, Arkansas, in the spring of 1945, he was just New York Fats, on account of his portly constitution. That's all he ever was till they made that movie *The Hustler* in 1961, which was based on a novel by a guy named Walter Tevis. When New York Fats saw the movie, he threatened to sue Tevis, because it showed a character named Minnesota Fats, played by Jackie Gleason, losing a match to a hustler named Fast Eddie Felson, played by Paul Newman. Newman's character was said to be based on my buddy from Oklahoma City named Ronnie Allen. Similar to how he was portrayed by Newman, Ronnie used to say, "I'm called Fast Eddie 'cause I shoot fast, talk fast, and bet fast. I'm the best one-pocket player in this country. Bar none. I'm so good I can't even get a game unless I promise to give it away first."

Fats claimed that he never lost a cash match in his life, much less to a nobody named Fast Eddie, and he let people know he was going after Tevis for defamation of character. When word got out to Tevis, he had a pretty good answer for Fats. "I wrote the book while I was working nights in a poolroom and going to school to get my degree. I completely invented the character of Minnesota Fats. He doesn't exist. I resent anyone capitalizing on my imagination. I once heard of a second-rate pool hustler named New York Fats, but I never saw him play."

Fats backed down real fast, especially when strangers started fawning all over him wherever he went, calling him Minnesota Fats and telling him how much they liked that movie *about* him. You talk about dumb luck; next thing Fats knew, every newspaper in America wanted to interview him and by the late sixties he had two TV shows—*Minnesota Fats Hustles the Pros* and *Minnesota Fats Hustles the Stars*—and was hobnobbing with James Garner and Zsa Zsa Gabor. Shoot, before long old Roodly legally changed his name to Minnesota Fats, and at the Jansco pool tournament at the Stardust in 1968, he even showed me his Social Security card, which read: "Minnesota Fats." Sometimes it's funny how legends are born.

To the real pool hustlers, Fats was kind of a joke by then, and a guy named Bill Staton, one of the top pool hustlers from Virginia who everyone called "Weanie Beanie" on account of the restaurants he owned, said to Fats, "Have you actually ever been to Minnesota?"

"I colonized the place," Fats said.

The truth was that Fats's home was in Dowell, Illinois, a town of three hundred about a hundred miles southeast of St. Louis. He moved there from New York to live with his wife, Evelyn, who he met at a restaurant (imagine that) called the Perfection Club. Fats was five-eight, and he weighed close to three hundred pounds and had a fifty-four-inch waist. Shoot, I could've used one of his belts to rope cattle. He said that he spent a hundred dollars a day on chocolate and claimed that he could "eat eight gallons of ice cream without batting an eye."

Fats's most important asset was not his stomach but his mouth. He could talk to people in a way that made them want to beat him, and as a high-school kid in 1945 I was in awe just watching the man. Back in those days, all the pool hustlers got together and played in Hot Springs during the horse-racing meet down at Oaklawn Park from February through April. And, boy, I thought I was a smart-ass, but Fats made my arrogance look like a slice of humble pie. The first thing I ever remember him saying to me was, "Son, every time a bird flies over my Cadillac, I buy a new one."

While Fats and I looked like a ball and a bat standing next to each other, he was the first hustler I patterned myself after and he's probably the reason I'm such a talker when I gamble. I learned from Fats that the more you can get someone to want to beat you, the more likely you are to make him emotional, so that his ego gets in the way of his brain. I also decided that I'd better get me a nickname fast, and since some of my friends called me Slim anyway, I took a page from Fats's book, and from that day forward, I became known as Amarillo Slim.

The fact that I was actually *from* Amarillo wasn't the only difference in how Fats and I went about our business. Even though I learned gambling talk from Fats, our hustling styles were completely different. Fats was always looking for a sucker, and I was always looking for a champion. Fats's strategy was to find anybody with a little money, bust him, and then kick him while he was down. The problem with that was, you could only win so much off a working stiff, and once you took his money, you couldn't show your face again in that town. That's why I went looking for wealthy champions and treated them with respect.

I like to leave a good taste with the people I play. Elmer once told me, "Slim, you can shear a sheep many a time, but you can skin him only once." And he was right. If you shear one of 'em, he'll grow some more wool, and next week you can shear him again. That sheep will make an awful lot of sweaters but only one coat. And while that sounds like simple cowboy talk, it's the most important part of my philosophy as a professional gambler.

Rather than try to take advantage of the ignorance of a sucker for a few dollars, I take aim at the ego of a millionaire and try to win me a few thousand. If there's one fatal flaw, the Achilles' heel of every gambler, it's hubris. I guess you could say that hubris is a fancy word for excessive arrogance, and I'd be lying if I told you I was never guilty of it myself. No gambler ever wants to lose face, and I have used that psychological edge to my advantage. All I have to do is play to a wealthy man's ego, and not only can I get him to gamble, but I can get him to gamble with me *for life*.

I never did get to play Fats on that trip to Hot Springs, but that would come later. As a sixteen-year-old in 1945, I went home with a nickname that would stick for life and the desire to be the best pool hustler who ever lived. Of course, most people think that being a pool hustler is all about the art of the hustle, but they seem to forget that you also better know how to *play*. And, boy, did I work on my game like a sonofagun. I practiced a lot with funny types of instruments like a cue without a tip or a broom (which later came in handy). Soon I had all the angles and gimmicks and the talent to go with it.

When I started making a name for myself around the country, wise guys would say to me, "Yeah, but you're that Amarillo Slim. Give me twenty points."

I always had a reply for those kinds of guys: "Give *me* twenty and I'll play without looking at the ball." I'd tell them that I'd turn my head before I'd shoot, and if they determined I could see the ball, that shot wouldn't count.

"Get your ass up here," they'd invariably say.

I'd bet even money that I could break and run a pool table without ever looking at the ball. I'd bring the cue back two strokes, turn my head, take two strokes, and shoot. I had as many propositions for pool as there were states in America. At some point or another, I played every sonofabitch that had three hundred dollars and could run ten balls, and 99 percent of 'em got the same results—they ended up scratching their broke ass. Remember, Amarillo Slim never makes a bet unless the bet is already won.

Showing off at the United States Constabulary in Stuttgart, Germany, when I entered the Special Services of the United States Army. *(Courtesy of the author)*

2

Serving My Country (and Myself)

Even though I spent most of my time in high school hustling pool, I still managed to make pretty good grades. At the end of 1945, the U.S. military sent recruiters to our school, and everybody that had a B average was eligible to receive his high-school diploma early if he joined the navy. Boy, that suited the dickens out of me, so I signed up for it. Not only was I ready to serve my country, but, with the education I had received as a gambler, I was ready to serve myself.

I graduated early from Amarillo High, on Polk Street, in December 1945. The school later burned down and was rebuilt on the southwest part of town, and my kids ended up graduating from there as well. I turned seventeen on December 31, 1945, and on January 30, 1946, I was sworn into the United States Navy and sent to San Diego for boot camp. Not long after I arrived, I was in the dayroom when one of the officers saw me shooting pool and asked if I would like to give pool exhibitions.

Because of his intentions, he had me assigned to about the cushiest job in the navy. I became a captain's yeoman and chauffeur for Captain Len C. Petros. Technically, the captain's yeoman was to assist the commanding officer (CO) in day-to-day duties like filing and delivering sensitive messages, but since it seemed like all Captain Petros wanted to do was to go fishing, my job consisted of not doing a damn thing.

The first place I was stationed was on the LST 10-97 (a landing ship tank), based out of Honolulu. Just a few months later, I volunteered to go to the Bikini Atoll to witness an atomic-bomb testing. On July 1, 1946, the AAF B-29 *Dave's Dream* released an atomic bomb over a cluster of targets anchored in Bikini lagoon to measure the effect of an atomic outburst on unmanned ships and aircraft. All of us were topside on a ship several miles away, wearing goggles, and we sat with our heads between our legs. The blast created a forty-foot tidal wave, and, boy, did we feel the shock. The first time I looked, all I could see was this big white mushroom cloud about a mile high, and it scared me something fierce.

While it wasn't part of my formal duties (as it would later become in the army), I gave several pool exhibitions to my fellow shipmates and got to see a good part of the world as a teenager. I gave most of my exhibitions at the Hickham Air Force Base in Hawaii and a few in Guam and the Philippines, with a world champion named Irving Crane.

I came back to the contiguous United States on another LST, which docked in San Francisco. My ship was decommissioned, so we took it up to Astoria, Oregon, to the Nineteenth Naval District at the Tongue Point Naval Air Station, about a hundred miles from Portland. We prepared it, along with three other ships, to be abandoned.

As luck would have it, Petros was the CO of the base at the time, and he was happy to have me around as his captain's yeoman. Being Petros's right-hand man wasn't a hell of a lot of work—so, with all that free time, I put my gambling experience to use.

It wasn't long before I had dice games going on four different troop carriers. I had seventeen or eighteen "employees" working for me—and I'd go from one carrier to the other to monitor the action. About the first two weeks after payday, which was once a month, I stayed busy; it took about that long to break the whole base. If a guy got emergency leave, he didn't go to the Red Cross for money; he got it from me—gratis. I just looked at it as part of the overhead for taking care of my customers.

When I wasn't busy with the craps games, I'd take Petros's vehicle and drive a hundred miles to Portland. I had already learned from John and Elmer that in any event where the outcome is in doubt, somebody will want to speculate on it. Well, it didn't take me long to figure out that the guesser usually *loses*, and I wanted to be on the other side of those bets.

When I was in Portland, I spent most of my time at the Criterion Club, a high-class joint with a bunch of pool tables and a card room. It also had a chalkboard, and anybody could put a number up on the wall and book any sporting event. As a gambler in those days, I felt like the world was just giving away money, and I didn't think I could lose. I was at the Criterion Club for the seventh game of the 1946 World Series between the Boston Red Sox and the St. Louis Cardinals. Between all the people who had bet on the Cardinals to win the Series and the people who had bet on them to win Game Seven, I was $30,000 long on St. Louis. I became a Red Sox fan in a hurry.

My seventh-inning stretch wasn't too goddamn fun, as the Red Sox were down 3–1. But I guess all them years my parents made me go to church paid off, because the Red Sox scored twice in the top of the eighth to tie the score at three.

In the bottom of the eighth, Enos "Country" Slaughter, an outfielder for the St. Louis Cardinals, led off with a single to center. When Whitey Kurowski and Del Rice made outs, it looked like Slaughter was gonna be stranded on first—right where he belonged. With Harry Walker up to bat, Slaughter was running with the pitch, and when Walker hit a liner to left-center, I tell you, Country looked like somebody was chasing him with a bat as he headed for third. Everybody in the world thought he'd stop at third, and when he ran through the third-base coach's stop sign, I could not have been more pleased. A man can't *possibly* score from first on a hard-hit liner, and I would have much rather seen an easy out at the plate than men on the corners with two down.

Even better, old reliable Johnny Pesky, the shortstop for the Red Sox, handled the throw from center fielder Leon Culberson and—but wait— Pesky hesitated just long enough for Slaughter to beat the throw to the plate. I wanted to strangle the sonofabitch, but when the Red Sox got out of the eighth down 4–3, there was still hope.

And, wouldn't you know, it was my lucky day. The first two Red Sox hitters reached base in the top of the ninth, and it looked like I was gonna draw out again. What followed were the three most painful outs of my life; I think I might have cried—or at least thrown something at the radio—as the Cardinals were celebrating their World Series victory.

Not but a few weeks later, Pesky, who was born in Portland, came to the Criterion Club and we played in a poker game together. And *every* time—not some of the time but *every* time—he came into the pot, I raised. One time he had bet fifty dollars, I raised him five hundred, and when he folded, I turned my hand, which was a complete bluff, faceup and said, "I suppose you had this beat." I really needled him but good.

Pesky asked me what I had against him, and I told him about how his hesitation had cost me thirty grand and I was gonna try like a sonofabitch to get some of it back from him. Then I asked him if he still had the glue stuck on his hand from the game. He insisted that he had done his best, and we all wound up getting a big laugh out of it. Truth be told, even the press had exaggerated how long Pesky had hesitated. It was more aggressive baserunning by Slaughter than anything Pesky did wrong. But that didn't make me wanna strangle the sonofabitch any *less*.

Pesky, who I believe inspired an adjective, moved to third base in 1948 (so he wouldn't have to deal with being the cutoff man, I suppose) and later went on to manage the Red Sox in 1963 and '64. To this day the right-field foul pole in Fenway is called "Pesky's Pole." The 1946 World Series was one of the greatest World Series of all time, and most people remember it by the words "Pesky holds the ball." But for me it will forever live in my mind as "Slim loses thirty grand."

Like I do all my losses, I shrugged it off and kept doing my thing at the Criterion Club. In May 1947 I booked the Kentucky Derby, and most people liked one of three contenders—Phalanx (the 2–1 favorite), Faultless Home, and On Trust (which were both a little more than 6–1).

On the morning of the big race, a bookmaker from Terre Haute, Indiana, with whom I had become friends in Hot Springs, called me and asked what I was doing in the Derby. I told him that I had taken action on everything—booking bets for everyone on the base and at the Criterion Club—so it didn't make much difference to me who won the race.

"I know Phalanx is a pretty good horse, and he's a deserving favorite," this bookmaker from Indiana said to me on the phone, "but that horse Jet Pilot likes the slow going. You could put a bucket of oats and a bucket of mud in his stall, and he'd kick the oats out."

"So you're telling me he likes the slop?" I asked.

"Yeah, and it's going to rain today at Churchill Downs."

That was just a good example of the gambler's code—that if you do right by folks in gambling circles, it comes back to help you. This bookmaker, who I'll do right by now and keep his name to myself, had taken a liking to me in Hot Springs, and simply because of that, he turned me on to a great bet. Word must have gotten out a little that this colt liked the mud, because at post time the horse went off at about 5½–1, and I bet $8,000 on Jet Pilot to win.

Thanks to heavy rains, the track was slow, and the three-year-old son of Blenheim II came out of the gate like he knew I had bet on him. That was the good news. The bad news was that the rain didn't seem to bother the favorite, Phalanx, who was closing like a banshee. I said about twelve Hail Marys while the horses were entering the stretch, and, sure enough, Jet Pilot took it home, earning me about $45,000.

I'll tell you what it was like to be that rich and that cocky while I was still a teenager. I'd go to the theater and buy up the whole front row so me and my gal could sit there. Now, that's a kid who was rich and full of himself. There wasn't any need in doing that, and less than a year later, when I was near broke, I learned that a gambler can't get too high or become wasteful when he makes a score. But back then I'd take the *whole front row*.

At the end of 1947, after twenty-two months in the navy, I got what was called a "convenience of the government" discharge. I hung around Portland for a little while, hustled my way playing pool through California, and after a couple of months, headed home.

Back in Amarillo, I hit the pool halls. The problem was, I could hardly get a game anymore, so I paid a visit to Prairietown to see good old Bobby Turner—the cat I had broke in 1945 on that trip with John and Elmer. I wound up beating Bobby out of a 1941 Ford convertible.

I was enjoying life in Amarillo with my convertible and my own apartment. How could I not? At age nineteen and still too cocky for my own good, I thought I had all the money that had ever been minted. From running craps games, booking bets, and playing pool, I had more than a hundred grand when I came out of the navy. But after giving a bunch of it to my parents, trying to impress the girls, and buying horses, it didn't last me three months.

Most gamblers—and most people, for that matter—have leaks, personal weaknesses that poke holes in their pockets. It's not uncommon for a world-class poker player to show incredible discipline to make a nice score, only to go over to the craps table and blow it on one roll of the dice or bet $10,000 on a football game between two teams he's never even seen play.

I don't have any of the typical gambling leaks. I wouldn't put a red cent in a slot machine, and the only time you'll see me at a craps table is when I'm running it. As for sports, I'll only bet a game when I've researched the game and feel like I know something that the public doesn't. Like I said before, I gamble to win—not to feed some habit.

If I had to say I had one leak, though, it would be horses—not betting on them, but *owning* them. Sir Winston Churchill once said, "There's something about the outside of a horse that's good for the inside of a man." Old Winston had it right, but what he left out is something that has cost me a pretty penny over the years: You should never have a hobby that eats. I had bought a couple of horses when I got back to Amarillo, and, while I treasured them animals, I missed the action of life in the service. Besides, my bankroll was whittling away to nothing, and I wasn't gonna find too many millionaires in Amarillo who hadn't already heard of me.

ARMY SPECIAL SERVICES IN THE EUROPEAN THEATER

At the beginning of 1948, my buddy Wendell Cain and I decided to join the army, with the agreement that we were going to Germany. At that time you could choose where you wanted to go. The war was over, but the United States still had plenty of troops in Europe, and I figured it'd be fun to see some more of the world and try to hustle pool in places where nobody had heard of me.

Wendell—who went on to become a famous television announcer back in Amarillo—and I went to the receiving station at Columbia, South Carolina, to start our tour. We took the AGCT—Army General Classification Test—along with all our physicals and aptitude exams, and I made an exceptional score. It turns out Mama was right about my mathematical ability. So here came the bosses—my word for them was the "gendarmes"—and they explained to me how lucky I was and what a good career I had ahead of me in the good old U.S. Army.

They wanted me to go to Quantico, Virginia, just outside of Washington, D.C., to go through training for the FBI. I did some research into their offer and found out that they wanted to use me to break code and do all sorts of investigative and undercover stuff. I declined, since my intent was to do what I had done in the navy—not much of anything—and the FBI didn't appeal to me much. I've always sided with the bad folks, so it probably wouldn't have made much sense to put me in charge of catching 'em. I'd probably end up trying to help 'em. Honor among thieves, I guess you'd call it.

I'll tell you more about our trip over the pond in just a minute, but when we arrived at the receiving station at Marburg, Germany, I was just piddling around in the dayroom showing off with a pool cue, and this big shot, Colonel Gardner B. Gross, saw me and asked if I was Amarillo Slim.

He had seen me in either Guam or the Philippines, giving exhibitions with Irving Crane, and the next thing I knew, the Special Services man on the base said, "Why don't you let us put you in Special Services, and you can tour Europe giving pool exhibitions. I think you'd have a lot of fun, and it'd be entertaining for the troops."

Naturally, I accepted the position and was sent to the headquarters of the United States Constabulary in Stuttgart, Germany. Special Services is a division of the army used for entertainment—Bob Hope, Jake La Motta, Joe Louis, Jimmy Stewart, and even Bobby Riggs all had done some entertaining for our troops over the years. Wendell ended up going to Augsburg, Germany, and did guard duty on the Russian border, but he was a good sport about it. I told that sonofagun he should have spent more time practicing pool!

Being in the Special Services meant that I was on *permanent* TDY—temporary duty—and wasn't stationed anywhere. I'd go to a base to give a pool exhibition, and when I got through, I'd make my way to the next one. I was classified as an entertainment specialist, and I traveled with folks like Bob Hope and Irving Berlin to such exotic destinations as Tripoli, Algiers, and Casablanca. I tell you, I had it real tough.

BUILDING A BLACK-MARKET OPERATION

On my way to Europe in early 1948, I was aboard a troop carrier, and I was having a meal with George, one of the mess cooks. I might have spent most of my money after the navy, but I wasn't too broke to pay a bribe and eat with the ship's crew. I never was one for waiting in lines, plus, I knew the cooks always ate better than everyone else. When George asked me if I was going to Germany, I told him that I was, and then he asked me if I smoked.

"Excessively," I said, which was true back then, before I gave up that nasty habit. Then he uttered these words, which I will never forget, because they were to make me a very rich man: "You shouldn't smoke cigarettes, cowboy, you should sell them. They're bringing between thirty and thirty-four dollars a carton overseas."

I thought, good Lord, I've got to find me a way to get plenty of cigarettes. They sold for fifty cents a carton on the ship, and everyone was allowed to buy a carton and a half. A lot of the guys couldn't afford their full share, so I'd pay for 'em, give them half a carton, and keep a carton for myself. To make room for my loot, I threw all my clothes over the side of the ship. When I got off the ship in Marburg, Germany, I had the clothes on my back and one little ditty bag with some socks and drawers in it—and, of course, all my cigarettes.

It didn't take me long to find the German black-market operators. I sold my stash of cigarettes, and these fellas told me that they'd buy *anything* I could get my hands on. Cigarettes, penicillin, coffee, syrup, nylon hose, and gasoline all went through the black market. In Germany back then, everything was rationed, and you could hardly get a bar of soap.

Most of them GIs were broke, so it was easy enough to buy their cigarettes, but that got too slow. So the first thing I did was to cook up some counterfeit ration tickets and started buying cigarettes by the case. Then I bribed a government official and had a fix with the main PX (Post Exchange) in Frankfurt, and I could get all the cigarettes I wanted. Let's put it this way: instead of selling a carton for thirty dollars, I would sell a case for six thousand dollars.

There was a shortage of gasoline, and that, too, was rationed, even for civilians. But if you had a bunch of ration cards, you could get all you wanted. So I made some counterfeit gasoline ration cards—not that it mattered much, since the people I bought the gas from were getting a piece of the action as well.

With the money I earned from selling cigarettes and gas, I was able to buy several vehicles and build a big crew of folks who worked for me. The more money I made, the more my operation grew, and at one time I had thirty cars in one convoy carrying contraband. Most of the guys working for me were Germans, and they got paid well. Even though most everybody there spoke English, I wanted to be able to relate to them, so I learned how to speak German. *Sprechen zie deutsch*, neighbor?

Of course, this little operation wasn't without its risks, and it got to where every time I'd make a trip—even if it did pertain to my billiard exhibitions—I had company. I'm greedy, but I'm not stupid, and I could always feel when the heat started getting on me. Besides, I had discovered some more traditional ways to make money over there—more in line with what I was used to anyhow.

MONSIEUR CONTI SAID THE WRONG THING

Even though people in America use the words "pool" and "billiards" like they're one and the same, they're about as similar as Ping-Pong and tennis. I think people get confused because pocket billiards is just another name for what most people call pool, and it's the game that is most played here in America. Snooker is similar to pool, and even though it's more popular in England than it is here, I played it every day for two years at Peabody Academy.

Before I went to Europe, I had never seen a billiards table—and I'd bet a lumberyard against a toothpick that most Americans hadn't either. It doesn't have any pockets and has only three balls on it—my cue ball, your cue ball, and a red ball. The object of the game is simple: You hit the cue ball, it has to go three rails, and then it hits the other ball. It's a game of touch and strategy, and while I picked it up pretty quickly, I didn't have enough time to master the game the way I had mastered pool and snooker.

In addition to traveling with the big-shot entertainers from America, I would travel to different countries with the pool and billiards champions of Europe. In France and parts of Holland and Luxembourg, I played with Monsieur Conti, a Frenchman who was the European three-cushion-billiards champion. Playing with him showed me just how much I had to learn about this game of finesse. I traveled all over Germany with Eric Hagenlacher, the international European pocket-billiards champion. We'd do trick shots and then play each other before playing against the troops. I toured England with Joe Davis, the world-champion snooker player then, and, in my opinion, one of the best players who ever lived.

Prior to our arrival, the soldiers would have a tournament to determine the best player on the base, and whoever won it played me after the exhibition was over. If the soldier won, he received a $100 war bond. Whether he beat me or not, he still got $25 worth of PX tickets and a three-day pass to go wherever he wanted, which was something special in the European theater.

You might think that I'd have let them boys beat me, but like in anything I did, I always wanted to win. I probably couldn't have kept my job if somebody beat me; heck, they would have given *him* my job. Plus, those soldiers were a proud lot, and I don't think that any one of them would have respected me, or themselves, if I let them off easy. So I took no mercy on those GIs.

While I had fun in just about every country I visited, the most frustrating thing about my time in France was that they spoke a different language than what I was used to: billiards. I couldn't find a table with pockets over there, and I was getting awful tired of being thrashed by Monsieur Conti. I couldn't beat him more than I could fly a jet. I hadn't played but ten games of billiards in my life, and here I was playing the world champion. We'd play twenty-five point-exhibitions, and I don't think I ever made ten points against him.

So one day I said to him, "Say, Conti, this is an exhibition; it's just to entertain these people. You oughta let up on me a little. Hell, there ain't no way I can run six or seven and get out on you, if that's what you're concerned about. Make it interesting. Let's at least give these GIs a rooting interest."

I wasn't trying to hustle him or nothing; I just knew that it wasn't gonna be fun for nobody to watch a mismatch. But Conti was a smart-ass, stuck-up Frenchman, and only because he was a champion did I respect him. But, boy, did he say the wrong thing: "Yeah, but you just can't play."

I was only nineteen at the time, and I didn't want to hear that I couldn't play. I had won my fair share of money playing pool, and the U.S. government didn't have me on their payroll for *not* being able to play. I was hotter than a firecracker when he said that, and the rest of the day I didn't think about much other than how I was gonna make that French-man eat his words.

By accident—or fate, I guess—it wasn't two weeks later that we were in Luxembourg giving a billiards exhibition at the Berdeback Galla—which, like our city halls in America, is where the mayor had his office. I was walking down the street, and I heard *click, click* coming from the open door of a café. I had known that sound all my life, and when I walked in, sure enough there was a snooker table in the basement. I played five games by myself just to develop a feel for the table and get my snooker touch back. Then I went to do my job.

Before we started the exhibition at the Berdeback Galla, I went up to the billiards champ and said real loud, "Conti, is there any place in these godforsaken countries around here where they've got tables that have pockets in them?"

"*Je ne sais pas,*" he said in that annoying voice of his.

But one of the Luxembourg officials, who overheard my question, answered, "Well, yes, it's not a regular billiards room, but there's a snooker table in the basement of the café just up the street."

"You're kiddin'," I said, acting as if it was the biggest surprise since the Alamo. "I didn't know they had a table with pockets in these parts. Conti, how come me and you don't play some snooker?"

"What do you mean?" he asked.

"Shoot, as bad as you beat me playing billiards, I'll let you go beat me somewhere where you gotta at least shoot a ball in a damn pocket."

"It would be my pleasure," he said.

"Good. Now, whatever money you've got—and I don't care what type of currency it is—you can post it and you can play me in snooker for *all* of it."

The official who had set up the exhibition match, figuring that I'd be no match for Conti, said, "What about the rest of us?"

"The rest of you can bet whatever you can pay off. Or get to a figure where I can't pay off—and, gentlemen, that is a *big* figure."

By that point the black market had given me a big bankroll to match my big mouth.

"That suits me," Conti said. After all, the guy had dominated me in every cotton-pickin' billiards match we had played.

So off we went to the local café to play some snooker—me, Conti, the mayor, and everyone else who wanted to put their money on Conti. And who could have blamed 'em for wanting to bet on a champion?

But Conti wasn't used to playing a game with pockets. Now he was in *my* ballpark, and, boy, did I thrash him. After I won the first bet, he said, "I'd like to play some more." So I put the same thing on him that I put on everybody else. "That's fine, Conti," I said, "but now we're playing Texas rules."

He didn't know Texas rules from the Texas two-step, so I explained to him that Texas rules means that when you lose one, you bet two. In other words, you double the bet. That's the way we do it in Texas—where size *does* matter.

"I'll have to get a marker," he said, which was his way of saying that he wanted me to take him at his word, like a casino giving a line of credit to a customer.

"No, you don't need to get a marker. Get this *Burgermeister*"—which is their word for mayor—"to stand good for you. I trust him."

"What do you know about the mayor?" he asked.

"I know he owns these banks around here," I said, "and that's all I need to know." I had done my homework, like I always do. If you're going to survive as a gambler, you *have* to be ahead of all the other folks. I wasn't gonna trust Conti to pay me back, so the mayor stood good for him. We played again, and I won. We kept playing until I wore him plumb to a nub and broke half the damn country.

I took a page out of Fats's book and needled Conti every second of those matches, and, boy, did he deserve it for what he had said about my game. If you beat me straight up, then I'll take my lumps like a man. But if you try to rub my nose in it, then as sure as the day is long, I'm going to find a way to get the best of you. Conti found out the hard way, and I hit him where it hurt that pompous Frenchman the most—in his wallet.

The next exhibition we played was in Holland. We were playing his game—three-cushion billiards—so of course I didn't bet any money on it. I'm a gambler, not a fool. The first exhibition we played, he beat me 25–19, and I thought, maybe I can do something with this game of billiards. The next one we played in Düsseldorf, Germany, and he only beat me 25–21. Then it hit me: Up until then, I had never scored ten points against him, but after that sonofabitch got broke playing snooker, he was as sloppy as a wet dog.

KEEPING THE BALL IN THE INFIELD AT THE GI WORLD SERIES

Arnold Rothstein, a gambler who New York police referred to as "the J. P. Morgan of the Underworld," was best known for fixing the 1919 World Series between the Cincinnati Reds and the Chicago White Sox. The "Black Sox" scandal is one of the most famous in all of sports, and it involved "Shoeless" Joe Jackson, probably the greatest player never to make the Baseball Hall of Fame (and that's including Pete Rose). I wasn't alive when it happened, but as I had learned in the navy, anytime there's an event in which the outcome has yet to be determined, there are gonna be plenty of guessers looking to piss away their money.

Now, let me say this straight off the bat: While I might be a cold-hearted sonofagun when it comes to breaking men at the gambling game, I'm not a mean-spirited person, and some of the stuff I did when I was in the Special Services, I'm not real proud of. I already told you about running the black market, and while I made a lot of money doing it, that doesn't mean it was right. There were, of course, some other no-nos. I don't know whether there's a statute of limitations on this kind of thing, but since more than fifty years have passed, I'm hoping that we can let bygones be bygones.

All the branches of the services have championships for their sports, and in October 1948, in Frankfurt, Germany, I attended the GI baseball World Series. It was *the* event for everyone serving overseas, and there might have been forty thousand people in the stands, all set to watch one of the best forms of entertainment these soldiers would ever see. This series had all the passion of an Army-Navy football game. In 1948 the 547 Engineers, an all-black team stationed in Gellenhausen, Germany, had earned home-field advantage and were prohibitive favorites against the 101st Airborne, a group out of Fort Benning, Georgia.

I was ready to book some action on the series, and there were plenty of folks itching to bet. The only problem was that everybody wanted to bet on the 547 Engineers, and I just couldn't see them losing a game. Just like in the major-league World Series, this one was the best out of seven. After the 547s dominated the first game, even more folks wanted to bet on them in Game Two. With all them people dying to get their money in play, I knew I had to find a way to give them an opportunity.

I got to talking to the three best players from the 547s and invited them down to my suite at the Excelsior Hotel. Even though I don't drink, I made sure I had the bar stocked with the finest of liquors so I could demonstrate to these hardworking soldiers, who were making $29 a month, what it looked like to live high on the hog.

The key to getting them to do what I wanted them to do was to prey on their egos a little bit. So after chatting for a while, warming up to them and all, I said, "You all could certainly lose one game and still win it, *couldn't you?*"

"Sure, Mr. Slim."

Well, naturally they were going to say "sure." These were competitive, world-class athletes; do you think they were gonna say that they couldn't spot a team one lousy ball game and still win it?

So I tested them again. "You all positive about that? One game is a lot to spot another team."

"Surely we can still win. What do you mean?"

"You all wanna make some money?" I asked.

"Certainly. What do we gotta do?"

"All you gotta do is lose the second game. It's that simple."

"But how can we guarantee that? We're only three guys. What about the rest of the team?"

"You're right," I said. "You can't guarantee that you'll lose the second game, and I can't guarantee it either, and I won't say nothing if you end up winning. But every time any one of you come up to that plate, I don't want the ball hit out of the infield."

"That ain't hard to do."

"Why, certainly it's not hard to do. Now, you know that you'll still beat 'em in five games to win the World Series, so what's the harm?"

I knew they were gonna do it, but to help justify it in their own minds, I put the words in their own mouths. In any hustle—or any legitimate sale, for that matter—you have to make a person think that it's *his* idea. It also helps to confront head-on any objections that may come up later and prevent any second thoughts.

So they talked among themselves for a little bit while I fixed each of them a drink. When I sat back down, they asked for a certain figure. Now, if there's one thing I learned in life, it's never to say yes to the first offer. If you agree to a deal too early, a person is always gonna walk away thinking he could have gotten more out of you. But if he has to work for it and you cave in a little, he'll think that he really got the best of you. Why do you think a car dealer starts with such a high sticker price? He wants every person to walk out of there feeling like he's the smartest fella since Howard Hughes.

So we went back and forth on the figure a little bit and finally settled on $600 each. Then I said, "Here's the kicker. If none of you hits the ball out of the infield for the entire game, I'll give you each six hundred more. But if one of you does, no bonus money for anybody."

If any of them was gonna have a change of heart, I was giving 'em eighteen hundred more reasons not to. What $29-a-month soldier was going to say no to $1,200—and just for taking a little batting practice instead of playing full out?

I don't remember how much action I took on the second game of the GI World Series, but I made a bet with everybody I could. I cooked up some story about having a sweet little girlfriend back in Georgia who swore to me that the guys from Fort Benning were just slow starters. Guys were putting up their car titles just to get action, and I'd put up cash. Folks from the Pentagon—I'm talking about fully decorated generals—were coming up to me and placing their bets!

The game was pretty close, but the 547s just couldn't seem to get any run production from the middle of their lineup. Oh, sure, they'd swing real hard at the ball, but they always seemed to be a couple of inches on top of it. None of those three guys ever did hit the ball out of the infield, and it was just the cushion the Fort Benning boys needed to win the game. Now, if the 547s had won the game, I still would have paid my three guys for living up to their end of the bargain. Smart gambling is about putting the odds in your favor, and sometimes the result isn't always what you want—that's why it's called gambling. In this case, however, things went as smooth as a spanked baby's ass.

The 547s, sporting the three highest-paid players in military baseball history, ended up winning the series in five games. I won fourteen cars, mostly converted Jeeps, and sweaters full of money. Like I said, that bet was nothing more than a swindle, and despite all the money it earned me, I still feel bad about it to this day. A lot of generals would like to know about that, and I hope that more than fifty years later we can all forgive and forget.

MY OWN MISTAKE SENT ME BACK TO AMERICA

I wasn't the only American GI who was making a small fortune in the black market in Europe. It seemed like the higher the rank, the greater the odds were that a man had his hand in the cookie jar. Naturally, these big officers played in some big poker games, too. At that point in my life, I wasn't a great player, but I had learned to play pretty well at the Criterion Club in Portland. So when a big officer in the military offered to get me into the game for 25 percent of my winnings, it didn't take me long to accept.

This colonel had arranged to get me a captain's uniform, which, because of my age, was a bit suspicious. He should have given me a second lieutenant's uniform, which would have been more appropriate. But anyhow, I went to this officers' club in Gellenhausen, where they played high-stakes draw poker.

During a break in the game, I went to make a phone call to a Special Services hostess that I had met in Stuttgart. To place a long-distance phone call, I had to fill out a form, and, without as much as thinking about it, I signed it "Specialist First Class T. A. Preston Jr." instead of "Captain T. A. Preston Jr."

A few minutes later this operator came over to the table and said, "Specialist First Class T. A. Preston Jr., your phone call to Stuttgart is ready."

I had ratted my own self out, but as dumb as that was, I wasn't about to make another mistake. So without even looking up, I said, "Wait just a minute," and I could feel seven faces staring bullets at me.

I casually grabbed some of my money, but I left a few hundred on the table so they'd think I was coming back. Instead of stopping at the telephone, I ran down the stairs straight to my hotel room at the Excelsior. A few hundred dollars was a small price to pay for not getting caught—and, even better, it seems like that hostess figured out why I was calling and met me at the Excelsior the next day.

Between the black-market risk and this poker game, I knew it was time for me to go. The only trouble with my getting back to America was that a hundred-dollar money order was the biggest thing you could get, and I had no way to get my money back to the States. It was my good fortune that Wells Fargo had just opened a branch in Frankfurt, and I was able to have most of my money wired to Denver, Colorado—the closest branch to Amarillo. I kept two bags full of currency—about $300,000—

that I could exchange in America. After being in the Special Services of the army for less than a year, I went back to America in November 1948 as a nineteen-year-old millionaire. But winning money and keeping money would prove to be two different things.

Helen, Becky, Tod and I in front of the $1 million display at Binion's Horseshoe. *(Courtesy of Binion's Horseshoe)*

3

If You Want Some Publicity, Set Yourself on Fire

My first stop back in America was in Perth Amboy, New Jersey, the discharge service for the army, and who wasn't there waiting for me but old New York Fats. Well, not just for me, but any GI looking to match a game of pool against America's finest. In fact, Fats didn't even remember me from Hot Springs, which I took as an insult.

It shouldn't have surprised me that I ran into the Fatman. After all, he was always looking for suckers with a few dollars in their pockets, and with all them boys coming back from the war with their soldiers' pay, Fats was there like a hawk circling a bunch of chickens. It also didn't shock me that he was running his mouth like an outboard motor on a fishing boat, and even though I should have known better, Fats hit all the right buttons. With my pockets full of cash and my ego the size of a water-melon, I talked a big game, and Fats called me every name in the book.

"Don't go flapping your fat gums in front of me," I said, "unless you want to put your money where your mouth is."

Like he did to many wannabe pool hustlers before and after, Fats shut me up in a hurry and beat me out of twelve thousand dollars. Considering what I had made in Europe, and that I was carrying about three hundred thousand with me, Fats really blew a chance to break me. When he caught wind that I had a lot more money where that twelve thousand came from, it occurred to him that he sold out too cheap and he sent out word to try to put together another match.

By that time, though, I had already moved on to the big city in search of some transport back to Amarillo. Since I had all this money burning a hole in my pocket, the first thing I did was visit a Cadillac dealership on Fifty-second and Broadway in Manhattan. When I pointed to a shiny black Cadillac on the showroom floor, the salesman asked me, "Son, how do you propose to pay for that?" Now, remember, I wasn't quite twenty yet, and I didn't look much older than a freshly scrubbed kid out of high school.

"Y'all *do* take cash, don't you?" I asked, and I was soon on my way. I remember the exact price, $3,738, because a few years later I got into some tax trouble, and a judge asked me if I could recognize my own signature as he furnished the bill of sale on my car.

On my way back to Amarillo, I stopped in Johnson, Arkansas, to see my mama and share the spoils from my time in Europe. I know that "professional gambler" wouldn't have been her first choice as the occupation for her only child, but maybe because I was in such good spirits and flush with cash, she was more understanding than I thought. After a week with Mama, my next stop was downtown Hot Springs, to play poker at the Southern Club, right across from the Arlington Hotel on Central Avenue.

I went in there ready to show everyone that there was a new boss gambler in the South. I put $70,000 in my pocket and stashed the rest of my money in the back end of my Cadillac. That's something I've always done over the years—one, to keep from going broke, and two, if I got robbed, they could only get what was on me.

When I walked out of the Southern Club fourteen hours later, I didn't have two nickels to rub together. What can I say? Even old Slim had to learn a few lessons—seventy thousand, to be exact—the hard way. But I will tell you this: I never had to learn the same lesson twice. From then on I tried to keep my confidence in check. Sure, my arrogance sometimes got the best of me—winning a bunch of money gambling at an early age will do that to a man—but I was always aware of how easy it was to lose if I was *too* confident.

LET'S GET US A DIFFERENT KIND OF WEAPON

It seemed like just as soon as I got back to Amarillo, Fats was there waiting to gobble me up like a gar does a minnow. He came running down to Amarillo with two backers—one from New York and one from Woodward, Oklahoma. As much money as Fats made in his day, he'd just as soon play with somebody else's. Besides food, he also had a weakness for dice. He even said himself that had it not been for craps, he would have been a millionaire by the end of World War II. But it didn't make no difference what he won, he never could keep it.

I reckon that the most popular variety of pool in this country is eight ball, which I think everybody knows how to play. No real gambler plays eight ball. And straight pool, where you can hit any ball in any pocket until you miss? Shoot, the only guys who played straight pool for money were the "youse" guys—that's them guys from New Jersey, New York, and Philadelphia—who might play up to a hundred points for two bits or something. As far as I'm concerned, straight pool is for people looking for a trophy or to get their picture in the paper. Even Fats had it right when he said, "Straight pool was about as obsolete as washing clothes on a rock in the river. One-pocket is the game that kept pool alive."

One-pocket, which was my specialty, is a game where you rack all the balls and each player is assigned a pocket and must hit all his balls *only* in that pocket. So if you have the left corner pocket, I'll have the right corner pocket, and the first one to hit eight balls in his pocket wins. Fats called it "the most elaborate, the most scientific pool game in the world," and I couldn't argue with him on that either. The only other game worth anything to gamble on in pool was nine ball. In nine ball the balls numbered one through nine are racked, and the object is to clear them in order of their number.

Fats had beaten me in Perth Amboy playing one-pocket, and I don't think I ever made six balls against him before he sank his eight. So when he came to Amarillo, I wasn't in the mood to play—especially after what happened in Hot Springs. I told him as much, and Fats said, "Well, come on, Slim, I'll give you a chance to get your money back."

"I'm through with that," I said. "You treated me like a redheaded stepchild."

"I came down here to play," said Fats, who was always a sore loser and known to pout when he didn't get what he wanted.

We went back and forth on some different propositions, but Fats wasn't giving in much, and I wasn't about to get my butt kicked *again* by that fat sonofabitch. So finally I said, "Let's get us a different kind of weapon."

Fats nodded, and I said, "Play me eight to four and I'll play with that broom over there in the corner."

"Just a minute," Fats said, and he went to go look at the broom. Now, I know you're probably thinking that, like my Ping-Pong wagers, there was some gimmick to it, but there wasn't much to this one. I told you that I used to practice using all sorts of funny instruments, and shooting with a broom was something them GIs in Europe always got a kick out of. In fact, I did it so often that it got to be where there wasn't much difference for me between a pool cue and a broom.

Fats, of course, thought it was some sort of trick, and he inspected that broom like he was Sherlock Holmes until finally he said, "Rack 'em, cowboy. I'll spot you four."

The handicap was that I only had to knock in four balls before he knocked in his eight, and while I wish I could tell you there was a great story behind this hustle, the truth is that this match was over before it even started. Heck, if it were a fight, they'da stopped it. I didn't so much outplay Fats as I outhustled him, and I trashed his goat-smelling ass pretty good.

I played Fats twice more after his trip to Amarillo. Once in Atlantic City, where he got the best of me, and then in Reno in 1969. After I beat him in

Reno—in front of a bunch of casino executives, no less—he pulled me off to the side and snarled, "If you want some publicity, go set yourself on fire, you skinny fuckin' cowboy." That was the last time I played Fats (Fats died on January 18, 1996, at the age of eighty-three) and while I would never call Fats a good friend, he did teach me an awful lot, and I have to give the man his due. He was a hell of a player and an even better showman—he could attract a crowd, and he knew how to work the room, making all the suckers want to challenge a man who they *knew* was a champion.

THE LOVE OF MY LIFE: HELEN ELIZABETH

When a man returns from overseas, he does what every proud, red-blooded, tough sonofagun does—he goes running like a baby to his best girl.

Since I didn't have one, I went stag to a dance—this was 1949, at the tail end of the big-band era—at the Nat Ballroom, which is still standing in the west part of Amarillo. A buddy of mine named Calvin Stock was there with a brunette named Helen Elizabeth Byler. She was about five-six, which made her taller than most of them other gals, and she was as pretty as a speckled pup under a red wagon. In fact, I thought she was the prettiest girl there, so I short-sheeted my buddy Calvin and wound up dating Helen the next day.

We went to the Palo Duro drive-in on our first date, and I knew I was in love. But our second date was when Helen really proved her stripes. Once I had arrived back in Amarillo from the service, it didn't take me long to find people looking to speculate on sporting events, and, brother, people down in Texas live and die for high-school football. That Friday there was a big game in Waco, Texas, and I chartered a light airplane to go down there and book the action. I was too important back then to drive a new car 420 miles to Waco. So while I was gone, I showed off a little and lent Helen that shiny black Cadillac.

Helen was the youngest of eight kids, four boys and four girls, and was born and raised in Claude, Texas, about thirty miles east of Amarillo. You didn't think I'd be courting a woman from Arkansas, now, did you? When I met Helen, she was working at Southwestern Public Service Company as a secretary, and she took the Cadillac to work while I was in Waco. I guess she wasn't used to a car that big, and she ended up attracting the attention of the police when she double-parked it. When the policeman asked her to open the glove compartment, parking tickets poured out like water over low land. I suppose I never did pay much attention to details— at least ones that didn't apply to gambling.

Since Helen didn't give me a hard time about going to book a high-school football game, I knew I had found the right woman. And, believe me, I always wanted a family. I even remember when I was in the service saying that I wanted a pretty wife and a little cotton-headed boy.

Weddings weren't such a big deal in Texas back then, and, like a lot of couples, we went to Clovis, New Mexico, for the same reason a lot of folks go to Nevada to get married today—mainly because you didn't have to bother with any medical records or background checks like you did in Texas. We had a small wedding at the justice of the peace on July 20, 1949. I never did have the heart to break away from my new wife and try to find Tom Christensen at Mexican Tom's joint for a little pool action in Clovis. Instead we had a real nice honeymoon in Ruidoso, New Mexico, at a swanky resort called the Inn of the Mountain Gods.

It was a minor coincidence that the horses were running at the race-track in Ruidoso during our honeymoon. Helen just thought I was showing her a nice time at the racetrack and that, because I was such a friendly cat, all these folks kept stopping by my box to spread their good cheer. Come on now, neighbor, you didn't think old Slim would let a little old marriage stop him from booking action!

When we came back to Amarillo, we moved into a ranch-style brick apartment on Tenth Street in Amarillo, and then, when she got pregnant, we bought a house in West Hill Trails. On February 1, 1951, it was sixteen degrees below zero in Amarillo when Helen told me that I better take her to Northwest Texas Hospital. And, wouldn't you know, I got my wish—a little cotton-headed boy, who we named Thomas Austin Preston III, was born to me and my darling wife. When I looked at him, the first thing that came out of my mouth was, "There's my little Bunky," and he still signs his name that way to this day.

Helen was a year older than me—and don't think I don't give her hell about it—but I swore I didn't know her at Amarillo High School. After Bunky was born and she started putting together some photo albums, she found her proof that I had signed her high-school annual:

Dear Helen,
As you go sliding down the banister of life, remember me as a splinter in your career.
—Austin "Curly" Preston

Most people didn't know that I had curly hair back then, because for one thing, "Curly" was no kind of nickname for a hustler, and besides, it was rare to find me without one of my Stetsons wrapped in snakeskin, which, along with my cowboy boots, have become my trademark. In his book *Big Deal*, a fine Brit named Tony Holden called me the "Imelda Marcos of poker footwear," and he was right: I own more than thirty pairs of boots made of calf, alligator, lizard, ostrich, kangaroo, and anteater skin. I've got a pair of white alligator boots made by Willie Lusk out of Lubbock, Texas, that cost me $3,800. Most of them say "Slim," along with clubs, diamonds, hearts, and spades around the name.

A MAN NAMED ELMO SANDS

From 1951 through 1959, when I was between the ages of twenty-two and thirty, I went around the United States hustling pool. Being on the road for months at a time, I would miss Helen and Bunky, and sometimes I would load up the family station wagon and hit the road. My family got to see some interesting parts of America, and I got to ply my trade the only way I knew how.

Bunky, who's got a little bit of his old man's sense of humor in him, will tell you that I was such a bad pool player that we barely had enough money to eat. Back in those days, we'd just get in the car and take off to where I heard the action was. Most of the time, I'd put our boat behind the car so we could stop and fish along the way. It was a good life.

The part Bunky remembers, of course, is pulling up to a pool hall in that station wagon and having to sleep in it while I went in and played. He thought I was too cheap to pay for a motel, but what he didn't realize was that I just didn't know how long I was gonna be in there. Sometimes it got dangerous inside and I always wanted to be prepared to make a quick getaway. But even more important, it helped me hustle a game if I could pull into a place, family in tow, and say something like, "I was just taking a trip with the family to the Grand Canyon and looking to find me a game of pool." You think anyone's gonna suspect a man traveling with his wife and kid to be a pool hustler?

On one of my trips with the family, I was in Portland and found myself back at the good old Criterion Club, when one of the wise guys said to me, "Have you ever been to Provo, Utah, to meet that Elmo Sands? It'd be a good score; somebody like you is liable to win a real big figure off of him. He likes propositions, and he likes to play high, and you'll accommodate him on both things."

They told me that Elmo Sands owned a chain of cleaners called QuickPress. Back in the fifties, they used to have this quick press at the cleaners where, for fifty-nine cents, you could just step into one of them machines and come out with a perfect crease in your pants. At fifty-nine cents a pop, Elmo had made himself a small fortune, and—just my luck— he was a good pool player. A real good player.

We left Portland and went straight to Provo. I spent the mornings fishing with Bunky and Helen, and every day at about 2:15 P.M., I'd go into the poolroom up there (it had snooker tables and pool tables) with a golf tee stuck over my ear, wearing dress golf slacks, brown two-tone shoes, and a good-looking golf shirt. The first day I played snooker for fun, I got beat, of course, and made it look like I was there just for some recreation.

The next day I decided to make my spread. A guy asked me if I wanted to play snooker for $2 a game, and I said, "That's about right." So we played four games for $2 each, and, naturally, he won every one of 'em. Then he asked me to raise it to $5, and I lost about six games at this price. I started to quit, and he said, "C'mon. I'll give you ten and play you for ten dollars."

It's a little confusing to describe the scoring in snooker, but let's just say that I could give anyone in that room a twenty-point spot and still win.

So, with him giving *me* a ten-point spot, I lost four more games to this cat, at $10 a game, and I left. My whole buildup that day didn't cost me but eighty bucks, including a Coca-Cola.

The next day I came in dressed in my golfing outfit and the same guy said, "C'mon, friend, you wanna play some more?"

"Yes, sir," I said, "but I like your rules. I'll take fifteen for fifteen."

Do you see the idea of doing that kinda thing? It put everybody at ease. Here I was joking around with this guy and acting like I was just there to have some fun. So he agreed, and I got the kinda spot where I could put one hand in my hip pocket and win. Naturally, I lost four straight to him and paid him my sixty dollars.

"Man," he said, "ain't nobody ever had twenty for twenty."

I was down sixty dollars and I told myself that this would be a perfect spot to make it an even hundred. So I took a twenty-spot for twenty dollars, and of course I didn't come close to winning either of our next two games.

The next day when I turned the corner on my way to that poolroom, there were about twenty of 'em out front. I could hear them whispering, "Here he comes. Here he comes." Shoot, they've got themselves a walking gold mine. These guys were wanting to play snooker for a dollar a game, and here was a tourist that was playing for twenty a game—and he couldn't play!

So I walked in, and the guy tried to get me to go twenty for twenty again, and I said, "You've thrashed me long enough. It's obvious I ain't got no chance."

"My buddy here doesn't play quite as good as me," he said, "he'll play you some."

Well, I knew he was lying, but I didn't want to be no sharpie, so I said, "Damn, if he plays less than you, then I oughta be a favorite against him."

I'd always say something like that at the end so they'd figure me for a rich guy who thought he was better than he was. I played his buddy twenty for twenty, and after I lost one game, I said, "That's all for me," and I left.

You're probably thinking that this was taking an awful long time to set up, but the key to hustling is patience. Like I've said many times now, I never did want to just *beat* someone; I wanted to *break* the sonofabitch. I knew that the more I showed my face in that joint, the more believable it would be when old Elmo showed up—and, believe me, I knew it wouldn't be long.

You hear all these stories about how tough life on the road is, but I always enjoyed it. On this trip Helen and Bunky and I stayed in a nice hotel, ate at the best restaurants, and I'd always be home by nine o'clock to read my boy a story (or usually just make one up) before he went to sleep. I think the reason I was so patient was that I was truly enjoying myself and didn't see no reason to be in any hurry. The money I was losing was nothing more than an investment for a bigger payday down the road.

The fifth day I went back and I saw a guy wearing an expensive shirt, dress slacks, argyle socks, and a pair of alligator loafers. I'd never seen this man in my life, but there was no doubt who he was. I'd just seen Elmo Sands.

He came over to me and said, "You've been helping the local pool economy, young man. Are you a good player?"

"Well, I thought I was," I said. "Really and truly, I'm the fourth-best player in Tulia, Texas. There's not but three guys in Tulia that can beat me playing snooker, and one of them gives me thirty and the other two give me twenty-five."

Sure enough Mr. Sands, one of the richest men in Utah, took the bait and said, "I'm a pretty good player myself."

"I thought I was, too," I said, "but I may not be."

"Do you wanna play some?"

I knew it was time for me to put him down or insult him a little to get his juices flowing, so I said, "Say, mister, you don't realize, but I'm more than a two-hundred-dollar loser around here playing pool."

"What are you trying to say?" Elmo asked.

"I'm not looking to play no twenty-dollar pool. Do you know somebody around these parts who will give me a game?"

"Wait just a minute," Elmo said. "I'm not a twenty-dollar bettor either."

Now he's a goner, you understand? He's already answered my question. I wouldn't have taken five thousand in my hand for what I had right then—a millionaire with a lot of talent but not *that much* talent. I knew he was fixing to throw off some quick presses.

"What do you want to play for?" he said.

That was when I used one of my favorite lines, one that I still use today. "I'm not on no budget. Make me feel it."

"What about two hundred a game?"

"Depends upon the conditions of the game."

"Well, everybody else gave you twenty. I'll give you twenty."

"I'm afraid you're a shark. I reckon you're a better player than they are."

Well, he was, and he knew it, so he said, "What do you wanna do for twenty-two?"

"I want to put four more points with it," I said. "And I don't wanna play for two hundred a game—I wanna play for four hundred a game."

"That's twenty-six," he said. "You got twenty-six for four hundred a game, boy."

Naturally, I had my personal cue out in my car, but I couldn't go get it or nothing. So I turned my back to him, and I walked over to the rack to get me a cue—so I looked like a big-ass sucker—and while I was looking at the cues out on the rack, I heard Elmo say, "Amarillo Slim?"

I just kept looking at the cues, still with my back to him, and he said, "Hey, Slim."

By this point in my life, my name was pretty well known in pool halls across America, and that's why I had to change my cover from time to time. Rather than showing up in my Stetson and cowboy boots and playing the part of a country cowboy, I had to be somebody else.

So I just kept going through the cues, and I said, "Boy this looks like a self-shooter to me," and I just kept acting like I was looking for the right one. When he asked me to be scorekeeper, I went over to the table and wrote, "Me and him." And Elmo said, right out loud, looking right at me, "Tall, skinny, and blond-headed."

He had heard of an "Amarillo Slim," and he just described me, but I wasn't paying him no mind. He *knows* I'm not Slim, but I guess he just wanted to give me one more test, and he said, "Where are you from?"

"Tulia, Texas," I said. "What difference does it make?"

Oh, shit, I thought, but not another word was said. He chalked his cue, we legged for the break, and here we went. He would have bet his life I wasn't Amarillo Slim. He had given me some good tests, but I could have earned an Oscar for my performance.

He gave me twenty-six for $400, and we started playing. The world champion couldn't give me eighteen at snooker, and here was a guy giving me twenty-six who probably couldn't have beat me if *I* had given *him* a spot. Talk about being up shit's creek without a paddle—this man was gonna be tasting it before long.

I thought the best thing I could do to try to bust this sonofabitch was to break even for the day, or be up one or down one. It didn't much matter. He was a rich man, and if I won a game, he'd think he was unlucky, and if he won one, he'd know he could win. So it ended up being even after a couple of hours, and I quit, like I always did at 8:45 P.M.

The manager, who now realized that I always quit at the same time, said, "Why do you quit at this time every night?"

"I go eat," I said, "and I go back to my hotel to talk to some associates on the phone."

"What do you mean, you talk to associates?" he said.

"I'm involved in sports," I said. Now, I'm substantiating that I had money. In a different situation, I might have said that I was with my family, but I wasn't playing the family man against Mr. Sands. No, I was playing the rich bookmaker from Texas who had more money than ability. When I left, at least he had enough sense not to ask me if I was coming back. He knew I was.

The next day I turned the corner and there were about sixty people outside. It seemed like half the town was waiting for me. Shoot, nobody there played snooker for $400 a game. It might have been the biggest moment of the century in Utah before the Jazz moved there from New Orleans in 1980.

Mr. Sands and I didn't waste much time with pleasantries and started with the same bet as the day before, $400 a game with a twenty-six spot for me. I beat him the first game, not by much, and he said, "Isn't it about time to raise it?"

Now it was time to be a smart-ass and get his britches all knotted up, so I said, "I thought you'd never ask."

I knew if I kept beating him at twenty-six, he wasn't gonna get broke on that number. But if we moved the spot down, he'd keep gambling with me, thinking we would be on more even terms. So we raised the stakes to

$600 a game and changed the spot to twenty-four, and I just barely beat him again. Still, when it got to be 8:45, I quit. The folks on the rail couldn't understand how a guy playing for those kind of stakes could quit, but I told 'em I had to tend to my business and left. I quit about a $4,800 winner for the day. The few hundred I had lost from my first few days had paid off more than twentyfold.

The next day, don't you worry, they were all there waiting for me. Heck, there were people from Salt Lake City, Denver, Portland, and everywhere in between watching us. I didn't much care for that, because sooner or later one of them folks was gonna know who I was. I was just hoping that it would be a hustler with enough sense not to say anything— just sit over there on the side and bet on me and keep his mouth shut.

When I walked in the door, Mr. Sands said, "Our snooker's over."

"Good," I said, "it was getting to be too close anyway."

"I mean it's over at twenty-four. If you want to play twenty-two, you can play higher than you've ever played in your life."

I didn't have the heart to tell him that I had played awful high, so I just went along with him, and he said, "You can bet a thousand dollars a game if you'll take twenty-two."

"A thousand?" I asked. "That's a pretty good-size bet for a sonofabitch that don't have a job, but that's okay with me. I'm playing with your money anyway."

That got under his skin a little, and I knew it was working because *he* was the one who raised it to a thousand. It didn't look like he was getting hustled—it looked like he was hustling me. So we played, and you couldn't breathe in that poolroom. Everybody in there was betting something— and this was in Utah, a place where gambling isn't exactly embraced. And now it was time to really give him a whipping. I beat him real bad because I knew I could keep lowering the spot. At about 8:15, he said, "Goddamn, I wish that clock would hurry up. I'm sick of this."

Sure enough, at 8:45 he asked me if I was gonna keep playing, and I said, "You know I've got to quit." Even though I beat him for about ten thousand that day, I was still keeping up appearances.

Well, there isn't much more to the story from here. The next day it seemed like everybody west of Arkansas was in that joint, and I just kept lowering the spot and raising the stakes. Before long I was getting six points and playing for six thousand a game and just *barely* beating him.

Sure enough, someone did show up who knew me, a hustler from Oklahoma City named Buck Barrett. Old Buck was smart enough to keep his mouth shut, but when I went into the men's room, he got ahold of me and said, "Slim, why don't you take four and then two and really beat this man?"

I always had a pretty good reply for them wise guys. "Say, man," I said, "you're trying to tell Babe Ruth how to bat."

You'da thought that Elmo would have figured out who I was at some point, but I think he had gone so far that he was already *convinced* that I wasn't Amarillo Slim. When he had called my name a few days before, anybody in the world would have turned around and said, "Yeah? Uh-huh." I didn't even change expressions. If I had, we never would have played and Bunky really *would* have slept in that station wagon!

I know you folks want figures, but I've already learned my lesson with the tax man. Let's just say that by the time I was giving *him* a spot, about the only thing I didn't win from that man was his chain of quick presses, which was just as well, 'cause I didn't feel like sticking around Utah to liquidate them things.

AN INTERESTING STIPULATION IN INDEPENDENCE, MISSOURI

It doesn't take long for legend to spread in the pool world—especially about the bad guys—and the word was out about a guy named Happy Yaeger from Independence, Missouri, the same town where Harry S. Truman was raised and died in 1972. Everyone knew that Happy was a real good player, but even when he lost, he won. It wasn't much of a scam: If you beat him in pool, he'd just beat the hell out of you and take back his money.

Not long after playing Elmo Sands, I was playing pool at Thirty-first and Truce in Kansas City, when one of the old remnants of the Pendergast mob got a hold of me. It was no secret to anybody that the Pendergast mob was the strength of Harry Truman. They weren't so much killers as they were racketeers, and one of their guys—to mention his real name wouldn't be appropriate, so I'll call him Vinnie—came up to me and said, "There's a real good score to be made in Independence, Missouri."

I told him I knew what the score was down there—it was obvious who he was talking about.

"He plays real good, and he plays real high," said Vinnie, "but everybody who goes over there, he either cheats 'em or, if they beat him, they get hijacked."

Not one to back away from a challenge, I asked him what his intentions were, and he told me that he wanted me to go over there and beat Happy Yaeger at pool. So I told him that I'd go whip that boy, with the stipulation that if I won, it would be up to him to see to it that I kept a nice percentage of it—in addition to all my limbs.

Then he surprised me a little bit when he said, "That's exactly what I'm looking for." I kinda had an idea where he was going with this, but it didn't concern me. I just wanted to get my hands on some of old Happy's money—and, with Vinnie's protection, I knew I would keep it.

I drove to Independence, Missouri, which took about an hour from Kansas City, and there really wasn't much else to it. I just beat Happy Yaeger out of a bunch of money playing one-pocket, and, like Vinnie had asked me to do, I drove back to my hotel room at the Pilsner Hotel in downtown Kansas City.

Sure enough, Happy came to hijack me at my hotel that night. All I did was stay in my room and watch a ball game on television, but with Vinnie's boys on my side, I felt pretty safe knowing that Happy would never get to me. As far as I was concerned, Mr. Yaeger needed to get scolded for what he had done to all those other hustlers, and I didn't give it another thought. Let's just say that before old Happy made it inside the hotel, he got a little unlucky.

When I got back to Amarillo and started thinking more about what had happened, it wasn't sitting quite right with me. I was a family man now, and if making a living at pool meant putting myself in situations like that, I was ready to be done with it. By that time most people knew my reputation as a pool hustler anyway, and it was getting harder to find a game. That didn't mean I wouldn't keep my eyes open, but my days as a full-time pool player were over. It was time for me to find some more creative ways to make a buck.

I was introduced to the crowd at the Keeneland Select Sale in Lexington, Kentucky, wearing a black Russian wolf fur coat that is a piece of property that no one in their right mind should own. *(Courtesy of the author)*

4

Have I Got a Proposition for You: Titanic, Runyon, Moss, and More

On November 30, 1892, in the smoky back room of a general store in Rogers, Arkansas, a tough cat named Lee Thomas had just drawn to a full house and won the biggest pot of the night. He was running so good that he didn't bother to make it home to his three-room log cabin to witness the birth of his son, Alvin Clarence Thomas. Alvin—who later became "Titanic," because he sank every gambler he ever met with his famous proposition bets, and "Thompson," just because he damn felt like calling himself that—grew up in the woods at the base of the Ozarks. Rogers is only seventeen miles from my birthplace in Johnson, which makes me wonder if Ti might have been kin to me.

Ti died in Fort Worth, Texas, in 1974, at the ripe old age of eighty-two, and some say that before they put him in his grave, he handed me his torch. Quite a few folks have noted that the three slickest men this country has ever known were born in the Natural State (so called because of Arkansas's vast natural beauty). You figure out who the third one is, partner—but I'll give you a hint: It rhymes with Minton.

Ti's daddy left for good shortly after he was born, but gambling stayed in his blood. When Ti was just eleven years old, he was fishing at the twenty-foot-deep fishing hole where he used to spend all his free time with his cute little spaniel named Carlo. One day a man, who I'll call Eugene, came to the pond with a real fancy fishing rod and offered to exchange his rod for Carlo. When Ti said that he couldn't dare part with his little pup, Eugene added some cash to the deal, and when Ti said no again, Eugene demanded an explanation.

Keep in mind, Ti was only eleven at the time, and he explained that he had the smartest dog on earth. Carlo was so smart, in fact, that he could dive into the pond and retrieve the very stone that you threw in there. Eugene thought it was hogwash, and Ti told him he was so sure of it that if Carlo couldn't do it, the man could keep Carlo, and if he could, Ti would get the fishing rod. Naturally, Eugene said okay.

Eugene chose an average-size rock, and Ti marked it with an X. Eugene aimed for the deepest part of the pond, and Carlo went after it with everything he had. When Carlo came out of the water, he had a rock clenched between his teeth, and, wouldn't you know it, it had an X on it. Eugene wasn't too disturbed, though, figuring that he could get away with telling little Ti that it was only a joke.

I reckon Eugene was a little surprised when the little kid pulled out a .22! "Mister," Ti said, "I'm about as good at shooting this twenty-two as Carlo is at fetching rocks. If you don't believe me, just pick up that rock and throw it up in the air, and I'll make you another bet that I can hit it."

Ti got his fishing rod, and he sure as hell deserved it. After all, he had spent every minute of the past few days gathering all the rocks from that hole and marking 'em with an X before he threw 'em back in. Sharp kid, huh?

I had just been born in 1928 when Ti, who was also tall and slim but most would say better-looking than me, was making his way through the hustlers' part of New York City known as Jacob's Beach. Like Fats, Ti was in New York at the same time as Damon Runyon, and he was the man that Runyon used to create his character Sky Masterson, the legendary gambler who was later immortalized in *Guys and Dolls*. Even though most people connect Sky with Marlon Brando, the actor who played Sky opposite Frank Sinatra (as Nathan Detroit) in the 1955 movie, Runyon really made the character in Ti's image. It was Ti who Runyon had in mind when he wrote in "The Idyll of Miss Sarah Brown":

> Son, no matter how far you travel, or how smart you get, always remember this: Someday, somewhere, a guy is going to come to you and show you a nice brand-new deck of cards on which the seal is never broken, and this guy is going to offer to bet you that the jack of spades will jump out of this deck and squirt cider in your ear. But, son, do not bet him, for as sure as you do you are going to get an ear full of cider.

A lot of people have asked me over the years if Sky Masterson was patterned after me, but unlike old Mr. Wanderone, who ripped off the name Minnesota Fats after *The Hustler* in 1961, I told the truth for a change and gave Titanic Thompson his due.

Ti mastered the one thing that is the key to any proposition bet: understanding human nature. A poker author from England named David Spanier said, "It is the greed of the sucker that makes the hustler's skill pay," and I couldn't have said it any better myself. If you go to a person with a proposition, and if he's got any bit of larceny in him (and most men do), he'll go for it. You can't swindle an honest man, but those guys who *think* they know something are ripe for the taking. That's because the only man who's gonna make a bet is one who is looking to hustle *you*. See what I mean about turning a champion into a sucker?

I liked Titanic Thompson—most people didn't, because he did a lot of things that weren't on the square—but I was able to overlook that and respect him for what he was: the greatest proposition bettor who ever lived. I also thought he was the most talented man I've ever seen—*still do*. At the Ridglea Golf Course in Fort Worth, Ti once shot a twenty-nine on the back nine to beat a little old player that you've probably never heard of—a man who went by the name of Byron Nelson. Nelson, of course, was from *Texas* and won the Masters in 1937 and 1942.

Ti would play you right-handed and beat you, then stall a little bit and make you a bet that if you gave him a handicap, he'd play you left-handed, too. Well, heck, if you just got through playing a guy who shot par playing right-handed, you know goddamn well he couldn't play half as good from the left side. But Ti was also a scratch golfer as a lefty.

Ti could shoot a basketball, and he could shoot any kind of gun. He was also a champion bowler. Ti was the one who came up with the "hit a golf ball a mile" trick, and then he would take his suckers out to a frozen lake and that little dimpled ball would roll forever. I used that bet myself in later years—Ti had a good laugh when I told him about it.

I hate to admit this, but I couldn't hold a candle to Ti when it came to propositions. He would sit around for hours just thinking of ways to make money. One time in Missouri in the middle of the night, he dug up a signpost that said JOPLIN—20 MILES and put it back into the ground six miles up the road. The next day, just by chance of course, he rode by that sign with some gamblers and made a bet that Joplin couldn't have been more than fifteen miles away.

Another time, right before World War II, in Evansville, Indiana, Ti bought a whole truckload of watermelons from a guy on the condition that the driver would count 'em, put 'em back on the truck, and call Ti at his hotel with the exact number loaded in the truck. Then, at exactly 4:00 P.M., the man had to drive past the McCurdy Hotel, where all the gamblers gathered in the afternoons.

When the truck showed up, Ti boasted that for a hundred dollars he could guess within five the number of watermelons on the truck. Some wise guy said, "I'll give you two-to-one on that and pay the driver another ten to count 'em up." Ti guessed 413, and, wouldn't you know it, the driver counted 415.

There are a million more stories where those came from, but, as good as Ti was, the one thing I had on him was my respect for the law. Ti was reputed to have killed six men, served jail time, and got arrested as a material witness in connection with the murder of Arnold Rothstein after

Ti was found trying to collect the $475,000 that Arnie had lost to him at a poker game in New York.

Ti also had plenty of leaks. As much talent as he had, he was a sucker when it came to betting horses and playing pool—maybe because they were the only things he couldn't beat, and he needed the challenge. That old sonofagun, boy, if he would have just devoted his time and energy and effort to legitimate business rather than trying to swindle folks, he'd have made Lee Iacocca look like a coward.

THE TITANIC TRIES TO SINK THE GRAND OLD MAN OF POKER

Johnny Moss, the best poker player of his generation, was born in 1907 in the poor prairie town of Marshall, Texas, two hundred miles east of Fort Worth. By the time he was eight, his family had moved to East Dallas, and, to help support his family, Johnny took a job delivering newspapers. It didn't take him long to run into Chill Wills, who later became a famous actor, and Benny Binion, who opened the Horseshoe Casino in Las Vegas. Johnny, Chill, and Benny spent most of their time together, shooting dice in alleys and selling newspapers in the domino halls of East Dallas.

Like a lot of great poker players, Johnny, an average-size man who was bald as long as I knew him and wore thick, black-rimmed glasses, had his weaknesses—mainly that he just couldn't turn down any opportunity to gamble. I was probably still riding a tricycle at the time and didn't hear about this until much later, but in Lubbock, Texas, in 1932, at a local nine-hole course called Meadowbrook, Johnny was looking to gamble and he ran into—who else?—Titanic Thompson.

Ti had the perfect mark in Johnny, a golfer whose talent could be matched only by his ego, and sure enough, they made a $5,000 wager that Johnny couldn't shoot forty-six. Now, I know that ten over par doesn't sound like much on a nine-hole course, but there was just one itty-bitty stipulation. You see, the *only* club Johnny could use was a four-iron. Ever tried putting with one of them things?

After they posted their money and agreed to play the next day, all the money that Johnny had left in the world, $3,300, was in his pocket. Knowing her husband better than he knew himself, his wife, Virgie, a sweet little old thing, begged Johnny to at least pay the hotel bill before he went down to play the match. But Johnny wouldn't think of it. What Virgie didn't know—and, more important, what Titanic didn't know—was that Johnny had taken his four-iron to a blacksmith and had it bent in the shape of a two-iron. Sure enough, when Ti challenged him the next day to bet everything that Johnny had in his pocket, Johnny didn't hesitate. Keep in mind, now, Johnny wasn't some tourist. He had heard plenty about Ti but had so much confidence in himself that he bet all the money he had to his name. Don't get too wound up about it, neighbor. I can assure you it wasn't the first time.

With hundreds of gamblers there to witness the showdown, Johnny drove the ball a country mile with that freshly bent four-iron on the first hole and was putting for par from three feet away. Even with that four-iron, he hit it perfect, but just before it reached the hole, it bent off. Johnny couldn't imagine what had happened. He had already given the groundskeeper a hundred dollars to keep the cups in the same place they'd been when he was practicing the day before. When it happened to him again on the second hole, he couldn't figure out for the life of him what had gone wrong.

It's a sight to behold when two hustlers go head-to-head, and Johnny knew that Ti was capable of every trick in the book. After examining the area where he putted—looking for everything and anything—it finally dawned on Johnny that it couldn't be but one thing. Someone must have crept out there and raised up them cups so the ball would kick away. It wouldn't take but raising 'em an eighth of an inch, and that's exactly what Ti had done.

Some of you Square Johns out there might think that Johnny would have cried foul, but we hustlers live life by a different code. In fact, if someone is trying to cheat you, you put it on yourself that much more to whip him back. So Johnny sent one of his friends ahead on the third green to stomp that cup down—just as one of Ti's guys was raising it up on the fourth. It went like that for a hole or two, until Ti just kinda stepped out of the crowd with that old boyish grin spread over his face.

By that point they were both onto each other, and without either one of them having to speak a word, it was understood that they had figured each other out and there was no need to continue with the charade. That's what I mean about a code among gamblers. Sure, Ti wanted to fleece Johnny, but once his gimmick was found out, he knew to leave it alone. Now free to just focus on his golf game, Johnny tore that course up and sank the Titanic by shooting a forty-one. You can bet Virgie slept well that night.

While Johnny was a heckuva golfer, he became legendary for playing poker, mainly in Dallas, Fort Worth, and Birmingham, Alabama, in the thirties, forties, and fifties, earning the nickname "The Grand Old Man of Poker." I met him for a short time in 1950 at a pool hall in Amarillo, but because I had heard from my friend Benny Binion that Johnny was the best poker player he'd ever seen, I knew better than to mess with him. And let me tell you, that Moss was a tough sonofabitch. Some doctor once told him that he'd have heart trouble when he was older, and Johnny said, "Not me, Doc. I don't have no heart."

After he and Virgie got hijacked in Alabama one time, Johnny bought a scattergun and took to carrying it with him wherever he played poker. Back in those days in Texas, and even today in Texas, it's acceptable to carry a gun. Shoot, to tell you how much poker has changed over the years, right now at the Bellagio in Las Vegas, a man can't even smoke a cigarette while he's playing poker. Now, that suits me just fine, because I gave up smoking a long time ago, but just think about how drastically the times have changed.

SHOOTING SKEET, THE CASE OF THE DISAPPEARING GUN, AND A VERY SMART CAT

The first time I met Ti was at a golf course in East Dallas called Tennison Park but known by everybody as just Hustlers' Park. I had heard his name a lot and generally did my best to avoid him. Even Johnny Moss, who ended up partnering with Ti after that golf match, said that Ti wasn't loyal to anybody but himself and was a tough man to get along with.

Then I was in Tucson, Arizona, in the early sixties, playing a guy from New York—let's just call him Ira—some pool and golf. Ira was a little bit connected, but that didn't stop me from gambling with him. Ti had just turned seventy, but he was still going strong, fleecing people by pretending he couldn't shoot skeet, then picking them all out of a clear blue sky. I'm a hell of a shot, but I knew better than to get involved with Ti. Then, when Ira said that he wanted to back me, I figured I had nothing to lose. It was a real simple bet: All I had to do was knock down twenty-three of the twenty-five clay pigeons that they shot up into the sky.

I wasn't quite as good a shot as Ti, but I was still pretty damn accurate, and, since I was better than even money to hit at least twenty-four, hitting twenty-three seemed like a cinch. The first time I downed twenty-two of them. I could have sworn that I hit 'em all, but there wasn't much to argue about. Ira still had faith in me, and the second time he bet on me, I hit twenty-two again.

Well, I knew that what I could smell cooking wasn't on the fire, so I sent Ti off in the opposite direction, then went down to check on the skeet they'd been putting up for us. They all looked okay. It wasn't until I started kicking 'em that this one little fella jarred my foot good and proper. He was made of metal, and I found two others that were as well. Naturally, I switched the skeet and told Ira to make it Texas rules, and he managed to get his money back. Ti never could figure out how I downed those metal birds of his, but don't worry, he was already on to the next thing.

A few days later I was playing Ira some one-pocket for big money, and Ti showed up to put a little action on me. We played a few games, and then, all of a sudden, Ti started a squabble with Ira—and for no good reason whatsoever. Ti was way out of line.

"Ti, for Christ's sake," I said, "let up on this man. You're wrong."

"Don't try to let this sonofabitch off the hook," Ti said.

Like I said before, Ti wasn't the most docile cat in the world. So when he nonchalantly put his hands in the air while he was talking, you could see his .45 tucked into the front of his pants just as clear as Sunday. Everybody in the room saw it, but Ira didn't care none; he had some friends of his own who liked to pack heat. The argument between the two of 'em got a little more intense, until finally I told Ti, who had money on me in the pool match, "I've had enough of this bullshit. You're going to have to cut that shit out, or this game's over."

"You can't stop the game," Ti said. "You've got to play."

So I told Ti something along the lines of he could go have sex with himself and that I wasn't going to play under those kinds of conditions.

Ti started in on Ira again, and Ira said, "Sure you're going to raise hell. You're all rodded up. What do you think I'm gonna do when you got that big-ass pistol?"

This is where it got interesting. In a room full of people who had *seen* that gun, myself included, Ti said to Ira, "Man, I ain't never carried a pistol in my life."

"*What?*" Ira said.

"I said I ain't never carried a gun in my life."

Everybody knew better—Ti didn't have the best reputation when it came to sparing human life. And everybody had seen that .45! Ti had made it obvious for a reason.

So Ira thought he'd get smart and said, "I bet you've got one on you."

"You can bet whatever you can pay off," Ti said. "I never carried one in my life, and I wasn't about to start now."

Ti hadn't moved from where he'd been standing at the head of this pool table. Figuring he finally had his first cinch to beat the famous Titanic, Ira bet whatever it was he had in his pocket; I think it was $2,800. Being as I had seen that gun with my own two eyes, and that there was nowhere it could have gone, I was tempted to make a wager myself. But I'd been around Ti long enough to know that if I bet, I was liable to get an ear full of cider.

"Now we've got to search you, Ti," Ira said.

"Well, *suuuuuure*," Ti said.

Ti took off his coat and laid it on the pool table, and everybody there patted it down. Then they made him take off his pants. Then his socks—everything! After they'd stripped this boy stark naked, we looked in all the pockets around that pool table, under that table, all over the damn place, and it wasn't there.

Nobody had walked up to Ti during the squabble and taken it away.

Everybody in the room had seen it. He couldn't have thrown it in the wastebasket; there wasn't one around. And *I saw it*—and I wasn't drunk neither. I don't drink, and I don't hallucinate. We never did find that gun, and even years later Ti never did tell me how he did it. I reckon if he did, I could have made a lot of money making things disappear. But that was Ti—he took some of his best secrets to his grave.

Ira, on the other hand, had a knack for being on the wrong side of these bets. Not long after our pool match in Tucson, I had gone to New York to play him some golf, and when we finished on the golf course, we'd always go to this pub in Manhattan called the Office. This particular morning I had given a newspaper boy outside my hotel fifty dollars if he'd go catch me an ordinary cat—not a kitten—and throw it into the Office at exactly four o'clock.

That afternoon at the Office, I made sure that Ira had a seat facing the door. I knew that this bet would be a whole lot easier if he saw the cat first and I just sat there drinking my usual, a Coca-Cola in a six-ounce bottle. We'd been sitting there a little while, and this thin little yellow-and-white alley cat suddenly appeared.

Ira saw it, and he said, "What in the hell is a cat doing in a nice place like this?"

So I went out of my way to look at this cat, and I said, "I can tell you what he's doing in here. That's a real smart cat."

"What do you mean, that's a smart cat? That's nothin' but an old alley cat."

So I leaned over and looked again, and I said, "No, he's real smart."

"Well, what do you mean?"

"You can tell by the distance of the width between his ears that he's got a lot of brains. That's a smart cat."

"Shit, Slim, you're the craziest bastard I ever saw."

"Yeah, but I tell you he's smart."

"Like what?"

"Like I bet that cat would come over here and pick up my Coke bottle, take it out the door, and put it on top of your car."

Then it got *real* quiet in that room. There were a lot of people there—

very few sharp ones and a lot of rich ones, and Ira said, "Now, what is this?"

"I don't know," I said. "I just think that cat can pick up that Coke bottle and take it out there."

"Let me tell you," Ira said, "there's a lot of things he *can't* do."

Now I knew he was fixing to bet, and he didn't disappoint me. One of his buddies was a lawyer, and he got out a yellow legal pad and started writing down the stipulations. I bet Ira ten thousand, and I bet two others another grand each.

I had hid a pair of heavy welder's gloves in a convenient place, and I went and put them on. See, if you grab any cat by the tail and start dragging him, he'll turn over and scratch you. But if you grab him with both hands, right at the base of his tail, you can keep him off you. So if you grab him and drag him, that cat will grasp at everything there is. And, as you know, a cat lets his claws in and out.

If you drag a cat over that bottle, sooner or later, his claws are gonna grasp that raised edge on the bottle. As long as you got a hold of his tail, he'll hold on to it. It's one of those things that you kinda have to see to believe, but trust me, partner, I had tested it more than once.

So I picked the cat up by the tail and dragged him over the bottle, which he grabbed with his claws. I carried the cat out the door and found Ira's automobile. Just as we got there, I turned loose the cat's tail, and he turned loose the bottle.

That little trick created a furor—it was so much fun. Everybody laughed and laughed about it, and it wasn't even a hot score. Once word got out, it seems like everyone in New York City tried it, and a few days later the *New York Post* ran a story titled "A City Full of Sore-Tailed Cats."

TITANIC: A BETTER GAMBLER THAN HE WAS A MAN

Because our paths crossed a fair amount, I did a few things with Ti, but I never was comfortable around him. Ti was every bit as treacherous as his reputation—and that meant not even sparing people he called friends. If Ti told me that we were going somewhere to beat somebody playing dominoes, don't worry, we'd beat 'em, but on the way home Ti would be trying to position himself to beat me out of what I had won right there along with him. And he didn't care how he did it either—that's not speaking real good for a guy.

As for poker, if Ti couldn't cheat, he wasn't much of a player. He played, but he didn't think he was supposed to play on the square. And even though people knew he was a cheater, he still could always seem to find a game, because everybody wanted the chance to test himself against a legend. These folks also thought they could protect themselves, but Ti was up-to-date on every form of skullduggery, and most couldn't.

With all the money that Ti made in his life, you'd think he would have retired with a fortune. But that's where you'd be wrong. Ti never did retire, and by the time he was in the nursing home in Fort Worth, he was stone-cold broke. Even there—and you can read about this yourself in the book *The Unsinkable Titanic Thompson*—the eighty-two-year-old would journey out to the local pitch-'n'-putt course, where he would hustle a two-dollar game—and shoot par!

I never did tell anybody this, but in those later years Ti was so broke that his wife of nineteen years, Jeanette, had to divorce him so that her income wouldn't prevent him from qualifying for government assistance. Rumor has it that a skinny old pool hustler helped pay his other expenses, but I'll deny it to this day. It wouldn't surprise me, though, because gamblers do have a way of looking after each other, and, shortcomings aside, Ti was one of us—and a legend at that—and he deserved to be taken care of in his old age.

OUTHOOFING HORSES

Some would say that my proposition bets have allowed Ti's legacy to live on, but I'm not all that sentimental. I was just trying to earn a buck with my bets, and horses and footraces seemed to go hand in hand. I've probably run thirty footraces in my life for money—I've run barefoot, and I've run a lot of races where I started flat on my back and facing the wrong direction. I could run, and the novelty was that, since I'm a tall, lanky cat, no one thought I could run short races. But I was a dasher through and through, and anything beyond a quarter mile nearly killed me.

I also have a perfect record in my career running the hundred-yard dash against a racehorse. Jesse Owens couldn't beat a Thoroughbred on the square, but I sure as hell did. The key to this bet is to make sure that the hundred-yard race is fifty yards one way and fifty yards another—that's a hundred-yard dash! Ain't nobody said anything about it being a "continuous" hundred-yard dash. I would always finish the race before the jockey could turn the racehorse around. Mind you, I'm not talking about a cutting horse, but a *race*horse—a big, powerful Thoroughbred. Heck, it takes them big things so long to turn around that even Secretariat would have been drawing dead against me.

All these itty-bitty Texas towns, most don't have a real racetrack, an oval, but it's not too hard to find a straightaway for a match race. A match race is a straight-up race between two horses—the most famous one being the 1938 Pimlico Special, which pitted Seabiscuit against War Admiral. Those two descendents of the great Man o' War ran their eyeballs out against each other, but it was Seabiscuit, the people's champ, who crossed that wire first. I remember my daddy talking about that one when I was just a pup. You hardly see a match race at a big racetrack today, but in these Texas towns they're still all the rage. "Why, my horse is faster than your horse" and all that kind of big Texas talk can get a race set up in a hurry. Since I own, breed, and race horses, I was a regular at these straightaways, and every time I showed up, there was always somebody there to challenge me to a footrace. And after I'd win three or four of these races, they'd start bringing in faster and faster people to run against me.

One time at the San Angelo racetrack, which is about 250 miles south of Amarillo, I made a bet with a guy named Pinky Rhoden, one of the big wheels in the liquor industry in Texas, to race some guys he knew in the hundred-yard dash. A few weeks before the race, I learned that Pinky had tracked down a bunch of speedsters. One of the runners, whose name I don't want to mention, held a track record in the hundred-yard dash before it was broken by "Bullet" Bob Hayes, the famous track star who later went on to be a wide receiver for the Dallas Cowboys.

Since I wasn't going to be the fastest runner there, I knew I had to think of some sort of gimmick. You've seen horse races; the starting gate that the horses break from is an electric gate that swings open. So I went down to the track a few days before, put on some thick welder's gloves, and locked my hands on the front of the gate. Then I practiced having that gate open and shoot me out of it a million miles an hour. In the beginning I couldn't keep myself up and fell facefirst a bunch of times. But I practiced a long time breaking from the starting gate until I could keep my balance after that start and stay right in stride.

When I showed up at the track in San Angelo, I said to Pinky, "About that race today, since we're at a racetrack, why don't we do what the horses do?"

"Slim, what are you talking about?" Pinky said.

"Well, the horses break from the gate, don't they?"

"They sure do."

"Okay, then me and them runners should start in the gate."

What did Pinky care? He had a world-class sprinter ringing for him, and he had no problem agreeing to it. When that gate swung open, sure enough, it shot me out like a cannonball—just the way I had practiced it. I was ten yards in front while they were just getting out of their track stances. There weren't many people at that time who could give me three steps, but Pinky's champion could have spotted me four or five. But my being ten yards ahead before he took a step was far too much for him to overcome.

After I collected the loot, the guys got to talking about a bet in which you had to hold on to a horse's tail for a quarter of a mile. I knew this was all but impossible, but my ego got the best of me, and I ended up making a big bet that I could. I don't know what I was thinking, but fresh off my victory against a world-class sprinter, that hubris led me to believe that I could figure out a way to win that bet.

I practiced for a long, long time, and I fell down so goddamn much that I didn't have a bit of hide nor hair left on my elbows or chin or backside. After trying different strategies, mainly just trying to hold on for dear life and match that horse stride for stride, which got awful painful, I was all but defeated.

Then it hit me. What if I tied a knot in the horse's tail and put a little leather strap on it that I tied to my wrist? This way I'd be attached to the horse, but I wouldn't have to hold on to it, and I could concentrate on running. The first time I tried it, the horse nearly pulled me in two. Then I tinkered with it and figured out that, instead of trying to run, I should just let him pull me so I just kinda *bounced*. All I really did was get behind the horse and let him drag me as I sort of just hopped along. You'd get sour with me if I told you that you'd have to see it to believe it, but it was just one of them things, and, boy, did I practice.

I went back to the racetrack in San Angelo, and all them folks were lined up to see it. I don't know if they were more interested in seeing me get killed or taking my money, but it seemed like the whole town was there for it. Well, it was just like another practice run, since I had already done it dozens of times by now. I did hang on to that horse's tail for a quarter of a mile and made a nice score. To this day I don't know of anybody else *insane* enough to make such a proposition.

BROAD JUMPING IN AMARILLO
(AND I DON'T MEAN JUMPING OVER BROADS)

When word had spread around Texas about all my footraces, it seemed like everywhere I turned, someone else was trying to set a trap. And, like I've said many times, all trappers don't wear fur caps. I was playing golf in Amarillo with a friend of mine named Alex Phillips at the Ross Rogers Municipal Golf Course, which is still there in the northeast part of town. We played eighteen holes that morning and agreed to take a break and come back and play eighteen more.

Phillips is one of them real nice guys who wouldn't harm a fly and just liked to play for a few bucks to make it interesting. During our second round, I noticed on the third hole that we'd picked up not necessarily a spectator—we had a bunch of people watching—but a caddy who was following my opponent around. It was a young black kid who I had never seen before, which was unusual, since I knew just about every caddy in town, much less on this course. This kid looked like he just kind of floated when he walked, and with those long legs, he looked like he could outrun a gazelle. So I said to myself, Well, look what we have here. Chances are here's a sonofabitch who can fly.

We were on the fifth hole, and Phillips started to set his trap. "Slim," he said, "can you outrun everybody on the golf course?"

"And carry you piggyback. That wouldn't be no problem for me."

"I doubt if you can outrun everybody out here on the golf course," Phillips said.

So I started limping a little and told him that I injured my heel on the last hole and that I didn't think I could run too well. But if he'd like, I'd bet him that I could beat anyone on the golf course in the broad jump, or what they call the long jump in the Olympics.

So we got down to the sixth hole, and Phillips said, "I'm betting you a thousand dollars you can't jump farther than my caddy."

Against my better judgment, I agreed to the bet. This wasn't the first time that my mouth had gotten me into a spot my body couldn't back up. Then, as soon as we had posted our money, Phillips started to draw a line where you break dirt to start, and I knew I better think fast.

"No," I said to Phillips. "We're on the golf course, so we'll jump from a golf club. I'll just lay a two-iron down there." Then I said, "If you step on the other side of it, you automatically lose. No second chances."

"That's okay, isn't it?" Phillips asked, and the boy agreed.

Knowing that I needed to use some psychology to win this bet, I went over there to where the kid was putting on some track shoes. *Track shoes*, I said—seems Phillips came prepared and old Slim was looking like a sucker. Anyhow, I bent over to tie my golf shoes, and I said to this caddy, who looked like he could jump farther than a goosed frog, "You know who these people are?"

"Yes, sir, Mr. Slim."

"Young man," I said to him, "let me give you some friendly advice. Phillips and his buddies are some tough customers, and if you step on the other side of that golf club and lose them a bundle of money, they're liable to kick your ass all the way down to the creek and back. I reckon that you might not even make it off this golf course alive. Of course, if I just out-jump you, that's a horse of a different color."

"They'll really kill me," he said, "won't they?"

"Be careful, son, don't break dirt."

We tossed a coin, and because I won the flip, I made the kid jump first. He went back about forty yards, and he came flying down through there like hell out of the blue yonder, and I was glad that I hadn't challenged him to a footrace. But just as he started approaching the golf club, he got real tentative and took off about three feet before the marker. He wasn't about to step over that two-iron—not after what I'd told him.

When it came my turn, I got a running start, and, using that old Mineral Wells Junior High School form, I took off just as I reached the club and leapt like there was no tomorrow. Turned out that even with a three-foot handicap, I had only beaten him by two inches.

That was a perfect example of how, even when you're an underdog, you can use psychology to win. I know that lesson wasn't lost on Phillips when he handed me a cool grand.

DID YOU KNOW I COULD TRAIN A JAILHOUSE FLY?

When I would go back to Arkansas to visit my mama, who lived until 1986 (my daddy died in 1989), I would go to a town where there was always either a pool game or a poker game in the back of this bar. Being that it was a small town, I knew just about everyone there. This was in the early sixties, and I'd rather not get into where or what this place exactly was, 'cause it's one of those things that some folks could catch serious hell for. Anyhow, at this little bar one day, the sheriff said to me, "Slim, I got the biggest drug dealer in the South in my jail."

"Is he charged with anything?" I asked.

"No. We were advised he was around, so we're gonna book him for vagrancy, since he doesn't have no visible means of support."

"I imagine he's got *some* means."

"Yeah, Slim, he's got an awful lot of money on deposit—that's what I come here for."

I asked him if it was against the law to put me in there, and he said it wasn't, and for the first time and only time in my life, I was behind bars. So there were two people in this cell—me and this drug lord, who I'll call Lorenzo. We got to talking, and I said, "I got a little strength down here. If there's any kind of food you want, I can get it. You don't have to eat that prison crap."

"That's pretty nice," Lorenzo said. "I'm about a half-ass coffee hound."

"Damn, man, I'm glad you said it, because I am, too," I said, which was the truth.

So I hollered at the jailer that we wanted a couple of cups of coffee, and the jailer said, "Do you use cream and sugar?"

"Yeah," Lorenzo said, "I like sugar, but I'm kind of spoiled to it—I like that lump sugar."

"Well, hell, we got a box of it," the jailer said. All he was asking for was a sugar cube instead of granulated sugar, and the jailer brought over a dozen or so cubes on a paper plate. We kept chatting while we were drinking coffee, and I picked up five of the sugar cubes—it looked like I was just clowning around with 'em—and I put them about six inches apart on a bench, and I said, "I wonder if there are any flies around here."

"There was a while ago. Why?"

"In case there is, I can train a fly to do some tricks."

"You can, shit! I never heard of anybody training a fly."

"Then, you haven't seen me. If we can get us a fly around here some-where, I can make that fly land on a certain one of those sugar cubes."

He was a pretty sharp guy, so I didn't press it, but about twenty min-utes later, we saw some flies buzzing around. "Okay, man," I said, "it's a shame you ain't got no money, or I'd dust you. I'm gonna tell you where that fly's gonna land."

"I got money on deposit," Lorenzo said.

"That's what you say, but how do I know that?"

You see, neighbor, there's two elements of the hustle—preying on a man's ego and preying on his larceny. The larceny part is him thinking that he's got the best of it and he's gonna sucker me. Any guy that makes you a bet thinks he's gonna win it, or he wouldn't bet it. The ego part is questioning whether he's got any money.

"Call that jailer back here," he said, and when the jailer came over, Lorenzo said, "Tell Mr. Slim that I've got money on deposit."

The jailer wasn't in on it—the big boss was—and he said, "He's *really* got some money on deposit—thirty-eight thousand dollars, to be exact." Of course, I already knew what he had. By now, he was itching to fleece me, and I pointed at one of the sugar cubes and said, "Now, the fly's gonna land on *that* one—if it lands on any one of the other four first, you win."

"What's the price?" he said.

The actual odds were four to one, but unless he thought he was getting some sort of edge, I knew he wasn't gonna bet. The other side of it was, if I lay him even money, he would have woken up and known it was a swindle. So I said, "I'll take 3½ to 1."

He shook his head, and, being that he was a hustler and all, he said he wanted 2½ to 1.

"Well, sure you do. I'll go in the middle and make it three to one."

"No," he said. "I'll lay 2½ to 1 since you're so fuckin' confident."

By then I had put up enough of a fight to show that it seemed like I was just gambling with him, so I agreed to it. But then he said, "How do I know you got any money?"

So we called the jailer over again, and he told Lorenzo that I had plenty of money—in excess of $38,000—and Lorenzo said he wanted to bet every damn bit of it.

"You got a diamond or a Rolex out there?" I said, trying to play to his ego a little more.

"I don't know what you're trying to do," he said, "but do you wanna bet or not?"

So, just to keep the figures easy at 2½ to 1, he laid $37,500 to my $15,000 that I couldn't get a fly to land on the sugar cube second from the left. He was looking around for the flies, and while his eyes weren't on me, I put my pinkie in my mouth right quick and put it on the sugar cube I had picked.

Sure enough, there were two flies, and when they started coming over to that bench, we moved out of the way so they wouldn't be scared to land. These two flies dive-bombed—they just zeroed right in and fell on the cube I had chosen. That poor sonofabitch could not imagine how I did it.

As soon as I won the bet, why, all of a sudden the sheriff came back there and said, "Mr. Slim, we're ready to release you." I picked up my money, and I've never seen that man since.

If you're looking to swindle someone—and I've got a feeling you might be—that's a bet that you can do on anyone. Sugar, if you get it wet, will dissolve, and when it dissolves, it gives off an aroma. Naturally, a fly is gonna go to that aroma. Those other four sugar cubes were just like marbles sitting there.

By the time the story got back to Texas, it was $50,000, but I was happy to give the boss his half and still walk away with almost $20,000. Shoot, that experience nearly made me want to become a criminal.

A BOWLING CHAMPION MAKES ME A CHALLENGE

I was in Newark, New Jersey, playing in a high-stakes poker game that just happened to be located in a back room of a bowling alley. When the game broke up, I went to the bar to get a Coca-Cola, and I heard somebody ask, "Mr. Slim, do you bowl?"

I can bowl a decent game, but I was already wise to the fact that they were fixing to set me up in a match with a bowling champion, who I'll just call Billy.

So when Billy appeared, I told him that I didn't bowl, and he said, "Well, it's a shame that you can't bowl, because I'm a high player, but I don't play poker or pool. If you could bowl, you could win a good score off me."

"I don't know about bowling," I said, "but I do about everything there damn near is that you sit down and do. What else do you play?"

He didn't play nothing else, and then something popped into my mind that I had seen done several times. So I said to this guy, "Do you think you could bowl blindfolded?"

This was in a crowd of people, and it was but another example of larceny and ego at work.

"I could probably bowl a hundred and fifty blindfolded," this champion said. "Am I allowed to walk up and feel for the gutter?"

"Yeah, once you get your ball, you can reach down and feel for the gutter so you'll know exactly where it is," I said, and I saw that agreed with him. Even though he had said one-fifty, I didn't think he would bet at that number, and if I insulted him a little, he might make a big bet. "Well, do you suppose you can bowl ninety for some cash?" I said.

"Sure can."

"Then you need to taxi up to the line. I bet you can't bowl ninety blindfolded."

"Am I allowed to have somebody get my ball?"

That was the only other thing we discussed, and I told him that he had to retrieve the ball himself. So, Billy thought about it some more, and, figuring he could use a little insurance before he posted his money, we kept negotiating. After some more back and forth, we ended up making a nice wager that he couldn't bowl seventy blindfolded. Since he was a hometown hero, all his buddies wanted to back him, and I also bet just about everybody else in the room.

You see, neighbor, I had already seen this bet done with several other folks and knew that there was no way in hell he could do it. When he threw another gutter ball in the tenth frame, his total score was a forty-three. Another champion bites the dust.

When I was in Las Vegas not too long after that, I told my buddy Doyle Brunson about this bet, and he swore up and down that he could do it. You'll be getting to know Doyle real well before long, but I'll tell you that he was a world-class athlete at one point in his life, and, while he wasn't what he once was, he still *thought* he was. So we made a sizable bet, and I even gave him a break and made the number fifty rather than seventy.

We went to a bowling alley near the Showboat Hotel east of the Strip, and it was just by chance that the bowling alley had assigned us the lane on the very end—right next to the window. Well, it wasn't but about the fourth frame when Doyle was so disoriented that he wound up and threw that bowling ball plumb through a plate-glass window! And, no, partner, he didn't score fifty.

It never does take long for news to spread in gambling circles, and about six months later I was up in Boston to give a pool exhibition with Boston Shorty and Weanie Beanie when I heard that Billy had a big windfall. I didn't know how he got it and didn't care, but I never did feel right about letting a sucker keep his hands on cash for very long—even if it meant having to go back to New Jersey to get it.

Boston Shorty said that it was a shame I'd already beat him with the blindfold bet, and I really didn't give it too much thought. Then, after we finished playing pool, I figured it was only a four- or five-hour drive to Newark, and I'd think of something along the way.

I wasn't but fifty miles outside of Boston when it dawned on me what I had to do. So I drove right to Newark airport and called a friend of mine back home named Wayne. I told him to arrange for someone to get him a real fancy chauffeur's outfit and sit tight until I made it back home.

When I got back to Amarillo, I bought us a couple of round-trip tickets to Newark, and we were on our way. When we arrived at the airport, I rented a great big Lincoln, and we drove right over to the bowling alley. The first place we went was to the bar to order a couple of Coca-Colas, and the bartender said, "Slim, good to see you. There'll be action around here now."

We chatted a little, and then I pointed to Wayne, who was in his chauffeur's outfit and had on real fancy sunglasses. "I'd like to introduce you to Wayne," I said to the bartender. "He's my driver."

Well, I knew that it wouldn't take long before everybody in there was gonna know that Wayne was my driver. Sure enough, Billy came right up to us and started talking about how hard it was to bowl blindfolded, and I said to him, "Hell, it ain't hard. I bet my driver could do it."

"He can, *shit!*" Billy said. "I've been practicing for months, and I'm a professional—and I can't do it."

That old fool thought he was going to get the best of Slim. Shoot, if he, a champion bowler, could only bowl a forty-three, how in the world was some ordinary chauffeur off the street going to bowl seventy? So I got this boy—not to mention all the hangers-on—to bet every penny in his pocket that my driver couldn't bowl a seventy. I let Billy blindfold Wayne and even allowed him to choose the ball.

Wayne got up there and bowled an eighty-two. Game, set, match, Slim.

He could have easily bowled over a hundred—I'd seen him do it several times—but that would have awakened the dead. What I never told these boys was that my driver wasn't really my driver at all. He was a friend of mine from Texas who had plenty of practice. After all, he was blind!

Dapper Texan Crandall Addington shakes Sailor's hand at the 1976 World Series of Poker. Doyle Brunson, who busted 'em both, looks on. *(Property of University of Nevada–Las Vegas, Las Vegas, Nevada)*

5

Doyle, Sailor, and Slim: Three Peas in a Pod Who Liked to Book and Bet (but Not Among Themselves)

My son, Bunky, turned eight the year that I had my second child and only daughter, Rebecca Ruth, who was born on June 10, 1959. With two kids now, I wanted to be more of a family man and spend more time at home. Shoot, I couldn't haul my baby girl around in a station wagon halfway across the country just for some damned pool game. So, in hopes of living a more traditional lifestyle and settling down to a good clean life, I gave up pool and turned to a more noble profession.

Two professions, really—booking sports and playing poker.

In Brenham, Texas, a small country town about ninety miles west of Houston, there was a great poker game above a feed store. Not long before Becky was born, I came to know two gents by the names of Doyle Brunson and Sailor Roberts, who were both just a couple of years younger than me. I had never met either one of 'em before, but I knew by reputation that they were both honorable guys, good poker players, and that they booked sports together.

Adrian Doyle Brunson, known by many as "Texas Dolly," had quite a reputation as an athlete—bowling aside, of course. Born in 1933 to a religious Baptist family in a small West Texas farming town called Longworth, he set the state record in the mile as a six-foot-three-inch, 182-pounder and was almost good enough to make the Olympics. He could also shoot baskets and earned a scholarship to Hardin-Simmons in Abilene, where he was MVP of the Border Conference, which back then included schools like Texas Tech, Arizona, and Arizona State. The Minneapolis Lakers were after him, and then, right before he was about to go on to the NBA, he was unloading Sheetrock from a train and he snapped his right leg and was in a cast for two years. He stayed at Hardin-Simmons to get a master's in administrative education, but when he learned how much money he could win playing poker, becoming a Texas road gambler seemed a lot more desirable to him than being a high-school principal.

After his injury, Doyle put on a bunch of weight, and he's constantly making bets about losing it. I'd wager he's lost seven figures betting on himself to lose weight—like I said, even the best gamblers have a leak. Even so, Doyle was always a polite cat, which made him a good fit for Sailor, who cursed like, well . . . a sailor.

Brian "Sailor" Roberts was from San Angelo, Texas, where he was a star football player. He first learned to gamble shooting dice as a caddy at the tender age of twelve and then honed his skills in the navy during the Korean War. Sailor was only about five-seven and started to get pudgy as he got older, just as his hair started to thin. His trademark was these ugly-looking short-sleeved jumpsuits in all these crazy colors that looked like beach towels. Sailor was about as good a poker player as Doyle and me, but he was lazy. If he threw a hundred-dollar chip in the pot and it rolled off the table to where he had to bend his elbow to pick it up, he'd leave it there and just throw in another. And as sharp as he was, Sailor had plenty of gamble in him and seemed to have a hard time holding on to money. He probably got rich fifteen times in his life and was broke every time within a year.

During this poker game in Brenham, Doyle, who was always on the lookout for a game, asked me if I played poker in Amarillo. I told him that there wasn't much poker there, which was true, but if he was ever in town, he could call me, and if there was a game going, I'd take him to it.

Sure enough, about three weeks later Doyle got in touch with me at my home. He and Sailor had gone to play poker in Slaton, a little community outside of Lubbock, which is about 120 miles south of Amarillo, and by the time they arrived, the game had broken up. So I invited Doyle and Sailor to my house, and we played head-up Texas Hold'em. I played one of 'em for a while, and then I played the other. A few hours later, I had busted them both.

"Where are you all gonna go now?" I said.

Sailor, who was as honorable a sonofabitch that's ever walked down the turnpike, said, "Shit, we ain't gonna go nowhere. If we get a flat going home, we don't have enough money to change the tire."

I don't remember whether it was $1,500 or $2,500, but I handed them some money and said, "Take this and get you a game."

They both said, practically at the same time, "Slim, we'll take care of this."

Everybody says that, but I wished them good luck, and they left. It wasn't but ten days later when I got a call from Western Union, and there was my money. Then, the next time I went to Midland to play poker, Doyle was in the game, and he said, "You wanna swap twenty-five percent?"

He said it right out loud. There was nothing wrong with that—we weren't gonna show each other our hands. The deal was that if you lost, whatever you lost was on you, but if you won, 25 percent of the winnings would go to the other guy. So, when the game was over, there were two winners: Doyle and me.

When Sailor showed up after the game, we all got to talking. Those two were already partners as bookmakers in Fort Worth, and they played the same money in poker. We decided that if we all joined up, we could expand the booking operation and watch out for each other when we played poker on the road. The rest is gambling history.

While I had always taken wagers—from the Pesky World Series in 1946 to the Kentucky Derby in 1947 to the GI World Series in 1948—nothing was ever too formal. But in 1959, Doyle, Sailor, and I set up a bookmaking operation and opened an office in Midland. Our choice of cities wasn't an accident either. Midland is in the Permian basin—an area full of oil and home to more millionaires per capita than anywhere in the country. It's also adjacent to Odessa, where a lot of poker was played in the sixties. Plus, I liked that it was a good two hundred miles south of Amarillo, because I always tried to keep my gambling away from my family. While I'll argue with you until the day I die that gambling is an honorable profession, it wasn't a field of endeavor I wanted my family involved in.

Doyle, Sailor, and I made book all winter, and the rest of the year we'd play poker. I once went a whole summer without seeing the sun—I'd play poker all night, go to bed at dawn, and get up at sundown. Man, those were some good times, and I consider myself lucky to have run into those guys. They were as good as partners as they were friends.

Don't misunderstand, when I say we were "partners" in poker, very rarely would the three of us play at the same time, but even when two of us played, everybody knew we were partners, and we never made a signal to one another in our lives. We just shared each other's wins and losses.

We always had a hell of a lot of fun together and loved to gamble among ourselves. In our office during football season, we'd even bet on TV game shows. *The Match Game*, that show with Gene Rayburn, where you'd say a word and your partner had to match it, was probably our favorite. We'd bet for more money than they were playing for on the show. The only time there was an argument was when Doyle and I said the answer to a question was the White House—which was right—and Sailor, God love him, tried to argue that the Capitol and the White House were the same thing. It looked like there was gonna be a killing over that one!

All the while our bookmaking operation kept growing, and when we took over another man's book in Fort Worth, I went down there to oversee it. As I've said, football is religion to folks in Texas, and we never ran short of customers. People always ask me what kind of action we took, and I'll give you the same answer I gave to my customers when they asked what my limit was: "You can bet more than you can afford to lose." We'd let a guy bet ten thousand on a game if he wanted to—and that amounts to about thirty thousand today.

I'm not gonna lie and tell you it was always easy, that we won every bet we ever booked or that we didn't have no trouble with the law. Back then bookmaking was illegal, but it wasn't a felony, and we didn't have much trouble in Midland or Fort Worth. Then, out of the clear blue sky, I was in the office one day in Fort Worth when the cops raided us. While this was going on, Doyle had called in, and when he didn't recognize the voice on the other end of the phone—it was the chief detective—Doyle said, "This is Vern over at the Sixty-six service station. I was looking for that Amarillo Slim guy. We finished washing his car, and I was calling to see if he wants it greased."

This policeman said, "Sir, you just go ahead and grease his car."

Doyle about died laughing, the dirty bastard. That day ended up being one I'd like to forget. After getting raided by the police in the afternoon, I got hijacked that night by parties unknown. That's just the life of a gambler. Between the law, the hijackers, and the inevitable losing streaks, there was always some kind of challenge. But as long as booking wasn't a felony, we just kept taking more and more action, sweeping up the poker games, and laughing our tails off traveling through Texas.

ONE RULE: NO GAMBLING AMONG OURSELVES

I've always done a lot of hunting, and some time around 1960, Doyle and Sailor asked to go with me to Mexico to hunt blue pigeon and white-wing dove, maybe even get us a jaguar. I had just bought a new Pontiac

Bonneville station wagon, and we left from our office in Midland to pick up our permit to enter Mexico and get insurance on my vehicle before we crossed the border. Our first stop was El Paso, Texas, just outside of Juárez, Mexico. El Paso is an old border town that's filled with colorful characters and plenty of cats looking to gamble. Shoot, what else is there to do over there?

That day we went to the horse races at Sunland Park, and we played like hell, booking other people's bets, betting among ourselves, and betting at the windows. That night we went to the jai-alai games and bet on those, too. None of us could even spell jai alai, much less know who the best player was, but we just took the action that came our way and made some money doing it.

We got a good night's sleep in a nice hotel, got up the next morning, went through customs, and then headed down to Chihuahua, Mexico. Our plan was to catch the narrow-gauge train over the Sierra Madres and come out at Los Moches, the coastal town on the Baja California side—a good five-hundred-mile trek.

Knowing that we had a tendency to make wagers with one another, Doyle, Sailor, and I made a pact that we weren't going to gamble among ourselves. The way I saw it, gambling among friends could only lead to dissension, so we all agreed not to make any bets among ourselves and to concentrate on having fun. It was supposed to be just a simple vacation south of the border—a few days of relaxation with good Mexican food, hunting, and some crazy dancing. I always could waltz and do the two-step pretty good, but I never could figure out that damn jitterbug.

We had just started into the edge of the mountains after we left Juárez, and I was doing about ninety on this beat-up dirt road, when we saw a little old mountain out there yonder. Sailor was in the front seat, and Doyle was in back, and just like it was nothing, Doyle said, "Slim, how long you think it'd take you to shimmy up the side of that there mountain?"

So I kinda ducked down to look out the window, and I said, "Well, I could run up there before sundown." Sailor bent over to look up, too, and said, "I doubt it. You're not as young as you used to be, pops."

It was just the regular old banter, and nothing more was said.

Besides, I knew better than to stir things up. Then we were entering into the eastern side of the Sierra Madres, and some of those peaks were starting to get a little bit of size to 'em. So we saw this big old mountain a few miles up the road, and Sailor said, "I guess you could shimmy up that thing before dark?"

Just in jest, I said, "That wouldn't be no problem for me." We kept scooting down the road and getting a little closer to it, and it wasn't as big as we had thought it was, and Doyle said, "Hell, I could climb that thing in three hours."

"You could *what?*" Sailor said.

"I could climb it in three hours," Doyle said again. "Easy."

And, like I said, brother, I had that station wagon's ears back—I had to be doing close to a hundred by now—and when we got just about parallel to that mountain, Sailor leaned over, shoved my skinny ass to the door, and slammed on the brakes with his left foot. By God, we were all over the road before we came to a screeching halt—it's a wonder that car didn't flip upside down.

"All right, get your fat ass out of this car!" Sailor said.

"All right, for what?" Doyle said.

"It's a bet. You got three hours to reach the top of that mountain."

I raised hell trying to stop it, but when two gamblers both think they can make a score, it was gonna take more than 170 pounds of me to stop them. I didn't like it, but there wasn't much more I could do when both of them agreed to a $2,500 wager. The bet was on.

Thinking that it might be a little cool up on that mountain, Doyle took a jacket with him, and the signal was that if he got to the top, he would wave it. I had binoculars, so I knew we'd be able to see him.

Doyle . . . well, he wasn't over 300 pounds then like he is now—probably about 240 or so—and even with the leg injury, he was still a great athlete. I didn't think he could do it, but I knew he'd have a heart attack trying, because that competitive nature comes out when money and pride are on the line. So, when Doyle started hiking up that thing, I said to Sailor, "We're liable to lose our buddy."

"I hope the fat-ass faints and can't climb that mountain," Sailor said. "I ought to take the grande rifle"—he called my big seven-millimeter magnum the "grande rifle"—"and if he looks like he's gonna make it, just shoot around him up there and scare him to death. He'll come back down in a hurry."

We sat there waiting, and every once in a while we could see him. And, wouldn't you know it, Doyle shimmied up that peak like a mountain goat on a mission. I took out my binoculars, and there he was, waving his jacket. It probably didn't take him but an hour and a half, and when he came back down, just before getting back into the car, Doyle said, "Hell, I coulda done it in twenty minutes if the price was right."

Sailor was hotter than a peanut parcher, cussing Doyle up and down until Doyle finally said, "All right, you know what Slim says."

"Fuck, Slim," Sailor said. "He's got more sayings than a whore has diseases."

"Well, it don't really matter about Slim," Doyle said, "but he's right when he says that quick pay *does* make lasting friendships."

So Sailor, who was as stubborn as a mule, counted out the $2,500, but he wouldn't hand it to Doyle and instead just threw the green on the floor of the wagon. Now, that was an insult.

Doyle, another proud man, refused to pick it up. That money lay there for a long time, and every time I looked at it just lying on the floor-board of my wagon, I said, "No more gambling among ourselves on this here road trip." The last thing I wanted was any dissension among friends, and it was important that I lay down the law—again!

Later on we stopped for some gas, and I said to Doyle, "You oughta pick that money up."

"I'm not gonna pick it up," Doyle said. "That sonofabitch can either pay me or stiff me. I wouldn't have thrown his money on the floor."

Well, you know how that goes. Sailor cursed him out and told him to pick up the damn money. Finally, we arrived in Chihuahua, and I picked up the money and gave it to Doyle. We checked in to three different rooms at the Chihuahua Hilton and made arrangements to catch the train at 10:00 A.M. the next day. Before we headed up to our rooms to clean up before dinner, I reiterated our pact: "Let's all make an agreement not to gamble among ourselves anymore for the trip."

"Well, shit," Sailor said, "I'm twenty-five hundred loser to that fat sonofabitch. There ain't *no* agreement like that for me."

So now Doyle chimed in—this was more of a rib on Sailor than anything else—and said, "That's right, we're not gonna bet no more among ourselves. Your twenty-five hundred's gone, you sucker."

But I calmed them turkeys down, and we made an agreement that until the trip was over, we would not gamble with one another—period. I went to my room to get ready for dinner and got held up on the phone for a while, and when Doyle and Sailor came to my room all ready to go, I hadn't even gotten started. I went into the bathroom to shave, and every now and then I'd hear *click*. I didn't think nothing of it, and then again I'd hear *click*. When I finished up, I walked out of the bathroom, and Doyle and Sailor had my hunting cap layin' right up in the middle of the bed, and they were pitching pesos at it.

I didn't pay it no mind, and I said, "All right, men, it's time to get some grub."

"Get some grub, your fanny," Doyle said. "Go eat yourself, you sonofabitch. He's got me eight-thousand loser pitching at that hat. I'm not ready to leave for nothin'."

Then Doyle collected himself a bit and laid in on Sailor. "Naturally this sonofabitch wants to lose. He's got his mountain money back, and he's now about fifty-five hundred winner."

They were ribbing each other mercilessly, and Sailor said, "We'll just stay and pitch. I'll bust your fat ass, and we'll put you on a bus back to Midland, while Slim and I go kill that jaguar."

"I thought we weren't gonna gamble with one another," I said.

"Forget not gambling with one another," Doyle said. "I'm down eight grand to this piece of trailer trash pitching pesos."

So they pitched for a little while longer, and after Doyle got most of his money back, we finally left. Then, when we got to dinner, we took the oath once again—no more gambling among ourselves.

The next morning we went down to the train station, and I watched 'em put my station wagon on a flatcar before I boarded the train. This was a real famous train ride. It started in Presidio, Texas, then it went to Chihuahua, over the Sierra Madres, and came out on the Baja California side at Los Moches. So we were chugging along on the train, just making conversation, and I looked out the window and said, "Boy, let me tell you, this is real good grass."

"What do you mean 'real good grass'?" Sailor asked.

"Well, look at it. It's up five, six inches high, and I know it's got a lot of protein because it catches the snow that melts off those mountains, and that's high in nitrate."

So I was explaining why it was real good grass, and Doyle said, "How many head would that run to a section?"

"I think that it would run at least forty cows to a section," I said.

This was before I owned my ranch, but I've always been around animals, and I had a pretty good idea how many cows a piece of land could support—a section of land is six hundred and forty acres—judging from the quality of the grass. Sailor, on the other hand, didn't seem to think much of my ability to do so.

"You don't know a cow from a goddamn goat," Sailor said—and now I knew what was coming.

"Well," I said, "I'll bet that it will carry at least forty cows."

Damn it!

Here I had gone to all that trouble establishing those rules, and I was breaking them myself. But, as far as I was concerned, if Sailor wanted to give away his money, I wasn't gonna stop him. And there was no reasoning with them boys anyway, so the game was on.

We bet $2,000, and now we needed to find somebody to tell us who was right. We walked down to the next car and found some men with cowboy hats who were having a whiskey breakfast. Figuring they were cattlemen, we all agreed that whatever they said went.

Since Doyle wasn't betting, he was designated to go ask 'em. He went up there all polite like—Doyle's a real gentleman—and he identified himself and said that I was back there with him. It turned out the guys were from Pecos, Texas, and they knew me. So Doyle told them we had a wager on how many cows to a section that grass could hold. "I don't want to say what it is," Doyle said, "because, knowing Slim, you might favor him or something. And I'm not gonna tell you what side of it he's got, but give us an honest opinion on how many cows you think will run to a section."

So the first guy said, "It's a cinch they'll run fifty." Another man sitting there said, "Hell, if it was my country, I'd probably put between fifty-five to sixty head to a section."

Doyle came back and told us what those cowboys had said, and after Sailor paid me, he was really hot. So, *chuggity-chug-chuggity-chug*, the train started on a little bit of an incline, and we could tell that the train was slowing some. It was like a diesel truck—when it downshifted, the smoke got black. And I said, "Boy, we're getting on a pretty good climb. As slow as this thing is going, I don't know whether it can make it up that mountain or not."

"How fast you think we are going?" Sailor asked.

Now, this wasn't deliberate, but I just said, "I don't know exactly, but I can guess closer to how fast we're going than you can."

"You can't guess closer than *me*," Doyle said.

"You all are not betting with yourselves," Sailor said. "We're all three gonna guess how fast the train's going."

Well, shoot, at this point I had already broken the pact, and I decided to get in on it, too, and we each posted $1,000 to guess how fast the train was going—closest without going over the speed would be the winner. Then it came up again: How were we gonna prove it?

We agreed that we would take the conductor's word for it. So we all wrote down our guesses, and Doyle went and got the conductor, and he came back to our train car and said, "On this part of the train," he said, "we don't have a speedometer; it would be just a guess with me."

So we asked him if there was any way of being certain, and he said that up by the engine there was a speedometer. The only problem was that he'd have to climb over a coal car to get to it. Now, at that time, one dollar was twelve and a half pesos, so a hundred pesos was eight bucks. But I knew that wasn't enough to get this man to climb over a coal car to check the speedometer, so we each gave him a hundred pesos, and he was tickled to death. He went up there, and when he came back and told us the speed, Doyle was $2,000 richer.

Sailor was hotter than a pistol now, and he said, "Cows to a section, how fast the train's going? You all are the two luckiest suckers in the world. Anything that requires skill I could beat you at."

So, *chuggity-chug-chuggity-chug*, maybe an hour and a half later, you could feel the pressure in your ears—it was just like being in an airplane. We were obviously changing altitudes, so I said, "I don't know about you all, but my ears are popping something fierce. We are really getting high."

Doyle agreed, but good old Sailor said, "High, your ass. Don't either one of you do no fuckin' drugs. You all don't know what high is."

"Well, yeah," Doyle said, "I have a better idea about *high*, not being on drugs, than you do. You smoke the goddamn stuff and everything, and that's the only high you know." Unfortunately, what Doyle said was true. Sailor was the only one of us who ever messed with drugs.

"By golly," I said, "let's all bet." But I caught myself and said, "No, we've agreed not to bet, and the last thing we need is any more dissension."

By some miracle Doyle and Sailor let it go, and about a minute later we went by San Blas, the little old town where we were gonna kill that jaguar, and I was sitting on the seat facing forward, with Doyle and Sailor facing me looking the other way. And as the train slowed up, I looked up, and there was a little depot with the elevation posted on it. Every train station I'd ever seen has got the elevation posted on it. So just real casual, I said, "Damn that agreement. I tell you, I don't think either one of you knows how high it is."

Here it goes. Sailor instigated it 'cause he was losing. "I can guess closer to how high this sonofabitch is than you all can."

I already knew how high we were—I'd seen it. So I said, "Let's shoot it on up. You all keep wanting to gamble among ourselves. So let's just get this over with. I'll bust both of you, and we'll quit this gambling till we get back home."

So we made a pretty sizable wager, $3,000 each, and we guessed the elevation. But the same thing came up: How were we gonna know?

Believe me, Doyle is a sharp boy, and he said, "If we could get them to back the train up, we wouldn't have to ask anybody. There's gotta be a depot where we just stopped to unload the passengers."

Naturally, I wanted to do it—that little plan was going to make me a lot of money. By this time everybody on the train knew we were gambling on everything, and we were having a real party doing it—buying drinks for the other passengers and swapping stories. So when we asked the conductor, who was our buddy by now, if he would stop the train and back on up, three hundred pesos later he did just that—and no one on the train cared a lick.

So the conductor started backing up the train, and Doyle, Sailor, and I just sat there looking. As we were moving backward, about to approach the depot, it dawned on Doyle that I had already seen the sign when we went by it the first time. The minute it did, you should have seen the look on that fat sonofagun's face!

I was still facing forward and just sort of looking over my shoulder. When Doyle saw this sign, he said, "Oh, my God, Sailor, look what that skinny bastard has done!"

"What the fuck is it?" Sailor said.

"Slim," Doyle said, "you *dirty* sonofabitch."

Boy, did he and Sailor cuss me out but good for that one—while I collected their cash.

Now, there was a trip where we weren't gonna gamble with one another!

We never did get that jaguar, but we still had a hell of a good time hunting and fishing. It's a memory I won't soon forget—of my two best friends and the three things we enjoyed doing together: laughing, traveling, and most of all, gambling.

BOOKING SPORTS BY PLAYING INTO THE STUPIDITY OF THE PUBLIC

Since you're probably some kind of owl who bets on sports, I reckon I should give you a little insight as to how it all works. The first thing I'll say is, them folks who run the NFL are a bunch of hypocrites. They do everything they can to not talk about gambling, yet they know damn well that when the Steelers are beating the Bengals 35–0 in the third quarter, the only reason most people are still watching is to see if the game goes over the total or not.

A total, also called the over-under, is just another example of how the bookmakers are always looking for more options to give the guesser an opportunity to wager. Rather than choose a team, you can make a bet—and this goes for football, basketball, and baseball—as to whether the total score of the game will go over a certain number. The way sports booking works is that when you place a bet, you lay 11 to 10—pay 11 if you lose and get paid 10 if you win. That 10 percent difference is what the bookies call the vig or the juice.

To give you an idea what I mean about how the public bets on sports, one fine college Saturday, Sailor was manning the phones at our office in Midland. I was watching the early games on TV when I heard Sailor speaking very carefully, saying, "Just a minute, and I'll get Slim."

I went to see what all the fuss was about, and Sailor put his hand over the phone and said, "Slim, there's an oilman on the phone who asked for you."

I'm not gonna say what this man's name was—let's just refer to him as Lou—but I will tell you that he was a rich oilman who had gone to Notre Dame. I nodded to Sailor to leave his hand over the speaker on the phone, and I said, "Sailor, you tell him that Notre Dame is a thirty-four-point favorite over Purdue."

"Do *what?*" he screamed.

"Deal him Notre Dame minus thirty-four against Purdue."

"Thirty-four?" he whispered. "I'm looking at our sheet, and it says thirty."

"It doesn't make a difference. Quote him that game at Notre Dame minus thirty-four."

You see, Notre Dame was really only a thirty-point favorite, but I knew this man well enough that I could put the odds more in my favor. I wanted to play into the man's pride a little bit. You see, if you've ever met a Notre Dame fan, you know that they're rabid, and they like to put their money where their mouth is. You'd think Notre Dame was the only college football team on the planet after talking to one of them Irish boys. So what was an extra four points to this cat?

Sailor started reading all the lines to this fella, and when he got to the Notre Dame game, I could see he was grittin' his teeth; he didn't want to do it. Finally he said, "Notre Dame, minus thirty-four."

And Doyle, who by now had joined us, nearly hit his head on the ceiling he jumped so high. "What the hell are you doing?" he said. But, with Sailor's hand still covering the phone, I explained to Doyle exactly what was going down.

Lou made bets on a few of the games, and then he said to Sailor, "Damn, that's a big number on Notre Dame."

Sailor didn't say nothing, and then finally Lou said, "Oooh, it don't make no difference; they're gonna blow 'em out anyway. Give me Notre Dame minus the thirty-four for eleven thousand to win ten."

Lou ended up betting a total of $80,000 on that call, which was a lot of action for one player, but it didn't faze us none, given all the action we handled. After he hung up the phone, Sailor said to me, "Well, I'm a sonofabitch, Slim." And Doyle said, "You shoulda known something was up, Sailor, or Slim wouldn't have done that."

You see, I knew that Lou, as an alum of Notre Dame, might not have bet Notre Dame minus thirty-four, but you couldn't have put a machine gun on him to make him take Purdue at plus thirty-four. He wouldn't dare bet against his beloved alma mater. So now I've got four more points that might make the difference in Purdue covering the game.

I know you're waiting for me to tell you that Purdue ended up losing by thirty-three, but the truth is, I couldn't tell you whether Dan Devine or Andy Devine was coaching that game, and it don't matter either way. The point is that in gambling you need to put the odds in your favor. The result of one particular game doesn't mean a damn thing, and that's why one of my mantras has always been "Decisions, not results." Do the right thing enough times and the results will take care of themselves in the long run.

And let me tell you, that Lou is just like 90 percent of the fools who bet on sports. Right here in Texas, even though the Cowboys haven't been worth nine settings of eggs for the past few years, there are thousands of people who wouldn't dare bet against the Cowboys. If they're supposed to be a four-point favorite and you tell bettors in this state that the line is seven, they might pass on the game, but there's no way they're gonna take the seven points and bet against *their* Dallas Cowboys.

It's because of that mentality that I think I could make a living booking sports, right here today, without even taking any vig. Because—I've said it a million times, and I'll say it again—*the guesser always loses.*

It's a myth that bookies want to balance their books—that they want the same number of people on both sides of the ledger so they can just collect the vig and not have any risk. Well, sure, they don't want to have too much risk on any one game, but their goal is to take as much action as they can, knowing that the bettor is going to lose in the long run.

See, when I bet sports, I don't like anyone; I don't have no *favorite* team. I like just the opposite of whoever you like. If you call me and you love Texas, then I love Oklahoma. If you love Oklahoma, then I just love Texas that much more. Because the guesser loses, and believe you me, every year the bookmakers are buying brand-new Lincolns, traveling around the world, building new homes in Aspen, while the bettors are sitting at home scratching their broke asses. It's been that way ever since I've been alive, so why would it change now?

DEATH OF BOOKING SPORTS AND MOVING TO THE OTHER SIDE

I reckon Bobby Kennedy had a little bit of a different upringing than I did. Had he won $45,000 on the Kentucky Derby when he was eighteen years old rather than playing for the Harvard football team, maybe he would have come to view gambling differently. As it was, that aristocratic son-ofabitch who became attorney general during his brother's presidency had a vendetta against it. I knew we were in trouble on September 13, 1961, when, as part of his "War on Crime," the Federal Wire Act was passed, making it illegal to transmit across state lines any information that would be helpful in placing bets.

Fines don't bother me, but anything that's a felony . . . well, that's another story. Good old Bobby K took a lot of money out of our pockets, because as soon as we heard that you could go to the Crossbar Hotel for making book, Doyle and I pulled up from it. Sailor wasn't as cautious, and he learned the hard way that Mr. Kennedy took this racket seriously. Sailor got busted in El Paso, Texas, and did about a year in a mimimum-security joint in, of all places, his hometown of San Angelo. I reckon he didn't stop booking then either.

Since I quit making book in 1961, I've been indicted twice for it, but nothing ever did happen to me besides my pissing away a bunch of money on attorneys' fees. The truth of the matter is that after the Wire Act was passed, Doyle and I gave it up and started concentrating on poker.

I also continued to bet—if any of you John Q. Laws are reading this, I said "bet," not "book"—sports. From all those years of being on the other side of it, I put that information to use as a bettor. Most of it's nothing more than good old horse sense. People think it's all numbers and computers, but I still don't even know how to turn one of them things on. See, betting sports has *a lot* to do with understanding human nature. For starters, as I explained with Notre Dame and the Dallas Cowboys, the public tends to bet favorites. Fans like to root for their teams, and, psychologically, they think it's easier to just pick a winner than it is to bet on the lesser team, even getting points.

There are about six people in the whole world who can make a living betting sports—and I mean of those folks who don't book. I happen to be one of those six. Billy Walters, Chip Reese, Doyle Brunson, Dale "The Professor" Conway, and Billy Baxter are the others. If you don't think so, follow me around for a year and watch what I do.

One person who has seen it firsthand is my nephew Johnny Byler, a fifty-five-year-old businessman from Fort Worth. On October 26, 2002, Johnny came to town, and after I took him to the Country Barn for some of Amarillo's best calf fries (for all you Yankees out there, calf fries are bulls' nuts), we sat around telling hunting stories and betting college football. We went three for three in the morning, and when it came time for one of the late games, Alabama-Tennessee, I didn't have much of an opinion on who would win. But based on my research, I thought that, depending on the number, the under might be a good play.

I called two . . . let's just call 'em "sources" about the total on the Alabama-Tennessee game, and one had it at 45½ and the other had it at 50. I know this sounds unusual, and it *is* unusual. Generally, all the bookmakers will be within a half point, or at most a point, of each other. So I told Johnny I favored the under, and we bet a peanut, $800, on the game going under 50.

After we did, Johnny said, "Gee whiz, Slim, we oughta take a shot at that middle—there's four points for a win and one for a tie."

"Nah," I said, without giving it much thought. "It's hard to get the best of it and then give it away. That's for suckers." You see, in general, I think hedging is for tourists. If I liked the under at fifty, why would I want to turn around and make a bet the other way?

Yet at certain numbers, it's the right thing to do. I got to thinking about it, and I saw that there were a lot of numbers—46, 47, 48, 49—that the score could land on for us to win both bets, and another number, 50, where we would tie one bet and win another. It was simple percentages; we'd be risking $80—the vig—with four numbers to win $1,600 (20 to 1 on our money) and another number to win $800. The true odds on it landing on one of those five numbers were 6 to 1, and that's what a gambler calls a great "value." Anytime you can get paid 20 to 1 on a 6-to-1 shot, you're getting way the best of it. So I called my other source, and we bet $800 on over 45½.

With the score 7–0 with two minutes to go in the first half, it looked like a certainty that this game wouldn't make it into the forties, so we took a break and had some of Helen's famous chicken-fried steak for supper. Well, it turned out that Alabama scored a touchdown with a minute to go in the first half, and Tennessee turned right back around and returned the kickoff for a touchdown. I don't have to tell you the rest—you guessed it. The score wound up on 48, at 34–14. It doesn't make any difference who *won*, neighbor.

Hitting that middle got me thinking about a little experience I had just two years ago in Lubbock, Texas. I knew all of their bookmakers down there, and five of them got together to take my action. I made them a proposition that if they would allow me to move the line in college football a half a point, I'd guarantee that I'd make a string of bets every week. I'd bet five thousand, *minimum*, a game on five games. In other words, I'd start 'em off with at least $25,000 in bets every week, which amounted to $2,500 worth of juice. Well, $2,500 a week over the college football season is a lot of juice, especially since there were weeks that I'd bet as many as nine games.

They went for it because they knew that if a man makes too many bets, that 10 percent vig will get him. So, after I did it, I singled out one of 'em and I said, "Do you all deal with totals?"

"Sure do," he said. "Would you make a string of bets for $5,000 on totals?"

"I'd guarantee to bet at least five games on the totals if you let me move it a point and a half."

"Why a point and a half?" he said.

I explained to him that since totals are usually around 45 and the point spreads are usually around 6, one and a half points on a total was a much smaller move, *percentage-wise*, than a half point on a game. And, by golly, he went for it.

Then I went to another bookmaker who I've known forever. He's honorable, reputable, and he takes real big action, and I asked him if he'd let me move the games of college football a half a point if I'd make him a string of bets.

He thought about it for a minute, and he ended up going for it with the stipulation that I make at least six bets. So with six bets of at least $5,000 a week, he was getting $3,000 a week in juice right there.

Then I told him about these totals. He was reluctant for a while, but the more he thought about it, the more he realized that if I was gonna bet six games, moving a total a point and a half wasn't such a big deal. So he agreed to it.

Here's the kicker. As you already saw from the Alabama-Tennessee game, bookmakers don't always have the same number. One guy may have it 4 and the other one 4½, and so on.

So I played the middles on the games, but never was I middling with just one point. I usually had two, and occasionally I'd have two for a win and one for a tie. And, brother, that's stronger than Nellie's breath. Because if one guy had it 7 and the other one had it 6, why, I'd bet the underdog, +7½, and I'd bet the favorite, –5½. That gave me two numbers, 6 and 7, and the true odds of its landing on one of those numbers are 10 to 1. Since I was getting 20 to 1 that it would land on one of those numbers, it was just another one of them great values.

It was the same way on those totals, and, man, I didn't have a three-point spread on the totals. For example, let's say one bookmaker had the total at 38 and the other one had it at 39. I'd bet under 40½ and I'd bet over 36½. So I had 37, 38, 39, and 40 for wins. Now, you talk about knocking some tailfeathers. That only lasted one season before them guys got wise to it. And they say the bookmakers never lose.

MY BIGGEST SPORTS BET EVER

Everybody asks me about my biggest sports bet. My goodness, it was a long time ago, January 12, 1969, for Super Bowl III between the Baltimore Colts, coached by Don Shula, and the New York Jets, coached by Weeb Ewbank. This was still back when there were separate leagues, and the two years prior, in the first two Super Bowls, the Kansas City Chiefs and Oakland Raiders—the AFL champions from a league that had just started up in 1960—got their butts kicked by the NFL's Green Bay Packers.

In the 1968 season, the Colts had won their last ten games with a defense that had broken the NFL record for the fewest points allowed in a season. They looked like a damn juggernaut when they beat the Cleveland Browns 34–0 in the NFL title game. And since the Jets barely sneaked by the Raiders, 27–23, in the AFL title game, everyone figured it would be a blowout. No one even seemed to mind that the Colts' quarterback, Johnny Unitas, was questionable for the game with a sore elbow, and the line opened with the Colts favored by 17½. By game time, it was a 21½-point spread.

When the line starts at 17½ and goes to 21½, it means that everybody in the world is betting on the favorite and giving the 17½. You hear the expression all the time about the "smart money" moving the line. People say that because they think only the wise guys can place a big enough bet that will make the oddsmakers adjust their spread. The truth is that the only thing that moves the line is *money,* and it don't make a bit of difference where it comes from. There ain't nobody keeping score to sort out whether it's a wise guy or a guesser who is making the bet.

What I do is, before the line even comes out, I do my own research—and it's nothing you can't do yourself, looking at the team's statistics, common opponents, injuries, and all that stuff—and figure out what I think the line should be. For Super Bowl III, I thought the Colts should have been favored by twelve so I loved the Jets at +21½. I liked Joe Namath, especially because "Broadway Joe" was such a cocky son-ofagun. He kinda sounded like me at the poker table when he said the Colts defense was "predictable and easy to deceive." He really sounded like me on the Thursday before the big game in Miami. At a dinner honoring him as the AFL's MVP, Broadway Joe stood at the podium and said them famous words: "We're going to win Sunday. I guarantee you."

Well, shoot, Broadway Joe was *guaranteeing* a victory.

By this time the line had gone to 21½, and everyone couldn't wait to see Namath eat his words. Hell, I think what Joe said *made* people want to bet against him. And I didn't give two hoots in hell about the "smart money" moving the line. There are rumors that I made an awful big bet on the Jets—let's just say that you'd hate to go pay the income taxes on it—but I believe that it started with a four and had between four and six zeros after it.

Was I a wreck watching that game? Hell no! I knew I had already made a good decision and was getting good value, and if the result wasn't favorable, I'd just take my lumps like a man and that would have been that. As it turned out, the final score was 16–7, so the winner didn't make no difference to my wallet. But in case you've been holed up in a cave all your life, it was in favor of the Jets.

THREE RULES FOR BETTING SPORTS

My good friend Steve Wynn, that sharpie who built the Mirage and the Bellagio and who is now building a place called Le Rêve that may be the nicest yet, said about the smartest thing I've ever heard as it relates to gambling: "If you want to win money in a casino, own one."

For those of you looking for some sort of secret as to how to beat sports, I could save you a whole lot of time and say to just stay away from it altogether. The only way to beat it, of course, is to be taking bets, which even I had to give up in 1961. But since I know you just can't wait to get your money into action, I will give you a few pointers.

When I said earlier that a line was *supposed to be four*, what I meant was, that's the right number for the game, determined by the professional oddsmakers who really do their homework. It's also a known fact that in sports betting the public's gonna bet on the favorite for reasons I've already explained. Because of that, I know bookmakers who put a half a point on everything that comes. If it comes 6, they automatically make it 6½.

Rule number one is to bet on underdogs. For the average Square John out there, if you were just to bet every underdog, at the end of the year you'd quit a winner. It'd be close with the vig, but you'd still win a little. My expression for that has always been the same: There are a lot more mice than elephants. You don't ever go to the zoo to see a mouse, now, do you?

Rule number two is that if you're going to make a bet, you need to know something that everybody else doesn't. Concentrate on a conference or a couple of teams, and know their every move. If you bet a game without knowing that the team's quarterback sprained his ankle that week in practice—and somebody else does know it—then you're in trouble. I study the Big 12 and can always get information about teams like Texas, Texas A&M, Texas Tech, and Oklahoma because they're right in my backyard.

The third and final rule goes back to old Lou with Notre Dame and all these fools in Texas with the Dallas Cowboys: Don't bet with your heart.

Emotion is the greatest killer to any gambler, and if you wear your heart on your sleeve when you wager, those bookmakers will knock it off like a dead limb.

Now, if you don't mind, neighbor, I'm fixing to get back to telling stories about my life. And the next part of it, aside from nice scores at the poker table, is a chapter that I wish I could forget.

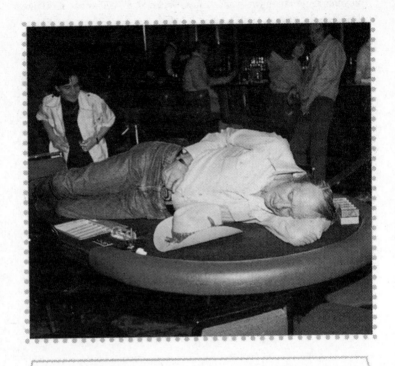

Taking a well-deserved nap during an extra-long session at the Sahara Reno during the Super Bowl of Poker. *(Courtesy of the author)*

6

It Takes a Tough Sonofabitch to Whip Me: Poker and Life as a Texas Road Gambler

$\mathcal{I}$didn't go to college, and I cut my fair share of classes in high school, but I always paid close attention to history—especially United States presidents. I can tell you, for example, that George Washington kept a ledger page headed "Cards and Other Play," and from 1772 to 1775 it showed that he was ahead more than six pounds. Tricky Dick won six thousand dollars in his first two months in the navy playing poker and used it to finance his first political campaign for Congress in 1946 against Jerry Voorhis. I played with Nixon before Watergate at a private club in Washington, and he wasn't as tricky as advertised. Nice enough fella, though.

I also played with Lyndon Johnson in Johnson City, Texas, in the early seventies, not long before he died in 1973. Joe Batson, a good friend of mine, had dated one of LBJ's daughters and arranged for me to play in a game with the thirty-sixth president. I think I told LBJ after I bluffed him out of a pot that he made the right decision by going into politics.

Dwight Eisenhower? He sure could play, but he didn't have enough killer instinct for my tastes. "When I found officers around me losing more money than they could afford," he said, "I stopped." That wasn't the case with Harry Truman, who played day and night with the press aboard the *Augusta* on his way back to the States from the Potsdam Conference in 1945. Apparently, deciding whether or not to drop the atomic bomb on Japan was weighing on him a little bit, so he relaxed by busting all them reporters. It's too bad I was in Europe at the time, or I would have voted for him—shoot, I would have campaigned for him! I think Truman was one of the best presidents this country has ever known.

In the nineteenth century, the Wild West was a gambler's paradise. Every town had a saloon where a man could find himself a good meal and a live poker game. Throughout the Midwest and the South, you couldn't find a riverboat along the Mississippi River without gambling. The cheaters set people up at three-card monte, and the real men played poker. Folks like Wyatt Earp and Doc Holliday became famous, but the cat I always looked up to was James Butler "Wild Bill" Hickok.

When Wild Bill won his first gunfight in 1861, he became the 1800s version of a road gambler: a touring sharpshooter with Buffalo Bill's Wild West Show. After a showdown against the McCanles gang, when Hickok shot down three of them, and another one against gambler Phil Coe, Wild Bill Hickok became an American legend. But just like earning a reputation as the best pool player in my town worked against me, being known as the deadliest gunslinger in the Wild West had its hazards.

Wild Bill set the standard for guys like Titanic Thompson and me when it came to looking the part of a gambler. With his long, wavy hair and "stallion-tail" mustache, Wild Bill wore waistcoats of the finest brocade and sixty-dollar calfskin boots, and he carried pistols with pearl handles. And don't think they were for show either.

Wild Bill liked to play poker in the town of Deadwood, South Dakota, and on the afternoon of August 2, 1876, he headed down a street full of miners to the No. 10 saloon. Wild Bill had a custom of always sitting with his back to the wall, and it had kept him alive for thirty-nine years. When he went to sit down to play cards with Carl Mann, one of the owners of the joint, Charles Rich, another famous gunman, and Captain Frank Massey, a Missouri River pilot, Massey had decided, just for shits and giggles, to sit in Wild Bill's regular seat against the wall. "Nobody is going to shoot you in the back," Massey joked.

They started playing at about 3:30 P.M., and Wild Bill asked several times to change seats, but being that these guys were his buddies, they just went on teasing him about his little superstition and kept him in a seat with his back facing the door. It's a wonder he didn't shoot them cats, and he wound up being so nervous that he lost his fifty-dollar stake and had to buy more chips at four o'clock. Then, on the next hand, Wild Bill was dealt a pair of aces and a pair of eights with a queen kicker. Just as my man was fixing to bust these cats, Jack McCall, a twenty-five-year-old wannabe gunslinger from Louisville, stormed through the door and fired his Colt .45 revolver at Wild Bill.

One shot was all he needed, as the bullet went plumb through the back of Wild Bill's skull, came out under his right cheekbone, and still had enough zip on it to get imbedded in Captain Massey's left forearm. I reckon Massey deserved a little worse than that for his poor choice in seating. As for Jack "Crooked Nose" McCall, as he was called, he was lynched for his sins. To this day aces and eights is known all over the world as the "Dead Man's Hand."

Boy, have times changed. Nowadays you can walk into the Bellagio in Las Vegas or the Taj Mahal in Atlantic City or just about anywhere for that matter, any time of day, and you can be sure that there's a game going. You can also be fairly certain that you're not gonna get shot, and when you go to cash your chips, you'll be paid. You can even leave your money at the casino cage or put it in a safe-deposit box and not have to worry about getting hijacked. I'd say the players today have got it pretty good.

When I was traveling with Doyle and Sailor around Texas—and other parts of the South, like Louisiana, Alabama, and Georgia—catching good cards was the least of our worries. As a road gambler back then, you had to do four things:

1. Find the game

2. Beat the game

3. Not get arrested

4. Not get robbed

The two biggest hazards back then were cheats and stickups. And it wasn't like we had much recourse: What were we gonna do, go running to the police and tell them a man kept an ace up his sleeve or that an illegal poker game got robbed? Let's just say that being subpoenaed by Bobby K would have been a pleasure compared to some of the things we were up against.

People who watch too many movies always ask me if we played with our guns on the table. I hate to break this to you, partner, but that's a myth. We didn't keep guns on the table; we kept 'em on our bodies! I can't remember playing in a poker game in Texas and not having my snub .38 loaded in my hip pocket, and just about everybody else in the game carried a gun, too. We weren't looking to do nothing to one another; we were worried about somebody coming through the doors.

To give you an idea what it was like, Johnny Moss and Titanic Thompson were playing in a game in the early thirties in a town about a hundred miles from Houston called Beeville, Texas. They were playing high-stakes Kansas City Lowball, and by Johnny's account he and Ti each had about fifty thousand in front of them when they got some unexpected company. When Johnny felt the sting in his eyes of the tear gas—which was shot through a window by a bunch of robber cowards—he looked outside and saw six thieves wearing gas masks and carrying scatterguns.

Johnny hid his money up in the divan in the coils, and Ti hid his in the freezing compartment of the icebox. And this is what I mean by "surviving" on the road. Here you had two of the sharpest road gamblers that ever lived, and they weren't smart enough to find a hiding place the robbers wouldn't find. In fact, the only person there who kept his money was a cat who had a rubber band around his bankroll, and hid it in the plunger on the inside of the toilet—a move that saved him twenty grand.

I remember like it was yesterday, when Johnny told me that story at a card game in Odessa back in 1962. "Slim," Johnny said, "keep a rubber band around your roll so if you get held up, you can throw it somewhere before you get mugged. A rubber band's saved me a dozen times from losin' my roll."

I still do use a rubber band to carry my bankroll, but let me tell you, it wasn't always enough. And damn it if most of it wasn't my own fault. You see, a road gambler's biggest asset is his friends, and it seemed like whenever I made the mistake of traveling without Doyle and Sailor, I got just what I deserved.

SO MUCH FOR TEXAS HOSPITALITY

In the early sixties, not long after we quit making book, when I wasn't home with my family, I was playing poker. In Houston, Texas, there was an old, run-down nightclub with a poker game in the back room, and just about everybody at the game was some sort of racketeer or drug dealer or assassin. Let me put it to you another way: It wasn't a real good environment to be in. Several friends told me I should avoid this place, but that hubris of thinking that I was invincible got to me again, and I decided to make the nine-hour drive.

I played, and invariably, every time I got involved in a pot, it was always with the boss—*unbelievable!* And I don't know why it is, but it never fails to happen to me: Everywhere I go, it always seems that *every* time there's a great big pot—and I mean a decision pot, one that's going to make or break a guy for the night—I get locked up against the boss.

Let me tell you, I did not want to thrash this boss, who I'll call Diego. I didn't get to be seventy-four by making foolish decisions. So one of them decision pots came up, and it was just me and Diego, who was a great big sonofagun. He bet first, and I raised him, moving all my chips in (about $10,000 or so). I'd been watching this guy play, and I wouldn't have paid a blind chauffeur a nickel to sit behind him and tell me what his cards were. I just *knew* he was bluffing.

Diego just kinda moved back a little, stared at me, messed with his chips, and said, "Man, let me tell you. I'm thinking seriously about calling, but if I do call you, and you got the best hand, you'll never leave this room alive."

Now, that was pretty definite, wasn't it? I really and truly didn't know what to do. I was hoping he wouldn't call me, and I'da been happy to take the pot as it was. Understand that this man had a track record, and I knew I needed to think of something to get out of this. So I looked over at Diego and said, "You can call if you want, but there's just one thing you need to know: It takes a tough sonofabitch to whip me."

With that Diego stood up—and he was about three times as broad as me and outweighed me by about two hundred pounds—and I said, "Now, wait just a second. It might take a tough sonofabitch to whip me, that's true, but it sure as hell don't take him long!"

And Diego just cracked up. Everybody at the table got to laughing, and, sure enough, everything was okay. In fact, he did call me, and I won a nice pot—that's the irony. I think he called because he wanted to show off his authority, and he didn't want to be bluffed out. Then he said, "Take it, you lucky stiff." Not one threatening word after that, not one. Here was a guy who had intended to do me such bodily harm, and all of a sudden he was my buddy.

Much later, at about four o'clock in the morning, a motorcycle gang showed up. I guess I shouldn't identify them, because their enemies, the Hells Angels, are my friends. Anyhow, this one great big guy—with about nine hundred tattoos and a ring everywhere there was a hole—was wearing a big leather coat and a little old leather cap. He sat down and said to me, "I know you. You're that skinny prick from Amarillo who thinks he knows how to play poker."

So much for good old Texas hospitality, I thought. I knew he wanted to establish some fear or control over me, and I figured the best thing I could do was ignore it. But when he kept at it, as clear as day, like he was trying to pick a squabble with me, Diego said to him, "Get off that shit. He's my friend."

Boy, I tell you, I bellied up to the table and said, "Deal them cards. I'm ready to gamble."

So for the simple reason that I was able to make that boss man laugh,

I got to keep my bread that night—which amounted to a nice score. And, like I always do, I got invited back to the game. I'll spare you that old saying about attracting bees with honey, but I will tell you that a good sense of humor got me out of a lot more jams than my big mouth ever got me into in the first place.

DON'T FIND 'EM IN GEORGIA

Even though I had allies across the state of Texas, if I heard of a good poker game in another part of the country, it didn't take much convincing for me to go. I don't want to say exactly where this happened, but it's a big city where peaches grow and a certain cola is made in a bottle that doubles as a Ping-Pong paddle. I heard there was a real high-stakes game of No Limit Texas Hold'em down there, and when I couldn't talk Doyle and Sailor into coming with me, old stubborn Slim left his best assets in Texas and went anyhow.

After getting caught in a couple bluffs and losing a few thousand dollars, I picked up a pair of wired aces in one of them decision pots. Some people like to try to trap with their aces—just play real weak before the flop and then pounce on 'em later. But my good fortune was that, when the betting came to me, a guy had already raised it $30,000, and, with about $75,000 in front of him, I knew he was what I call "pot committed"—meaning that he had already put so much of his chips in that there was no way he was gonna fold. So I just moved in on him.

Sure enough, he called, and, with all of his chips in the pot and no more betting to be done, it's customary for both players to just turn their hands up. So we both flipped them up, and it was his bad fortune to have a pair of kings against my pair of aces. You can't blame him for playing the hand the way he did; it's the second-best hand you can have. And since I had already run a couple of bluffs and gotten caught, there was no way he could have pegged me for aces. So now he's got to catch one of the two remaining kings to beat me (or make a straight), and it didn't happen. I kept playing until I busted just about everyone there, and I wound up leaving at about seven o'clock in the morning about a hundred-thousand-dollar winner.

I went back to my room in a leading hotel—it wasn't that I cared about the quality of the soap when I was in the room, but I always chose a hotel based on safety. Figuring I was in a good environment, I was just relaxing, watching some television to wind down. Turned out that letting my guard down was what got me—served me right for not putting the safety lock on—and, you guessed it, four men picked the lock and busted into my room.

They stripped me naked and wired me up—I didn't say "tied" up, I said "wired" up. They used thin wire, a little smaller than baling wire, to bind me, and, boy, did it hurt. Then I was put in a bathtub, and in the back of my mind, I figured what was coming next was the water treatment.

Back in the fifties, there were two outlaws named Slim and Shorty who were known for robbing gamblers and holding their heads underwater until they told 'em where their stash was. If you hid something, you'd tell where it was in a damn hurry with the water treatment. Believe me you would. So I was getting prepared to try to hold my breath for fifteen minutes, but it turned out that wasn't it.

They had gagged me with electrical tape, and, believe it or not, that was when I knew I'd be all right. They weren't gonna turn the water on in the tub, or else they wouldn't have gagged me. Then they told me, "We're gonna take about a thirty- or forty-minute head start, and then we'll call and have 'em come up and turn you loose."

I was wired up, and the harder I'd try to get loose, the deeper I'd get cut. I started going, "*Mmmmmmmm*," but you can't holler very loud when you're gagged with electrical tape. You see, they had already gotten my money, but they didn't want to give me no chance to catch up to them. Hell, if I were them, I wouldn't have wanted to get caught walking out of there either—not after I had just taken a man and stripped him stark fuckin' naked and tied him up with wire and put him in a bathtub.

So I was trying to holler, but I couldn't. I thought, Well, shit, it's gonna be all right. Sooner or later they'll call back, and someone will set me free. The only thing in my favor was that I'd left half my stash in the car, but it didn't seem to have too much value to me at that point.

And then I heard a key—somebody was trying to come in my door. I thought maybe it was the maid—it was now about nine in the morning— and sure enough, it was. So I had to use my head, literally, and made the loudest racket I could by banging my head plumb against the side of the bathtub. Finally I heard the bathroom door click, and the maid opened it and walked in, and she screamed like her titty was caught in a ringer. There was blood all over the tub, and I was lying there naked and bleeding like a stuck hog.

A couple of minutes later, hotel security came up to untie me. First off the house detective came, but it didn't take him long to turn it over to the GBI—the Georgia Bureau of Investigations. It was all the usual stuff—there were three of them, two flunkies and the boss man, and they asked me some questions. Then one of the officers took out a little pad and a pen, and said, "Slim, you are T. A. Preston Jr.?"

And I told him I was, but I was thinking, what the heck, I knew they had already checked the registration, and they knew who I was. Then he asked me where I lived.

"At 4105 Virginia, in Amarillo, Texas," I said. Then he asked me my age, and I told him. Then my Social Security number, and I said, "Ah, you all don't need my Social Security number."

"Well, why would you object to giving us your Social Security number?" he asked.

"If you all are a stool pigeon for the IRS, I'm not interested in helping your investigation."

There's not but one agency in the world that uses your Social Security number, and that's the IRS. While I knew it was unlikely that these guys were with them, I didn't see no reason to take any chances by giving it to them. Anyhow, I caught a little bit of flak for it, but finally the boss let it go and asked, "How many people broke in here?"

"Now, I tell you," I said, "you're asking me a lot of questions that I don't know the answers to." But they knew that I was lying. I wasn't out cold, I wasn't drunk, and I certainly knew what had happened to me. Then he said, "How long do you think you stayed in here?"

"I just can't recall."

This line of reasoning might not make much sense to you, but, understand, I wasn't much interested in helping them get the guys that robbed me 'cause they weren't gonna do a damn thing about it anyway. If they caught 'em, they were gonna keep the loot themselves. Shoot, they were probably tickled to death that a big-time gambler from Texas got robbed in their hometown. Plus, I'm not a stool pigeon anyway, so I didn't say nothing.

It became pretty obvious to them that I wasn't going to play their games, so the boss man said, "Slim, you all right?"

"Yessir."

"Well, what about this robbery report?"

"Oh, man, if I was to see a robbery, I'd be one of the first people to tell you about it."

That really didn't go over too good. So he said, "In other words, you didn't see anybody get robbed?"

"No, sir," I said. "If I do, though, I'll be sure to tell you about it."

They were fed up at this point, so the boss man sent the two flunkies out of the room. He got up real close to me, looked me dead in the eye, and said, "Slim, do me a favor. If you find 'em, don't find 'em in Georgia."

That sounded like an awful interesting thing for a man from the GBI to say, but he had reason to. He knew that, me being one of the good guys—at least everyone thinks I'm one of the good guys—would mean there would be plenty of people out there looking for them guys who robbed me. Especially all them brokes, who are always looking for a handout—they knew that if they could find who got me, they were gonna get some reward, which they damn sure would. I'm a man of integrity, goddamn it!

Forget the fact that I still had about $50,000 in the car that I had just won—do you think it's fun to get stripped stark naked, wired up, and put in a bathtub, knowing that all of them hijackers in the South had gone to gamblers' houses and given 'em the water treatment? Let me tell you, neighbor, it's not a good feeling. But when I look back on something like that, I see it for what it was: one of the many hazards of being a road gambler. It's something that I accepted when I chose this lifestyle, and I didn't complain about it then, and I'm not feeling sorry for myself now.

I've told many an up-and-comer that gambling is a hard way to make an easy living.

♠ ♣ ♦ ♥

Just as pool has eight ball, nine ball, straight pool, and one-pocket, poker has draw, stud, lowball, Texas Hold'em, Omaha, and a million varieties in between. If you're interested in learning about poker games with wild cards, you'd best be served by putting this book down and getting yourself a tourist manual.

Five-card draw is probably the game you're most familiar with. You get five cards, bet, and then get to draw cards followed by another betting round. A variety of five-card draw is called Deuce-to-Seven or Kansas City Lowball. It works the same as regular draw, except the best possible hand is the worst in regular poker—2-3-4-5-7 of different suits. Aces are high, and straights and flushes count against you.

Back before Hold'em took off, Kansas City Lowball was the most popular game in the South, and I played quite a bit of this on the road. Sailor played it about as well as anyone, and the best player in the world is still probably a man from Augusta, Georgia, named Billy Baxter. Regular lowball, sometimes called California Lowball, is similar in that you get five cards and then can draw to try to get your best low hand. The difference is that there is a joker in the deck, which acts as a wild card, and straights and flushes don't count against you, so A-2-3-4-5—called a "bicycle" or just a "wheel"—is the best possible hand.

Five-card stud was a popular game up until about 1960, but the only time you're liable to see it played nowadays is if you rent a video of *The Cincinnati Kid* and watch Edward G. Robinson and Steve McQueen go at it. In five-card stud, each player gets one card dealt facedown and one card dealt faceup after the ante. There's a round of betting before the next three cards are dealt faceup, one at a time, with a betting round after each.

Seven-card stud is similar, except each player starts with two cards down and one up, and, after three cards are dealt faceup with a round of betting after each, the seventh and final card is dealt facedown. It's still probably the most popular game on the East Coast, and if you walk into the card room at Foxwoods in Connecticut or the Taj Mahal in Atlantic City, more games than any other will be seven-card stud. Seven-card stud can also be played for the best low hand, and that game is called Razz. You'll also see it played quite a bit as high-low split.

While all these other poker games are okay and all, as far as I'm concerned, there's just one real form of poker: Texas Hold'em. And, as the expression goes, I could teach you to play in a day, but it would take you a lifetime to learn. The game can be played with as many as twenty-three players, but most games are usually played with between seven and ten. For me, the fewer the better, and I like nothing better than playing one-person "head-up."

There's a lot of talk about where Texas Hold'em started; some say Corpus Christi, Brenham, or Waco, and even some say Oklahoma or Louisiana, but I'd bet on Texas. Johnny Moss said he played it in the late thirties, so I imagine that's when it really got popular. He also said that "Hold'em is to stud and draw what chess is to checkers," and that's about as good a way of putting it as I can think of.

Here's how the game works: Each player is dealt two cards, and a round of betting follows. If you're dealt two aces, which happens only once in every 425 deals, you've got the boss hand—for the time being anyway. The dealer then "flops" three community cards in the middle that any of the players can use to make their hand, followed by a round of betting. Then comes the fourth card, called the "turn," followed by a round of betting. Then—and this is where many a man has been drowned—comes the fifth community card, called the "river," which is followed by the fourth and last round of betting.

Omaha is a variety of Hold'em, the only difference being that you get dealt four cards, and unlike in Hold'em, where you use five of the best seven cards to make your hand, here you use five of the best nine to make your hand. You rarely play Hold'em high-low split but it's pretty common to play Omaha that way. Whoever makes the high hand gets half the pot, and whoever makes the low gets the other half. The place where you really make your money is when you make both high and low and "scoop" the pot. Got all that, partner?

Aside from all the varieties of games, what really matters more than anything is the rules of betting. Most friendly games across America and most games in casinos are fixed-limit—nickel-dime, dollar–two-dollar, or ten-twenty—where you must bet a certain amount on each round of betting. The power of a pure bluff is restricted in a game with a limit.

Here in Texas, and in all the major tournaments, the betting is no-limit—meaning you can bet anything that's in front of you at any time—or pot-limit—meaning you can bet the amount of the pot at any time. Don't get me wrong, limit poker can be a lot of fun—if you haven't got the guts of an earthworm or if you make your living as an accountant. As far as I'm concerned, if you can't "move in" on someone—meaning bet everything you've got in front of you—then it's not real poker. Naturally, no-limit Texas Hold'em is my game of choice, and it's what is played to determine the winner of the World Series of Poker.

LEARNING THE MEANING OF KAZAGA—THE HARD WAY

Not only are there a million varieties of poker, but it seems like every game has a different set of rules. In some friendly games you can't check and raise, and with that rule you might as well be playing Go Fish. These friendly games can be a lot of fun, but when people start losing, the game doesn't always stay so friendly. You also have to keep your eyes open for folks who tend to change the rules to their liking.

One time, out of the clear blue sky, I got invited to a house game in this place called Dalhart, Texas, about ninety miles north of Amarillo. It's a little old town, but there are some wealthy folks up there, and some of 'em played in this poker game.

Each player generally started with $100 buy-in, but I think that because I was there and these guys wanted to show that they were high-rollers or something, they had a $500 buy-in that night. Heck, I think some of them old folks wanted to make sure I brought a lot of money, because they were fixing to take it from me. So we were playing Omaha High-Low, and after winning a few big pots early in the night, I looked down and saw that I had about $2,000 worth of chips in front of me.

It was still fairly early in the game, and one of them decision pots came up, and me and this guy—I'll call him Tiger—just kept raising and reraising, raising and reraising. So I figured that it had to be a tie, which is something that comes up more than you might think when you play Omaha High-Low, and when the pot got to about a thousand dollars, I just called his last bet, and he said, "I've got a wheel."

"Me, too," I said. "We should have known we had the same damn thing."

The community cards were 3-4-5-9-10, and since we both had an ace and a deuce in our hand, we each had a wheel. There wasn't any possible flush, so the suits of the cards didn't matter. So I turned my hand faceup, and everyone just looked at each other, kinda quiet like, and I said, "All right, split the pot."

"No, no, no!" Tiger shouted.

"But I got the wheel, too! Cut it up—it's a split pot."

"No," he said, "you've got a Kazaga."

"I've got a *what?*"

Now, I've been around a poker table for a helluva long time, and I ain't never heard someone say that someone else has a "Kazaga." Sounds kinda like a disease to me.

But Tiger said, "You've got a Kazaga. You can't win a high-low split hand with the deuce of diamonds in your hand; that's a Kazaga. You've got a Kazaga."

"Bullshit!" I screamed.

But everybody else shook his head too, and Tiger said, "Oh, shit, Slim, that's one of our house rules. You can't win the pot on a low hand with the deuce of diamonds; it's called a Kazaga."

That was the goddamnedest thing I'd ever heard. But they were all good guys—I didn't think they'd try to cheat me—so I just let it go. It only cost me about five hundred, and it was a friendly game, so I laughed it off, and we just kept playing. Sure enough, after a while, maybe three or four hours later, me and Tiger—that's what's so bad about it—got involved in a decision pot again, and it was in Technicolor, like a repeat of the hand that had gone down earlier. We got to jamming and a-ramming it in there, ratcheting up the stakes with every round of betting. So, after he finally just called my bet, I showed him my flush for high and he showed me his wheel for low.

We turned our hands up, and you know what I was looking for—that damn deuce of diamonds. And sure enough, he had it. "Wait just a minute," I said.

"What the hell," Tiger said, "it's a split pot. You're high with your flush, and I got a wheel for low."

"Yeah, but you've got a Kazaga, or whatever the hell it is you guys call it."

"Oh, shit, Slim," his buddy said, "didn't we tell you?"

"Didn't you tell me *what?* Tell me, your ass! I had one of them Kazagas a while ago, and I lost the pot. Now you got one, and you're telling me I have to share my winnings with you?"

At that point he could barely hold back his grin, and he said, "Yeah, Slim, but we just have one Kazaga a night."

HOW TO WIN AT POKER

Doyle, Sailor, and I dedicated ourselves to becoming the three best poker players in the world. In my opinion—and you won't find many who will argue—Doyle is the greatest poker player who ever moved a chip, and he'll be the first to tell you that the most important part of his poker education was the discussions we had in many a motel room in Texas. After a long session, none of us could hardly sleep from being so wound up, and we would just stay awake for hours talking about the hands we played that night, the players in the game, and all different sorts of strategies.

Imagine what it would have been like if Paul "Bear" Bryant, Vince Lombardi, and George "Papa Bear" Halas traveled together for ten years and did nothing but talk football. Or if Warren Buffett, Peter Lynch, and George Soros went around the world picking stocks together and exchanging investment ideas. Let's just say there was a lot of knowledge changing hands, because from 1972 to 1977, we won four World Series of Poker championships between us.

There's an old expression that your character is defined by the company you keep and how you keep it. In poker it's much simpler: The company you keep will affect your bankroll. And while I can't go back and replay all those conversations for you, I pulled a page from that old hoot David Letterman and came up with a Top Ten list of my own. That Hoosier lists his in reverse order, but where I come from the number one comes *before* the number ten. And who are you gonna trust, a man who was educated at Peabody Academy or Ball State?

AMARILLO SLIM'S TOP TEN KEYS TO POKER SUCCESS

1. Play the players more than you play the cards.

2. Choose the right opponents. If you don't see a sucker at the table, you're it.

3. Never play with money you can't afford to lose.

4. Be tight and aggressive; don't play many hands, but when you do, be prepared to move in.

5. Always be observing at a poker game. The minute you're there, you're working.

6. Watch the other players for "tells" before you look at your own cards.

7. Diversify your play so other players can't pick up tells on you.

8. Choose your speed based on the direction of the game. Play slow in a fast game and fast in a slow game.

9. Be able to quit a loser, and for goodness' sake, keep playing when you're winning.

10. Conduct yourself honorably, so you're always invited back.

That's a nice list and all, but if you could master the first item on that list, it's the only thing you'll ever need: Play the *players* more than you play the *cards*. What they say is true: A man's eyes mirror his soul. Why do you think I always wear a big old brimmed Stetson when I play? A man's eyes show 90 percent of what he's thinking. When I'm wearing my hat, you can see my eyes only when I want you to. Besides what you can see from a person's eyes, you also can pick up something about his hand from other physical giveaways, known among poker players as "tells."

One player may talk a lot if he's got a strong hand, giving signs of being anxious to raise; while another player may become very quiet if he's holding something. I can say this now because he's no longer alive—Jack "Treetop" Strauss, a world-class player who won the World Series in 1982, whistled ever so quietly when he was bluffing. Shoot, neighbor, if you can pick up a tell like that on somebody, he might as well be playing with his hand faceup.

Tony Holden, that author who called me the Imelda Marcos of poker, described in his book *Big Deal* how I use words to pick up tells from my opponents.

Amarillo Slim is one of poker's great talkers. This is not just his natural joie de vivre. Table talk, to Slim, is a wily tactic, designed to throw his opponents off their game. Variations on such themes as "Hey, neighbor, you better call that big bet o' mine, ah got six little titties [three queens] down here," or "This man's slower than a mule with three broken legs," or (if there are no ladies present) "This sucker's tighter than a nun's doodah," have won Slim a handsome fortune for years, and helped him become the most celebrated poker player of his time.

I always notice that whenever people quote me, they always try to make me seem like some illiterate country cowboy, but if that's how they want to portray me, it suits me just fine. People say that I could talk the nuts off a motorcycle, and, believe me, it's not because I like to hear my own voice—which I've been told resembles the voice of that old cop from *The Dukes of Hazzard*, Rosco P. Coltrane. I just think that talking at the poker table and studying my opponents was the best thing I had going for me.

BETTY CAREY LIKED HER TEA

Jimmy Chagra wasn't the type of man I wanted to associate with, but it was hard not to gamble with him. A drug dealer who spent millions like most folks spend quarters, Chagra came to Vegas for his last hurrah while awaiting trial in Texas. His case was before a judge named John H. Wood, who had earned the nickname "Maximum John." By some strange coincidence, Maximum John was shot dead on the day of the trial, and even though Chagra got indicted for heroin trafficking and sentenced to thirty years at Leavenworth, he managed to beat the murder rap.

While Jimmy was in Vegas, he would play golf for half a million dollars a round and once tipped a cocktail waitress $10,000 for bringing him a bottle of water. Treetop said about Chagra's time in Las Vegas, "It was like having that TV program *Fantasy Island*. I kept waiting for Tattoo to come on and say it was all a dream: 'Look, boss! The plane! The plane!'" Chagra always wanted to beat me at something, so after I had fleeced him on the golf course and at the poker table enough times, he got ahold of Betty Carey to play me in a head-up poker game at the Las Vegas Hilton. Betty, an attractive woman from Cody, Wyoming, was the most aggressive player I've ever played against. She was also regarded as the best woman player in the world, and there ain't no question she was. Jimmy staked her $100,000 to play me head-up in a No Limit Texas Hold'em freeze-out, which is our term for "winner takes all."

We sat down to play and gave our money to the floor man, who went to get our chips. Betty and I were just sitting at the table with the dealer and the hangers-on, who were sucking around the rail and all, waiting for old Slim to get shown up by a nice little lady.

I was drinking coffee, which I usually did when I played, and I said, "Betty, I'm gonna have some more coffee. Would you like some?"

"No, thank you, Slim," she said, "but I will have some hot tea."

I wasn't thinking anything of it at the time, about how she said it, but as a poker player, you're *always* working, trying to learn just the smallest thing about an opponent that might make the difference in a big pot. Well, it took a while to get the cards and count out $200,000 worth of chips, and after I finished my coffee, just real casual, I asked, "Betty, how is your tea?"

"Oh, wonderful," she said, "this is real good tea."

And I knew she liked it. She had no reason to lie; it wasn't like she needed to convince me that the tea at the Las Vegas Hilton was just as good as the queen mother's. She could have been drinking rat piss as far as I was concerned, but the way she said she liked that tea, that got me to thinking. So I thought, Well, after a while I'll ask her something else and see how she answers.

About an hour later, a big pot came up—one that was so big a show dog couldn't jump over it—and she moved in on me. Here she was risking all her chips, and I smelled a bluff. I just didn't think she had anything, so, like we were having a normal conversation, I said to her, "Betty, how do you like your hand?"

"Real good hand, Slim," she said, but the tone of her voice was just a little bit different than when I had asked her about the tea. It lacked the same sincerity. Now I knew she was a lying ass! So I called her with a lousy pair of fives—and I won the pot. She didn't disappoint me one bit; she had nothing and had been making a stone-cold bluff.

After I won, I bragged to everyone there that a woman would have a better chance of putting a wildcat in a tobacco sack than she would of beating me at poker.

Of course, that only made Betty want to beat me more, and the next time I played her—again it was a $100,000 freeze-out—Jimmy staked her on the condition that she wear earplugs. Boy, that was hard! Talking to my opponents is my secret weapon, and I couldn't get much of a read on her or pick up any tells from her voice. Sure enough, she busted my skinny ass and made me eat my words. See what I mean about playing the *players* more than you play the *cards*?

I hope you got a pretty good understanding of poker, because we're fixing to go big time now—to a place in Nevada that most folks know as Lost Wages.

A pair of Texans: actor Chill Wills (left) and Benny Binion, in front of Binion's Horseshoe in the early seventies. *(Courtesy of the author)*

7

A Binion, a Greek, and How Las Vegas Became the Poker Capital of the World

"Tough times make for tough people," said Benny Binion, and, boy, was he about the toughest sonofabitch who ever lived. You wouldn't have known it by looking at that plump little devil, who, with his round belly and baby face, looked as sweet as Santa Claus. But if you crossed him, Benny was the type of man who would put a rattlesnake in your pocket and ask you for a match. Naturally, such a fine man could only have come from one place: Texas.

In 1904, Lester Ben Binion was born in Pilot Grove, Texas, a town with a population of 150 about sixty miles north of Dallas. He had a third-grade education, but it didn't hold him back from making a fortune from anything in Texas that wasn't legal—mainly running whiskey as a "hip-pocket bootlegger" back in the days of Prohibition. In 1928, the same year

I was born, Benny opened what he called a "policy"—a numbers racket that was like a mini-lottery.

In 1936, the city of Dallas was hoping to win the right to host the Texas Centennial celebration, which was like a state fair, and "unofficially" adopted a policy of tolerance toward minor vices. Benny took this as an opportunity to build these special crates that were mobile and could be used as craps tables. Even though the police wouldn't shut him down, they did raid his roving craps games from time to time (as did the bad guys), and Benny was always prepared to move out. "If we had half an hour's notice that we were going to be raided," Benny said, "we could clear it out."

That's where the term "floating" craps game comes from, and from 1936 to 1945, Benny ran these games throughout Dallas and had his hand in all the rackets. Benny said who got what and who didn't. He wielded a big stick and was one of the sharpest businessmen the state of Texas ever produced. I reckon that even with the tens of millions he made, he never had occasion to diagram a sentence either.

The first time I met Benny was in 1945, when I was able to sneak out of Amarillo for a weekend to shoot pool in Fort Worth. I had earned a little bit of a reputation by then, and it wasn't surprising that I ran into Benny down at a pool hall on Fourth and Main. Benny told me that I reminded him of another Slim, a famous crapshooter from Dallas named Slim Williams, and being that both me and Benny had a thing for gambling and horses, we just kinda hit it off.

Benny had a police record a mile long for bootlegging, theft, carrying concealed weapons, and two murder raps—one of which he beat on the grounds of self-defense and the other of which earned him a two-year suspended sentence. I'm not going to tell you that Benny was a saint, because he wasn't, but he did live by a certain code, and if you asked him about it when he was still alive, this is what he'd tell you: "I ain't never killed a man who didn't deserve it." As foreign as that seems to most people today, that's just how things were back in those days in Texas, when a shotgun wielded more power than an attorney. And why shouldn't it have been that way? Our great state always had a long history of gunslinging and gambling, and I still have more guns than I have grandbabies.

When I asked Benny why he left Dallas in a hurry in 1946 to go to Las Vegas, he said, "Slim, I *had* to get out. My sheriff got beat in the election." Benny was considered such a dangerous man that the Rangers had orders to kill him on sight—not to arrest him but to kill him. You've got to make a lot of enemies in Texas for the Rangers to take a bounty out on your head.

Well, as much as folks wanted Benny out of Texas, Nevada seemed happy to have him. When Benny arrived in downtown Las Vegas in 1946, there were only eighteen thousand residents, a far cry from the 1.4 million that it had in 2002, along with the 34 million annual tourists. Of course, gambling was legal, and most of the action was in downtown Las Vegas. Downtown, which is actually at the north end of Las Vegas Boulevard at the intersection of Fremont Street, is now called Glitter Gulch because all the casinos are right on top of each other and it's lit up like it's Christmas every day.

On December 26, 1946, Benjamin Siegel, who you probably know as Bugsy, opened a casino on the south end of Las Vegas Boulevard, about five miles south of Fremont Street. Along with the El Rancho and the Last Frontier, it was the beginning of what is now known as the "Strip." Backed by the famous New York mobster Meyer Lansky, Bugsy named his new place the Flamingo after his mistress, Virginia Hill, who I suppose reminded him of that lovely long-legged bird.

Virginia was a mighty fine-looking woman who had fancy tastes and not enough sense *not* to use the mob's money to cater to them. After she helped Bugsy go way over budget building the place, in June 1947, at age forty-one, Bugsy got assassinated by persons unknown at the house he had bought for Virginia on 808 North Linden Drive in Beverly Hills. Then two of Meyer's boys, Maurice Rosen and Gus Greenbaum, walked in and announced that they were taking over. To give you an idea of how much the times have changed, that hotel is now called the Flamingo *Hilton* and is still right there on the east side of the Strip, across from the Mirage and Caesar's Palace.

When Benny arrived in Las Vegas, he formed a partnership with a man named Kell Housells in a casino downtown called the Las Vegas Club. When Kell sold the building a couple years later, Benny, along with a partner named Emilio Giorgetti, built a casino on the same lot and called it the Westerner. But still homesick for Texas, and not too fond of having a partner to begin with, Benny sold his share to Giorgetti after a few years. When he sent word that he was moving back to Texas, Benny was told that he best stay out of the state for good, and he figured that he'd better start making Nevada feel like home.

With Las Vegas full of people itching to gamble, I reckon it wasn't such a bad spot for that cowboy. In 1951, Benny bought a place on Fremont Street called the Eldorado, mainly because it had an $870,000 tax loss. Even with only that third-grade education, Benny was a man who knew numbers and was always looking for ways to outsmart the tax man—which landed him in Leavenworth a couple years later.

He renamed the Eldorado the Horseshoe, and the first thing he did was hang a sign that said THE WORLD'S HIGHEST LIMITS. Then he spent $18,000 on the first carpet that was ever put in a casino. Everyone told him it was a mistake, until the man who put the carpet in lost $18,000 the first night the joint opened. After a $96,000 loss during the first night of play, the Horseshoe won more than $100,000 in its first twenty-four hours in business, and, in Benny's own words, he was "stuck forever."

Not only was Benny the first to put a carpet in a downtown casino, but what really got people's attention was his willingness to take high action. When he opened the Horseshoe in August 1951, the most you could bet around town at craps was fifty dollars, but that didn't stop Benny from setting the limit at $500. Once he built the place up a little, he boasted that he would take any bet, and back in 1980 a man named William Lee Bergstrom asked if he could really bet $1 million on one roll of the dice. Benny obliged him, and a few months later Mr. Bergstrom showed up with $770,000 and *apologized* that he couldn't raise a whole million. Well, that suited Benny, and he never even bothered to convert the money into chips. Instead Bergstrom just put the whole damn suitcase of cash on the "don't pass" line, and when the woman rolling the dice crapped out, the Horseshoe counted out $770,000 in cash to Bergstrom, and Benny's son, Ted, the casino manager at the time, escorted him to his car.

A man like that would certainly have been entitled to a nice suite and whatever he could eat and drink, if he had wanted to stick around. Casino managers know that the longer you stay, the more likely the percentages will get you in the end. The real big players, what the casinos call "whales," get a suite the size of the Cotton Bowl and Dom Perignon to wash their hands with if they want. Everyone comps the big players, but Benny comped just about everyone and made the Horseshoe a real friendly place. "If you wanna get rich," Benny said, "make little people feel like big people." Now, that's a businessman for you.

Let me try to explain how this man's mind worked. One time Benny took his family to Washington, D.C., for some sightseeing, and, according to Benny, "People lined up there for five blocks to go in the Treasury every day to see that money. So I had the idea of puttin' a million dollars in a glass cage of a thing." When he got back to Vegas, Benny put up a glass display in the middle of his casino of $1 million in ten-thousand-dollar bills. Talk about knowing how to get people in the door! Nearly every person who came into town wanted to have his photo taken in front of it—and don't think most of 'em didn't play a few hands of twenty-one while they were there. Benny wasn't worried about the money getting stolen—besides his reputation and the fact that the money was in a glass case with a security guard next to it at all times, ten-thousand-dollar bills weren't in circulation at that time, and they would have been impossible to spend.

Benny had what I guess you could call an "unusual" relationship with the law. Even though his felony convictions prevented him from owning a firearm, he carried at least one pistol all his life and always had a sawed-off shotgun nearby. In Las Vegas in the seventies, if the police needed a bunch of cash on short notice to set up a phony drug deal, Benny let 'em take it right from the casino cage. Yet there wasn't no quid pro quo. If a slot cheater or pickpocket was caught in the casino, Benny preferred handling that himself—and had his own security force that dealt with things in such a way that would make a cat think twice about doing it again.

Because the Horseshoe never went public, it didn't have to report earnings, but everyone knew that Benny ran the most profitable casino in Las Vegas. Yet even with all the money floating around town, I had no desire to leave my lovely Helen Elizabeth and beloved Texas to go out to some godforsaken desert—especially when I could gamble right here in the comfort of my own backyard.

But one by one my means of making a living in Texas started vanishing. First it was pool, since I couldn't find anyone to take a game. Then I had to give up booking sports when Bobby K passed that damn Wire Act. And finally the poker games became so treacherous, because of all the stickups, that I started to think that paying my old pal Benny a visit wasn't such a bad idea. At least in Las Vegas you didn't have to worry about getting robbed on your way home from a game, and you felt secure that you'd get paid, too, because everything there was on the level—or at least it appeared to be.

NICK THE GREEK FINALLY HAD TO LET MR. MOSS GO

As evidenced by that gimmick with the million dollars, Benny was a master of publicity, and in 1951 he hatched a scheme that would change the world of poker forever. Even though the Horseshoe didn't have a poker room in 1951—and not for almost twenty years after that—Benny was always one to listen to his customers. So when Nick "the Greek" Dandalos, the most famous gambler next to Titanic Thompson in those days, told Benny that he wanted to play no-limit poker in a freeze-out against the richest guy he could find, Benny was happy to accommodate him.

Nick the Greek was in his late fifties, a tall, good-looking guy with a college degree who loved cigars and had about the best manners of anyone you'll ever meet. He was so calm when he gambled that folks like to say that he looked like a guy sitting with an icicle up his ass. The Greek met up with Titanic Thompson in Chicago in 1921, where they were backed by Al Capone, and later traveled throughout the Midwest before making their way to New York in the late twenties. After claiming to have won and lost more than $500 million in his life, the Greek spent his last few years playing $5 poker in Gardena, California. When asked how it could be interesting to play such low stakes, he said, "Hey, it's action!" He died broke on Christmas Day in 1966.

Benny saw to it that the Greek shot craps in his casino while he went about the business of finding someone to go head-to-head with him. Thankfully, he knew just the player to do it: Johnny Moss. You see, I was just twenty-two at the time, and while I had made some big scores playing poker in the service, I was still green to the game and known more for shooting stick. So Benny tracked down his boyhood buddy, who at the time was blazing a poker trail in Texas that I later followed with Doyle and Sailor. In fact, we did all we could to steer clear of Johnny Moss—he was that damn good. If Johnny was in Fort Worth, we'd go to Waco. If Johnny was in Waco, we'd go to Austin. And if Johnny was in Austin, we'd go to Odessa!

"Johnny," Benny said when he finally reached him by phone in Dallas, "they got a fellow out here who calls himself Nick the Greek. Thinks he can play stud poker. Johnny, I think you should come out here and have some fun."

Seeing a chance to make some money staking Johnny and gain some publicity for his hotel, Benny set up a card table right smack dab in the front of the Horseshoe, just inside the door on Fremont Street in downtown Las Vegas. Johnny had been up for four straight days playing in Texas, but it didn't stop him from catching the next plane out of Dallas.

Johnny arrived on a Sunday, didn't bother to check in to his room, shook the Greek's hand, and sat right down to play no-limit five-card stud. Other than to water his horse, Johnny didn't leave the table until Thursday. For gamblers, staying up long hours is just a way of life. I once stayed up three days and four nights playing in Texas, and it hardly affected me at all. Fats said that in the thirties he once played pool with a man for 120 hours straight. Well, you know for sure he meant without sleep—but not without *food*.

Over the next couple of months, there was always a crowd ten feet deep to watch these two guys play, and anyone else was welcome to join them—as long as they were willing to buy in for $10,000. But mostly the action was head-up five-card stud poker with a $100 ante.

For the first couple of months, they played pretty evenly, but Benny sensed that it was just a matter of time before Johnny broke the Greek. Then, in what seemed like just another hand, Johnny was dealt a nine in the hole and a six up to start. On the third card, he was dealt a nine, giving him a hidden pair of nines. Nick had a seven and an eight of different suits showing, so even if he had one of those cards matched in the hole, he was way behind Johnny in the hand. What transpired next is the stuff of legend, and this here hand ranks as one of the most famous in poker history.

When he caught the nine on third street, Johnny bet five thousand, and, just like it was nothing, the Greek raised him $25,000. Well, an ordinary amateur in Johnny's shoes would have moved in on him, but Mr. Moss wasn't looking to win no $30,000 or $40,000 on this hand. Like any good poker player from Texas, he wanted to break this sonofabitch. So he bided his time.

On the fourth card, Johnny caught a deuce, and the Greek caught a trey. Well, at that point, Johnny felt even better about his hand. There wasn't no way that the Greek could make a straight or flush, and since he didn't have a card higher than a nine showing, Johnny had the lock. Shoot, the two hundred people or so that were packed into the Horseshoe watching knew it—it seemed like everyone did except the Greek.

Johnny had the high card showing, which meant he had to act first. He didn't want to scare the Greek out of the pot, so he checked, hoping to trap the Greek, and he wasn't disappointed. The Greek bet another $25,000, and Johnny saw it and raised him another $50,000.

The Greek called, and on the fifth and last card, which is also dealt faceup, Johnny was dealt a trey and Nick was dealt a jack. Johnny was showing 6-9-2-3, and the Greek was showing 8-6-3-J, and because the Greek was high, it was up to him to act. Greek just sat there for what Johnny later told me felt like a month, puffing on his cigar. Finally the Greek bet his last $50,000. I might have given my best horse to have witnessed this, but while I was in Amarillo at the time, Benny later told me that it was so quiet you could have heard a mouse piss on cotton in that room.

Johnny didn't have any decision to make. He couldn't raise him any because all of the Greek's money was already in the pot—which was now about $250,000—and he sure as shit couldn't fold. There wasn't no way in hell the Greek could have raised him $25,000 on third street and called a $50,000 raise on fourth street without at least a pair going into the last card. There was just no possible way Nick could have had a jack in the hole to beat him, so without as much as a thought, Johnny called the $50,000 and turned over his nine that was in the hole.

"Mr. Moss," Nick said, "I think I got a jack in the hole."

Thinks he's got a jack in the hole! Boy, I'da reached over and slugged him. A man puts all that money in the pot, and then he says he's not sure what he's got. But the Greek was always a gentleman, and to this day I don't think he was putting Johnny on. You see, great poker players—and the Greek certainly was one—play their *opponent's* hand, not their own. When the Greek made up his mind on third street that Johnny was on a bluff, he didn't look back at his own hand; he didn't need to.

The Greek figured that if he played back at Johnny, he could get him to fold, so what he was holding wasn't of any consequence. As it turned out, the Greek had made a terrible read, because old Johnny had a pair of nines. Despite the Greek's comment, Johnny wasn't fazed. It wouldn't have been the biggest pot he'd ever lost in his life, that's for sure. "Greek," he said, "if you got a jack in the hole, you are liable to win yourself a damn big pot."

When the Greek went to turn that card over, two hundred–some-odd people craned their necks, and, I tell you, I truly think it was as much a mystery to the Greek as it was to everybody else. Well, shoot, I wouldn't be telling you the story if it weren't but the jack of diamonds!

It just goes to show you that luck does have a place in poker. Johnny had set the perfect trap, and the other guy just drew out on him. In my lifetime I've lost approximately $30 *million* playing poker (you wouldn't believe me if I told you how much I've won), and very little of it came from making a mistake. It's not like chess, where the best players win all the time. In fact, at the 2002 World Series of Poker, of the 631 entries, there were 13 former world champions, including me and Doyle, and not one made it to the final 45 players. If that doesn't tell you that there's short-term luck in poker (the tournament only lasts five days), then I don't know what does.

All you can do is make the plays that have a percentage of success and put yourself in a position to win. But that doesn't mean if you start with two aces and your opponent starts with two deuces that he isn't going to beat you sometimes. If that were the case, you wouldn't be able to get them suckers to keep coming back.

In the long run, skill will prevail, and, sure enough, after about five months, Johnny finally did break the Greek. Rumor has it that he got him for $2 million, but, besides the Greek, the only two people who knew for sure were Benny and Johnny, and they certainly weren't gonna run their mouths off about it. As Johnny was scooping in what was to be the last pot of that five-month session, the Greek smiled, stood up from the table, and said, "Well, Mr. Moss. I guess I got to let you go."

AIN'T NO COWBOY GONNA BEAT ME OUT OF $100,000

On March 27, 1964, Tod Alan, my second son and the last of three children, was born. Like his brother, Bunky, who was a good enough golfer to earn a golf scholarship to West Texas State and then Texas Tech, Tod earned a golf scholarship to the University of South Alabama.

I know it seems like I've been telling mostly gambling stories, but I can't begin to tell you how much them kids mean to me. I guess I just feel like what happens at home should stay at home, so I'll keep most of those stories in the family. In just a little bit, though, I will tell you how Bunky's golf abilities came in handy.

Nineteen sixty-four was also the first time that Doyle and I went to Las Vegas together, and the two of us were ready to show everybody that Texas had the two best poker players that desert state had ever seen. There weren't but a handful of men back in Texas who hadn't been broke by one of us, so Las Vegas opened up a whole new world of suckers for us to swindle—at least that's what Doyle and I were thinking when we came to visit. Sailor, of course, was back in Texas booking, not paying Bobby K no mind.

The big games in those days were at the Dunes, right on the corner of Las Vegas Boulevard and Flamingo Road, where the Bellagio now stands. The Dunes opened on May 23, 1955, with Hollywood musical star Vera-Ellen providing the opening-night entertainment in a show billed as the Magic Carpet Review. Since the Dunes wanted to attract the Hollywood crowd it specialized in big-name entertainers. In 1961, Liberace got onstage with Pinky Lee. Other stars such as George Burns, Carol Channing, Frankie Laine, Eleanor Powell, and Tony Bennett performed there, and, in a move that seemed awfully fitting, in 1963 they showcased *Guys and Dolls* starring Betty Grable. During the 1960s and 1970s, the Dunes also attracted a lot of New Yorkers, mainly because of a junket man named Julius "Big Julie" Weintraub. Talk about a sharp cat, he was the one who said, "The guy who invented gambling was bright, but the guy who invented chips was a genius."

Even though this was our first time playing against the sharps in Vegas together, Doyle and I felt like those cats were soft as butter, and we arrived with more than $100,000 between us. Back then at the Dunes, the main game was Kansas City Lowball, which wasn't my best game, but at least it was no-limit.

I felt like I had these guys' tells down pretty good, but it seemed like every time I made a hand, it was second best. It didn't take but a few hours for them Vegas cats to break a couple of guys from Texas who thought they had hung the moon. After having been a human vacuum cleaner for so long in Texas, it was some strong medicine getting broke by those guys. To this day Doyle talks about how he didn't even have money to take a cab home when he arrived back in Texas. That boy swallowed a lot of humble pie when he had to call his wife and have her pick him up from the airport.

When I got back to Texas, I concentrated on rebuilding my bankroll by fleecing all them Texas folks. On my next trip to Vegas, with that whipping still fresh in my mind, I made up my mind to bring my "A" game at all times. By this time, there was also big poker action at the Golden Nugget in downtown Las Vegas, and because of my friendship with Benny, I always had free accommodations right across the street at the Horseshoe.

Bill Boyd, known as "Mr. Poker" in Nevada, was the card-room manager at the Golden Nugget, and I still think he's the best card-room operator that ever lived. He was friendly, organized, and fair, and because the players respected him, there wasn't any skullduggery going on. Boyd was also regarded as the best stud player in the world, but since he was the only man capable of raising a big enough stake to play me, it didn't stop me from challenging him to a $100,000 freeze-out.

I would have been the favorite had we been playing Hold'em, but Boyd insisted that we play stud. Shoot, *no one* played Hold'em in Nevada then. With a huge crowd around us, including Benny and most of the folks I knew over at the Horseshoe, we got it on right there on Boyd's home turf in the Golden Nugget. Immediately I started whipping that boy good. In fact, it didn't take but a few hours before I had him down to his last $200 in chips, and I was sure he would ask for a rematch.

Mr. Poker had a lot of pride, though, and he knew how much it would have damaged his reputation to lose $100,000 to a country sonofagun like me. Keep in mind that this was still eight years before I became world champion, and at that time I was known more, at least in Nevada, as a pool hustler than as a poker player. With his ego on the line, Boyd had to save face, and I would have laid 50 to 1 that old Bill was gonna do what most people do when they're losing—beg like hell to keep playing.

"Seems as though you're gonna need some more chips if you have any intention of getting even," I said. I was fixing to throw my usual on him—Texas rules—and try to take him for $200,000 more. But Boyd didn't take the bait. Instead he picked up his last two hundred in chips with one hand, shook my hand with the other, and before he walked over to the cashier, he said, as much to the railbirds as to me, "There'll never be no Texas cowboy who beats me out of a hundred thousand dollars playing poker."

I guess I had no choice but to settle for a measly $99,800!

Despite the many gambling opportunities, I never moved out to Las Vegas. It just seemed like there were too many folks out there who were liable to piss on your leg and swear to you that it was raining. For me Amarillo will always be home, if for no other reason than that I wouldn't want to go through the trouble of having to change my name. Aside from that, living here allows me to keep my head clear and makes me that much sharper when I do travel to Vegas—which was often then and is still often now. And let me tell you, poker in that city was just getting started.

MCCORQUODALE, MOORE, A REUNION, QUAIL, AND AN IDEA

There wasn't a game of Texas Hold'em to be found in Nevada before 1963. Then a guy named Felton "Corky" McCorquodale from Fort Worth, who

I'd met in Hot Springs, introduced Hold'em at the Golden Nugget. Bill Boyd went along with it, but it didn't take off right away. Then, a couple years later at the Stardust, a big hotel on the Strip, Johnny Drew, the card-room manager there at the time, let me spread a Hold'em game, and every big shot in town came and played. It was a game of action, with much more skill than stud or draw. And then Syd Wyman, the owner of the Dunes, who became a good friend, said, "Slim, that's the best card game I've ever seen. Bring it out to the Dunes, and we'll start playing Hold'em there." Sure enough, by the late sixties, most of the big poker in Nevada was Hold'em. And, gee whiz, anybody who knew how to play could win whatever he wanted to win, because them folks in Nevada had never played it.

In 1969, Tom Moore, a friend of mine from San Antonio, bought the Holiday Hotel in Reno and held what he called "The Texas Gamblers Reunion," even though it wasn't limited to Texans. As a courtesy to him, most of the gambling bosses, including Benny and his son Jack Binion, and several of the rounders agreed to support the opening of his new hotel and casino. Anytime a Texan asks for help, you can bet I'll do my part.

So we all went up there and played poker: Treetop Strauss, Johnny Moss, Corky McCorquodale, Aubrey Day, Puggy Pearson, Jimmy Casella, Bill Boyd, Syd Wyman, Long Diddie, Jimmy the Greek, Doyle, and even Minnesota Fats, who was in town giving a pool exhibition. There were maybe twenty of us, and we played mainly Texas Hold'em. We didn't declare a winner; we all knew that whoever wound up with all the money was the winner. It wasn't really a tournament back then, but it got Benny, that master public-relations man, thinking about turning this gathering of greats into something more.

One day over lunch, me, Benny, Tom Moore, and a bunch of other cats were sitting around telling hunting stories, and it must have put Tom in the mood for some exotic food. He asked me if I could arrange to have some quail brought in. He said he needed enough to feed about forty peo-ple, including Minnesota Fats, who was never one to turn down an oppor-tunity for a free meal.

I hunt quail quite a bit, and I had arranged for some friends to fly me out a bunch from Amarillo so that Tom could get his "exotic" fare. Doc

Ramsey, a bird hunter from Waco, Texas, said, "You know about the deal on the quail don't you?"

"Yeah," Tom said. "I know that attorney in Austin bet that he could eat one a day for thirty days, and he couldn't do it. I never heard of anybody that could."

"There's nobody alive that can eat a quail a day for thirty days," Doc reiterated. "The meat's so strong that you get to where you can't walk within fifty yards of where it's being cooked before you start regurgitating."

Benny, who was listening mighty intently to this conversation, turned to me and whispered, "Slim, are you sure about this?"

"I know maybe ten people that have tried it," I said, "and nobody can do it. Doc and Tom are right."

It's kind of like the old bet about not being able to drink a gallon of milk in an hour. I don't know nothing about stomach enzymes, but I know that there have been plenty of bets about a man trying to eat a quail for thirty days in a row, and the longest I had ever heard of someone doing it was seventeen days.

So, looking for an opinion by a man who knew a little something about food, Tom said, "Fats, what about it?"

"Hell, I can stuff a turkey with a quail and eat it three times a day for thirty days," Fats said.

Well, to tell you how confident Fats was, we couldn't get that fat sonofabitch to bet one nickel. Even *he* knew it couldn't be done. And speaking of old Fats, that was the night I beat him in one-pocket in front of all them bosses, and he said, "If you want some publicity, go set yourself on fire, you skinny fuckin' cowboy." Sorry if I'm repeating myself, but that one still makes me laugh like a schoolgirl! Fats always did have a way with words.

Anyhow, before we went to bed that night, Benny pulled me aside and said, "Slim, I got a little project for you. You need to find a way for somebody to be able to eat a quail a day for thirty days. Shit, there's no telling what that Tom would bet—at least a couple hundred thousand."

I told Benny it was impossible, and he said, "I know you, you'll find a way for a guy to do it."

Now, I sure as hell didn't argue, but I knew I wasn't the guy he had in mind, and I didn't give it another thought. Then, about four or five months later, I was in Roswell, New Mexico, looking to buy a horse. I rode this colt around the ranch, and he was doing pretty good. The owner said that I should take him out and show him some country to see if I liked the way he traveled.

One of the ranch hands helping us out was a big, strapping kid, not more than twenty. I didn't think nothing of it, because you expect to see a country hoss working on a ranch like that, but when I rode the horse about fifty yards up to the fence, the very same kid was there to open the gate for me.

Now, I've already told you that I don't drink and I don't hallucinate, and it just didn't make no sense that a fella could be in two different places at the same time. "I just saw you down by the barn, and now you're up here opening this gate," I said. "Man, you must be able to fly for you to get up here that fast."

"Don't think nothing of it," he said. "That's my brother. We're identical twins."

So I started riding, and then I said to myself, *Identical twins.*

I cut my ride short. I did a U-turn, went back down there, got the two boys together, and said, "You fellas want to make some money?"

"Sure, who we got to kill?" the twins said, just like it was something they did every day.

"No one. I can show you how you can get ahold of a lot of money, and all you gotta do is eat."

The first person I called was Benny, and it didn't take him long to invent an excuse for us to get up to Reno to see good old Tom Moore. We had dinner that night with Tom and a bunch of his buddies—we talked about hunting, of course—and the topic of quail happened to come up again. Just like an ordinary sucker, I told them that I knew a boy who could eat a quail a day for thirty days. Well, brother, they couldn't post their money fast enough—and let me tell you, it wasn't a number that had five figures in it.

I already had them twins checked into the Holiday Hotel and had made arrangements to have the quail shipped from Amarillo. Tom said they'd cook 'em right there at the hotel, and, just so it didn't seem suspicious, I went through the whole rigmarole about different stipulations and such. Tom agreed that "he" could have 'em fried, boiled, baked, stewed, roasted, raw, however he wanted 'em, but he had to eat 'em in front of people. He also had to stay for thirty minutes afterward to show that he didn't throw it up.

Our plan was for one boy to eat 'em for about three days. Then, he'd go to a movie, where his brother was already waiting, and once the movie was over, he'd stay in the theater and his brother would come out. So now you'd have a big old kid who hadn't eaten quail for three days come in and do it for three days while his brother was chasing girls in Lake Tahoe or something. A few days later, they'd make the switch at the movie theater again, and so it went. The kid would go back to the hotel and eat those quail for about three days. After seventeen days of this, it had attracted a lot of attention, and everybody kept sitting around waiting for this sonofabitch to pass out or start vomiting or hallucinating. They all just figured he was a freak of nature or something when he kept on eating a quail a day for the entire thirty days. Boy, am I glad I went to Roswell to buy a horse.

As much as Benny won from the bet, it wasn't quail that was on his mind when we got back to Las Vegas. "That was a good thing up there in Reno a few months ago," Benny said. "It sure brought in a lot of people, and I'm certain there will be even more next year. The more I think about it, that might be a good thing to have here at the Horseshoe."

I told him I agreed, but when Benny talked about the idea with his family, all of the other Binions told him he was crazy to put in a poker room. Their reason was the same then as it is now: A poker room barely makes any money for the casino, especially compared to them one-arm bandits. Floor space was too valuable to waste on a game where the money passed between the players with the casino only collecting a small vig for running the game.

A poker table takes in about a hundred dollars an hour in revenue, and between the dealers, the chip runners, the cards, and all them card players who'd just as soon take a drink from the toilet than tip a cocktail waitress, it isn't exactly what you'd call a profit center.

But all that didn't matter to Benny. I'm telling you, this man was as sharp as they come and way ahead of his time as a marketer. He then made a decision to bring poker to the Horseshoe the next year. After 1970, poker would never be the same.

This picture was taken in the poker room at Binion's Horseshoe in 1970. I'm way in the back left, but in the front row, from left to right, are: George Barnes, Curtis "Ironman" Skinner, Johnny Moss, Chill Wills, Benny Binion (standing), Titanic Thompson, Joe Bernstein, Puggy Pearson, and Jimmy Casella. That's a who's who if I ever saw one. *(Courtesy of Binion's Horseshoe)*

8

Another Greek, a Thackrey, and the World Series of Poker

$\mathcal{I}$ suppose if you were born with the name Demetrius Synodinos, you too would have come up with something clever like Jimmy "the Greek" Snyder. Whether or not he took the nickname from Nick the Greek, I don't know, but unlike Nick, who was trim and a gentleman, Jimmy was a big guy and kinda gruff. Born in 1919 in Steubenville, Ohio, the Greek dropped out of high school in tenth grade and, like Benny, built his stake running floating craps games. After World War II, he moved to Las Vegas to become a public-relations man, and at one point he even represented Howard Hughes.

I can't say I liked the man—truth is, I couldn't stand him—but I have to give him his due. Before the 1948 presidential election between the clean-shaven Harry S. Truman and the mustachioed Thomas E. Dewey, the Greek took one of the craziest surveys I ever heard of. According to him—and I wouldn't trust him as far as I could throw him—he polled nineteen hundred women and found that most of them did not like men with mustaches.

You won't see odds on an election posted in any casinos, but take my word that there's big action on 'em. I know firsthand about a big bet on a presidential election between a man from Texas and a man from Tennessee in 2000, but we're not quite to that story yet. Before the 1948 election, the bookmakers at one point had the Democrat Truman as a 60-to-1 underdog, even though he was the incumbent. As the election got closer, Truman gained a little ground, and, with odds of 17 to 1, the Greek ponied up $10,000 on Truman to win.

Had I not been in Europe at that time, I reckon I would have taken a shot on Truman, too. He and his wife, Bess, were just simple country folks from Missouri, and people seemed to agree with their ways. Dewey, the former attorney general from New York, didn't have much personality, and his mustache made him look a little like Adolf Hitler. It wasn't exactly the look you wanted in a president in those times—or in any time, for that matter.

Apparently the press didn't see it the same way. The *New York Times* titled a story "Thomas E. Dewey's Election as President Is a Foregone Conclusion." *Life* magazine ran a photo of Dewey on the cover with the caption "The Next President of the United States." Truman was such a strong supporter of civil rights that it led to discontent within the Democratic Party and the emergence of the Dixiecrats, and South Carolina governor Strom Thurmond ran as the party's candidate on the "segregation" ticket. When Thurmond celebrated his one-hundredth birthday in 2002, Congressman Trent Lott said the United States would have been better off if Thurmond had won, and he caught so much heat that he resigned as the Senate majority leader.

Anyhow, with the odds stacked heavily against him, Truman took to the road on his famous "whistlestop" campaign that drew ordinary folks out by the thousands, and the legend of "Give 'Em Hell, Harry!" was born. One of my favorite moments in presidential history (aside from bluffing Tricky Dick out of a pot) came when old Harry spoke like a poker player in his final campaign speech. "The smart boys say we can't win," said Truman. "They tried to bluff us with a propaganda blitz, but we called their bluff; we told the people the truth. And the people are with us. The tide is rolling. All over the country. I have seen it in the people's faces. The people are going to win this election."

On Tuesday, November 2, 1948, Truman and his family voted in Independence, Missouri, and when they went to bed that night at the famous Elms Hotel, Truman was losing the election. I doubt that Jimmy the Greek even went to sleep that night, and when he got a call from a friend in Chicago at the crack of dawn saying that Truman had lost, he was crushed.

"Are you *positive?*" the Greek asked.

"I'm reading the headline in the *Chicago Daily Tribune*," his friend said. "It says DEWEY DEFEATS TRUMAN."

"That damn survey cost me ten thousand dollars!" said a dejected Greek.

Well, it wasn't long before that mistake got corrected, and Truman hopped on a train to Washington for another term in the Oval Office. Someone handed him the DEWEY DEFEATS TRUMAN newspaper while he was on the back platform of the train, and one of the most famous photos in American history was taken of Truman holding up the newspaper.

The only person who was happier than Truman was Jimmy the Greek, who pocketed $170,000 and never looked back. Flush with a bankroll that was surpassed only by the chip on his shoulder, the Greek acquired quite a reputation as a prognosticator and became one of Nevada's leading men. He then went on to write a syndicated newspaper column and built a strong following.

Like Sailor, the Greek didn't take Bobby K too seriously about it being a felony to transmit information related to betting over the phone, and in 1962 the attorney general shut down his bookmaking shop, Vegas Turf and Sportsroom, and fined him $50,000. In Nevada it wasn't illegal to book, but the Greek got caught for giving odds to an out-of-state friend over the phone. President Ford later pardoned him for these violations.

As his column became more and more popular, the folks at CBS took a shine to the Greek and in 1976 made him the resident oddsmaker on *The NFL Today*, where Brent Musburger was the top dog. I got to know

Brent when he covered the World Series of Poker for CBS. He said that if I came up in the booth with him, I'd relax him—which was the same reason that in later years Johnny Carson would have me on his show with Bob Hope, my old traveling buddy from Special Services. I guess there's something about the banter of an uneducated country cowboy that sets these guys at ease. Besides, the viewers loved it. Everybody else would have said, "Well, Brent, that fine player is on a real hot streak." But I'd always say something like, "Texas Dolly is hotter than a widow woman's love," and he liked that style of commentating, so we got to be friends.

In 1980 the Greek and Brent got into a fistfight at a midtown-Manhattan bar. Since Brent was the managing editor of the show, the Greek wouldn't let up on him about getting more time on the air. This was a swank bar in New York City, you understand, not some smoky back room in Steubenville, Ohio, or Bumbleville, Nevada. So when Brent told the Greek to let it go, it didn't surprise me none that the Greek would go so far as to slug him for not being given more time to run his mouth in front of a national television audience. But what goes around comes around, and the running of his big mouth—making racist comments on the air in 1988—got him shit-canned by CBS.

A big *I* and a little *you* is how I always described the Greek, and I said it right to his face.

"Slim, that's not a nice description," the Greek said, "but it suits me."

With the Greek it was always "*I* like St. Louis plus three." Never "Who do *you* like? It was always *I* like, and *I* think. And *I* this and *I* that. It didn't even matter when he got on television and started doing interviews; he never did give anyone else a chance to speak. It was always the same routine: *I* like and *I* think. But even though he was an above-average handicapper, he was a poor gambler, and aside from that election he never did make much money hustling. I suppose that's why he went out and got himself a few "real" jobs.

But none of the things I just mentioned are the reasons I didn't like him. The Greek did a no-no with me—and for a man like myself, who makes his daily bread by wagering, it was an unforgivable offense. Up at Tom Moore's place in Reno in 1969, the Greek made me some sizable golf bets before the Tournament of Champions, which used to be held at the

Desert Inn, but was at La Costa Country Club, just north of San Diego, that year. I knew all the golfers back then, played with most of 'em even, and I could handicap their play real well.

We must have made fifteen bets on a variety of things, including which players would qualify, where they would finish, and all sorts of other propositions. Right before the tournament, I think I had already won nearly half the bets on who would qualify, and it was obvious that I had about 70 percent the best of it on the remaining ones. The Greek knew he was fixing to lose a big figure.

So old Demetrius—that's what I liked to call him from time to time, and, boy, did it really frost his shorts—made a rare visit to the Horseshoe to see me. The Greek always thought he was better than everybody else and felt like it was beneath him to go downtown. He preferred them fancier joints out on the Strip where the elite meet to eat. Now, I'll be the first to say that downtown Las Vegas has lost its luster compared to the Strip—and I don't think it's a coincidence that this happened after Benny died in 1989. But back in those days, the Strip was more of a place for the socialites to show their faces, and downtown was home to the die-hard gamblers. You didn't ever see no men in leotards make an elephant disappear at the Horseshoe—not with anyone named Binion running the place.

"Slim," the Greek said, not wasting any time with pleasantries, "about these other golf bets . . ." Now, mind you, I was involved in a no-limit Hold'em game at the time, and he didn't even have the courtesy of asking for a minute of my time before he spoke.

"Yeah," I said, "what about 'em?"

"I need to *off* them."

It didn't surprise me that his sentence began with the word "I," but I've always had a good reply for that one: "It takes two people to make a bet, Demetrius, so it takes two people to off it."

"You're not gonna let me out?"

"Let you out! The idea is, you bet to win. Did you bet me to try to *lose?*"

"Well, uh, uh . . ."

"What'd you bet me for? Didn't you bet me to win *my* money?"

"Well, yeah, Slim."

"Well I bet you to win *yours*. Now that I've got it won, all of a sudden

I'm a bad guy and I'm supposed to let you off? Not a fuckin' chance in the world."

Then he said, "I probably won't be able to pay you," and I told him, "You *will* find a way to pay me."

It wasn't enough money that it was gonna change my life, and if it had been someone else, someone with a bit more integrity, I might've let it go, but not this sonofabitch. So I gave him a look that would make a rattlesnake crawl back into a cave, and he headed back up to the Strip and started running his mouth off to some of his "classy" friends up there.

You see, at that time I had a lot of friends in Vegas, and whenever there was a to-do with me, word got around pretty fast. Without my ever saying one word to anybody about my conversation with the Greek, Syd Wyman, the very powerful man who owned the Dunes, cornered the Greek one day and said, "Listen, Greek, I understand you're trying to welsh on old Slim. Let me tell you something: If you want to stay in this town, you're gonna pay him if you lose."

Well, we didn't off the bet, and somehow the Greek found a way to pay me—I don't know how, and, frankly, I don't care, so long as I got my money. And when I took his money, I told myself that I would never let that man win a nickel off me—I'd just as soon die before I forked over a penny to Jimmy the Greek. Now, that was a proclamation that nearly ended me for good.

THE WORLD SERIES COMETH IN 1970—BUT REALLY 1971, THANKS TO THACKREY

After that trip to Reno in 1969, all Benny could think about was bringing the best poker players in the world to his casino. So, just like that, in May 1970, Benny opened up a poker room at the Horseshoe, sent out word through the gambling grapevine, and before you knew it, all the top players were there. I joined Treetop Strauss, Puggy Pearson, Johnny Moss, Bill Boyd, and Doyle, and we played poker nonstop for three days. Sailor was still back in Texas, and it wasn't until 1973, when he took a job running the poker room at the Horseshoe, that he moved out to Vegas for good. Doyle had already moved there and was quickly earning a reputation as one of the best players in the world.

Benny even invited Minnesota Fats and Titanic Thompson, just so the greatest collection of gamblers this country had ever known could be assembled in one place at one time. It's pretty remarkable when you think about it—it was a legendary moment for Las Vegas, and what Benny did forever changed the history of poker in America. But before I tell you more about that, let me just say that while it seemed like a wise move to get Fats and Ti there for PR reasons, it ended up backfiring on Benny.

Because Fats was a TV star by then and, as most folks thought, the man behind the movie *The Hustler*, fans wanted his autograph. But when it came time to sign his name, Fats couldn't do it. Instead he would just pull out a rubber stamp and press his John Hancock onto his picture. It was obvious that Fats couldn't read or write, and I said to Benny—who was trying to change the negative image of poker—"Hell, Benny, that ain't no good for us."

Here we were trying to legitimize poker, and Fats was making us look like a bunch of ignorant fools. And Ti wasn't any better. He was nearly eighty years old at this point, and his talent as a poker player was very much in decline—but his ability to cheat wasn't, and people wouldn't even go near him for fear of losing their shirt. The next year Benny had enough sense not to invite either one of them back.

Even though we just did what we always did—which was play poker—Benny called it the World Series of Poker. It got a little bit of publicity, but unlike what Benny had hoped for, it didn't capture the public's attention. Sure, gamblers knew about it, and everyone who stopped by got a kick out of who was there and what was going on, but Benny's plan of attracting the average Joe to poker and putting his casino on the map was a flop.

And here's why: There wasn't any structure to the tournament or anything. All we did was play for a while, and at the end we all voted on who was the best player. Well, hell, that was kind of a joke, since we all knew that the best player was the one who got the most chips, but we went along with Benny's plan and designated his old buddy Johnny Moss as the first World Series of Poker champion.

But, like most things with Benny, his idea of creating a World Series of Poker wasn't gonna fail even if it killed him, and he got just the break he needed. Ted Thackrey, that feature writer for the *Los Angeles Times*, was there to check out the event. After Johnny Moss was voted the winner, Ted introduced himself to me and said, "You know, Slim, if you all had some way to make this gathering a lot more competitive, it would be an interesting event."

"Competitive!" I said, "How could you be any more competitive than to play for tens of thousands of dollars?"

Here was a man that I didn't know from a grape, and he was questioning me about two things I knew best: gambling and publicity. It wasn't like he was yelling at me or nothing, but when he said, "You got to have a *winner, a real* winner," I shot right back at him and said, "Damn it, we know who the winner is: the person who winds up with all the money."

But he wasn't letting up. "You gotta find some way to make it a contest," Thackrey said. "If you want to get the press involved and turn the World Series into a real sporting event, you need to give it some structure, create some drama, and make it like a real tournament."

"Freeze-out," I said, and, brother, that one word changed the face of poker forever.

When Thackrey asked what I meant by that, I explained to him what a freeze-out was—that everyone would just put up a certain amount of money and one guy would get it all, just like I had done with Betty Carey, Bill Boyd, and dozens of others. Play until everyone got broke except for the best poker-playing sonofabitch.

"That'd get it," Thackrey said.

It got me thinking a little, and it damn sure made a lot of sense. How many people would watch the Kentucky Derby if a bunch of horses ran around the track and then all the jockeys voted on the winner? Or at the baseball World Series, who would give a damn if they just played a bunch of games without any structure and then crowned the world champion based on a ballot? All the times that poker had been played with a big crowd—like when Johnny Moss played Nick the Greek—it had always been a freeze-out. There wasn't no drama in seeing the chips pass back and forth—what got people excited was seeing a person get *eliminated*.

Well, hell, that settled it. It wasn't but ten minutes later that Thackrey, Benny, and I were breaking bread together, and Benny thought it was the best thing he had heard of since identical twins from Roswell, New Mexico.

The 1971 World Series of Poker was going to be an *event*.

♠ ♣ ♦ ♥

In May 1971, the first *real* World Series of Poker took place in a roped-off corner of the Horseshoe, and, with the help of Thackrey, it was set up in such a way that made it suitable to the press.

Jimmy the Greek had volunteered to promote the event for free, an offer that Benny couldn't refuse, and because of the publicity it brought to the event and Mr. *I* himself, it ended up working out well for everyone. If you go back and look at any of those old tapes that they still sell at the gift shop at the Horseshoe, the Greek was the voice of poker back then. Despite the lack of love between us, we were both natural-born show-men, and we set our differences aside to put on an entertaining display for the hundreds of fans who packed into the casino.

Jack Binion ran the tournament while Benny kept a low profile and just kinda watched over things, making sure nothing went wrong. What with his reputation and his fondness for keeping a pistol on him, all he had to do was be there to guarantee that. The players were similar to the year before, and with six players each putting up $5,000 to enter, the win-ner would go home with $30,000. Most folks had their money on Johnny Moss, who was the defending champion. I wouldn't say I was a long shot, but very few people gave me much of a chance. But this year there wasn't gonna be no vote—Johnny was gonna have to bust all of us if he was gonna win it.

The tournament lasted for two days, and, like they should have been, the final three players were all from Texas: Moss, Treetop, and a lanky cat from Amarillo. We called Jack Strauss "Treetop" because he was six-seven and had been a star basketball player at Texas A&M. At sixteen he won a car in a poker game, and although I mentioned before that I had a tell on him, it wasn't something I picked up until years later. And let me tell you, that tall sonofagun was fearless. Probably the smartest thing he ever said was, "If the Lord wanted you to hold on to your money, he'd have made it with handles on it." Amen!

Well, that day apparently the Lord didn't want me to hold on to mine, because that giant busted me, and there were no prizes for third place. Too bad for Treetop that there weren't any for second either, because Johnny busted him to become the 1971 World Series of Poker champion and took home all $30,000. You can't say that Johnny had "defended" his title, because he hadn't really won it the previous year. But now there was no denying that he was the *world champion*, and, damn, did I ever want those words after my name. May 1971 to May 1972 might have been the longest year of my life.

WAS BUNKY FIXING TO GET AN EAR FULL OF CIDER?

From 1971 to 1972, while I tried to keep my mind off the World Series and my desire to become world champion, I spent an awful lot of time playing golf. With my son Bunky now in college on a golf scholarship, I'd bring him out to Vegas so we could play some of them nice courses together. There are rumors that both he and Tod played some high-stakes golf matches when they were just teenagers, with their old man backing them, but I can't substantiate those. I do remember, though, one time at the Las Vegas Country Club when Bunky was with me watching a big match that I had bet on. Shoot, I think everybody in Nevada had bet on it.

Tommy Fisher, who's still alive, was not only one of Nevada's best poker players but also a heckuva golfer—especially with money on the line. Over the years I had won quite a bit of money betting on him in different golf propositions. On this day he was playing the number-one golf hustler in the whole world, a man named Leon Crump.

When Tommy heard that my money was on Leon, he came up to me and said, "Slim, you've bet on me thirty times playing golf, haven't you?"

"Yup," I said.

"How many times you won?"

"The same number as the amount of times I've bet."

"Nobody in the world can beat me like this guy's trying to play."

What he meant was that even though there wasn't any handicap, Tommy was playing from the ladies' tees. But even with that big advantage, I kept my money on Leon. Between the two of them and all the hustlers on the course, there must have been more than a half a million dollars at stake. When they got to the seventeenth hole, a man we called Squirrel said to me, "You think Leon can hit a golf ball on top of the Hilton hotel?"

"If he says he can, I think he can," I said. I'd been involved in enough of these propositions to know when I was being hustled. Leon was the best golf hustler in the world—if Squirrel was asking me if he could do it, then it looked to me like Leon had already told him that he could.

I had already bet a huge figure on the match, because it seemed like nearly everybody had bet on Tommy, and I was happy to take their action. So we were sitting there waiting for them to play the last hole, and Bunky pulled my coattail and whispered, "Come here, Dad, I want to talk to you."

So we walked away from the crowd, and Bunky, who got real serious all of a sudden, asked, "Dad, would you say I'm a pretty good golfer?"

"I reckon I would, son."

"Good. Then listen to me when I tell you that there's no way Leon can hit that golf ball on top of the Hilton Hotel from here."

"Bunky," I said, "you are a damn good golfer, but let me tell you something: If a guy tells you that he can hit it on top of the hotel, he *knows* that he can."

I told Bunky about the time in Hot Springs, Arkansas, in 1917 when Titanic Thompson got 3-to-1 odds on a hundred dollars that he could throw a walnut from the porch of the Arlington Hotel over a five-story building across the street. Once he made the bet, he switched a regular walnut with one filled with lead and looked like Walter Johnson as he cleared the building with ease. Years later in downtown Amarillo, I was there when Ti made the same switcheroo and threw a walnut on top of the twenty-two-story Herring Hotel.

Bunky, who not only has a little bit of his old man's sense of humor but also has his stubbornness, said, "I know what you think of him and everything, but I'm telling you, it's not humanly possible to hit a ball from here to the top of a thirty-story hotel."

There wasn't no telling Bunky that there had to be a gimmick, but I did manage to convince him to at least wait for the end of the match before we did anything. If Leon didn't win, I wasn't gonna have any money to bet with anyway.

Well, not only did Leon win the match, but he also won the front nine, the back nine, and a few side bets to go with it. Both of us now had plenty of money to gamble with, and Bunky wasn't letting up. "As long as he uses a regulation ball," said Bunky, "you can't lose. You didn't raise no sucker."

I was sure that there had to be a gimmick but figured that it would build a little character for my son to get him an ear full of cider. Squirrel and Leon were counting their money, and I said to Squirrel, "How much do you want to bet on Leon hitting a golf ball on top of the hotel from that spot you asked about earlier?"

"I want to bet all I've got in my right front pocket," he said.

Now Leon couldn't count what he had in *his* front pocket, but when he said he was in for another $10,000 to go with the $26,000 Squirrel had in his pocket, it was a bet. I was still uneasy about it, because when it comes to propositions, I like to be the one *proposing* 'em, not *accepting* 'em.

We agreed that he would have three chances using balls that Bunky and I would get to inspect first. We shook on it, and Leon teed up his first ball. By now it seemed like 82 percent of Nevada was there waiting for me to get fleeced.

Leon swung the club back with that golden swing of his and hit the ball about as cleanly as you could. But as the ball was on its way *down*, it hit about the eleventh floor. Just when I was thinking that he was fixing to raise the stakes, he shocked the hell out of me. "Pick up the money, Slim," Leon said. "I can't hit one any better than that. Ain't no need to hit these other two."

I know you're waiting for the gimmick, but there wasn't one. I guess because Leon had played about the best round of his life, he thought he was superhuman and simply made a bad bet. Bunky never did get that ear full of cider, and when he went back to college, I don't remember him ever asking me for pizza money again.

IT FEELS BETTER IN: THE 1972 WORLD SERIES OF POKER

Thackrey was right that the freeze-out structure of the tournament was just what the press needed to latch on to the World Series of Poker. There was a pretty good turnout in 1971, and by the time the 1972 event rolled around, the press flocked to Vegas to see if Johnny Moss, the Grand Old Man of Poker, could defend his title.

Here I was, back at Binion's Horseshoe for the 1972 World Series of Poker, and in my mind I had a big old bull's-eye painted on Johnny Moss's forehead. Twelve players had signed up, but four of 'em got so caught up in the side action that they never made the tournament. Then, and now, during the World Series, with poker players from all over the world, there are side games, also called "ring" games, that go on nonstop, and in some of those games, the buy-in can be more than a hundred thousand dollars. It's the greatest smorgasbord in the world for anyone who's ever drawn to a flush, but it's also a great temptation, and some men get broke before the real tournament even starts.

Just like the year before, all the characters were in their places. Jack Binion was running the show, the Greek had the microphone, and Benny was telling tales to all the newsmen that Thackrey had set up in a special section. As far as everyone knew, all eight players had paid $10,000 as their entry fee—$5,000 more than the year before. What everyone didn't know was that Benny had decided that for every player who was willing to put in $5,000, he would add another $5,000 to the pot. Listing the buy-in at $10,000 made for better headlines, and it was another example of Benny knowing that to make money you had to spend money.

With $80,000 worth of chips on the table, we were roped off on the casino floor of Binion's Horseshoe. Above us the silent, watchful eye of a camera was there to relay the action to closed-circuit TVs placed all over the casino. Benny, always the marketer, wanted to accommodate the thousands of gamblers that came to watch over the course of what turned out to be a two-day affair. You could hardly breathe in that joint, and the crowd had me more excited than a sore-tailed cat in a room full of rocking chairs.

Of the eight players, five were Texans and three weren't. Going around the table, the players were Johnny Moss, Treetop Strauss, and Doyle, all guys you know by now. Aside from yours truly, the other Texan was Crandall Addington, a dapper millionaire from San Antonio who changed his entire outfit three times a day. In fact, in the 1973 World Series, he laid the Greek fifty dollars to one dollar that he wouldn't loosen his tie the entire event. And while Crandall didn't win the tournament, he was so happy to win a bet from the Greek that he had Demetrius sign the bill and said he was gonna frame it. Crandall was a heckuva nice guy, but no one was giving him much of a chance.

The youse guys were represented by Jimmy Casella, a real tough player from New York. He yakked about as much as I did at the table and, just like me back then, was rarely without a cigarette while he played. In the late fifties, Jimmy had moved to Las Vegas and knew more about Hold'em than the rest of the youse guys combined. Another non-Texan was a man from Missouri named Roger Van Orsdale, who we all called Jolly Roger. He was a quiet guy who dealt in farming equipment and couldn't play a lick. He might as well have just sent in his $5,000 and not even bothered showing up.

Even though Casella could play, the only player not from Texas who I was worried about was Walter Clyde Pearson. Pearson's trademarks were the Cuban cigars that he always chomped on and the flat nose that had earned him the name Puggy, or just Pug. He was born in southern Kentucky, just a couple months after me in 1929. His daddy was a sharecropper and moonlighted as a whiskey bootlegger until one of his competitors shot off his pinky. Talk about childhood memories. It's not too hard to find Pug in Vegas these days, and he'll tell you about the time he was six years old and helped his daddy bury that finger. One of nine kids, Pug moved with his family to Jackson County, Tennessee, where he started hustling pool, pitching pennies, and playing cards when he was eleven. At age thirteen he hitchhiked to Tampa to play pool with three dollars in his pocket, and in two weeks he made it look like a thousand—kinda like my trip with John and Elmer to New Mexico when I was in high school. It was all Pug needed to know that he could use his wits to make a living. In

1945 he joined the navy and came out with $20,000 from playing poker. Twenty-five years later he had become one of the best poker players in the world, and aside from Johnny and Doyle, he was the cat I was most worried about.

Each player started with $10,000 in chips, and the ante started at $10. The minute two players got busted, it went up to $25, then to $50 with four players, and $100 when it got head-up.

About four hours into the tournament, Jimmy Casella and Pug got locked in a big pot. The first three community cards put in the middle, which we call the "flop," were the six of clubs, the six of diamonds, and the queen of diamonds. Jimmy had a king and a ten of diamonds in his hand and was drawing to a flush. Figuring that any of the nine diamonds left in the deck or one of the three remaining kings would give him a winner if Pug had a queen in the hole, Jimmy made a sizable bet.

Little did he know that Pug had *two* queens in the hole—a hand we now call "Siegfried and Roy"—and with a full house, he was setting a nice little trap. Jimmy didn't know it, but he was in a position that we call "drawing dead"—trying to make a flush, but even if he made it, he'd still lose to Pug's full house. The fourth community card, which we call the "turn," was the four of diamonds. Now Jimmy really thought he had something with his flush and made an even bigger wager. Again Pug just called, figuring he could break the sonofagun after the fifth community card was dealt, which we call the "river."

The river card was the deuce of hearts, which didn't change anything. Jimmy was first to act and thought for a while. He figured either that Puggy had a big hand and was setting a trap or that he had nothing and was fixing to make a big bluff. Jimmy checked, and Puggy moved in on him. Well, let me tell you, neighbor, when you're sitting there with a king-high flush and a guy moves in on you, it's not an easy decision.

Jimmy thought for a while more, and after counting his chips he saw that calling the bet would mean putting in the last of his stake. Finally he called—and exited stage left when Puggy made them three queens magically appear. Not long after, Treetop busted Crandall, and we were down to six. Remember, in a freeze-out, once you lose the chips in front of you,

you're out of the tournament. You can't buy more chips, and you can't cash in what you have in front of you and quit during the tournament. You play until there's one man standing for $80,000.

After about six hours of play, we took our first break. Just by looking at everybody's stack, it appeared that Johnny Moss had the most chips. Not long after we started playing again, three of the Longhorn State's finest got locked up in one of them decision pots.

Doyle was first to act. Holding a pair of aces, the boss hand in Hold'em before the flop, he made a small raise. Some players would move in with a hand like this, while others wouldn't raise at all and try to set a big trap. Doyle, though, knew that just calling tends to raise the most suspicion, and he figured that a small raise would add some deception to his hand. I knew his moves pretty well after all those years playing together, and, smelling a rat, I folded a queen and a king, which is normally a strong hand. Treetop and Johnny called, and a good-size pot was building.

The flop came nine, seven, deuce of different suits, and Doyle made a small bet. Treetop, holding a nine and a jack, called. Then it came to Johnny, who made a sizable raise, enough that it would put Doyle all in. I'm telling you, poker isn't for the faint of heart. Here Doyle had started with the boss hand, and he had to risk all his chips to find out if Johnny was bluffing. I read Johnny for having either two pair or three of a kind. After deliberating forever, Doyle finally called and said, "Well, if this hand's not any good, I'm ready to go home."

Treetop folded. Because it was down to two players, there was no more betting, and they both turned their cards faceup. As I suspected, Johnny had pocket deuces, giving him three of a kind. Doyle's only hope was for one of the two remaining aces to hit.

By this point Doyle was standing up ready to leave, and Johnny started going through the discards and found one ace. In other words, there was only one ace out of the thirty-five cards left in the deck. The turn card brought a ten, and now Doyle started putting on his jacket.

Then, on the river, with the last card being dealt, the dealer turned over an ace! Doyle hit a 34-to-1 shot and scooped in a huge pot. Had the state of Nevada allowed pistols, it wouldn't have surprised me if Johnny had stood up and shot him. It was like Nick the Greek catching the jack of diamonds all over again—only twenty-one years later in the very same casino.

Johnny still had some chips left, but not long after, he had the misfortune of being dealt a pair of nines in a hand where Pug was dealt a pair of kings. And to make things stranger, Jolly Roger had the two remaining nines in his hand. As it turned out, both Johnny and Roger ended up getting all their money in before the flop, and their only prayer was to make a straight. In sort of a funny way, I was rooting for Johnny to win the pot. I guess ever since I put that bull's-eye on Johnny's head, I was hoping to be the one to bust him. But when Puggy's kings held up, Johnny and Jolly Roger said *adios*.

Remember now, there was $80,000 on the table when we started, so with four players left, $20,000 would mean average chip position. Treetop had $11,000, I had $13,000, Doyle had about $26,000, and Puggy had the rest, which was about $40,000. Texas may have had more players, but the flat-nosed cat from Tennessee was certainly the boss. We took a break, and I went over and schmoozed all them press guys. Thackrey had really helped attract a crowd, and while some players used breaks to get away, I got right in there with 'em and hammed it up pretty good.

To give you an idea what I was up against, Puggy and Doyle will probably go down as two of the five best players that ever lived. As for Treetop, he's in my Top Ten, and he sure as hell was the least predictable.

So with four of America's finest going at it, it wasn't long before I picked up the queen and ten of spades. The flop came ten of clubs, seven of spades, and four of spades, giving me a monstrous hand with the top pair on the board and nine more spades out there that would make me a flush. I bet $5,000, and Treetop moved in all his chips, which was $11,200, to be exact. I called, and Treetop, whose card selection often defied sanity, had a seven and a four in his hand, giving him two pair.

Even though he was ahead of me, I still had fourteen "outs" to beat him. Outs are cards that will make your hand, and in this case any of the nine remaining spades, the three remaining queens, and two remaining tens would give me a winner. It was about an even-money proposition with two cards to come, but when the turn brought the nine of diamonds, it was looking like trouble. Now my odds were worse than 2 to 1 against me, and you could have just stuck a fork in me when the river brought the ace of clubs. With exactly $1,775 of the $80,000 worth of chips on the table, I had a better chance of getting a French kiss from the Statue of Liberty than I did of winning that tournament. A spectator on the rail who was taking odds on players throughout the tournament made me a 25-to-1 underdog at that point. When Thackrey told me this, I said, "Well, I'm taking a hundred dollars of that." I said it with a grin, but I knew it was a sucker bet. The real odds against that field were probably more like 40 to 1, but I wanted to portray an image of confidence.

It wasn't long after that a pot came up where Doyle raised $700, Puggy and Treetop called, and, with $1,700 in front of me, I looked down and saw that one of my cards was a king. I shoved back my Stetson and said to the boys, "Well, there ain't no need of me looking at that other card. I can get action for my money *now*. It makes no difference what that other card is."

When I pushed all my chips into the pot, the Greek was narrating and had the crowd all whooped up. He was droning, "Amarillo Slim's a-movin' in."

"It feels better in!" I yelled, and the crowd cracked up.

Chill Wills, the western actor who grew up with Benny and Johnny down in Dallas, hollered to the crowd, "Who are we rootin' for?" and they yelled back, "Amarillo Slim."

The reason I moved in all my chips was that I was getting such a big overlay on my money. If everyone called, which they did, I was risking $1,700 to win $5,100, and with any hand in that situation, it was the right play. The flop came five, five, three of different suits. Doyle bet $4,000, and Treetop and Pug folded. Since I was all in, Doyle turned up his cards, a pair of tens, and I wasn't liking it too much. Then I looked down at my other card, and damned if it wasn't the five of hearts!

That pot picked me up, and, with a little less than $7,000, I was starting to feel like I could win this sucker. Sure, I got lucky in that pot, but to win a tournament like this, you have to catch some breaks. You've already seen several times that the best hand at the beginning often gets drowned at the river. At about three in the morning, we broke the game and arranged to meet at two o'clock the next day. Even though it was late,

I took a couple of glasses of milk up to my room and called Helen. Her pretty little voice gave me encouragement, and when she told me that the kids were rooting like hell for me, I knew I had to give my best effort the next day.

The second day of the tournament, we played for four hours without any significant hands. I was able to win a few small pots and slowly but surely build my stack up to about $20,000. Then Doyle and Treetop got locked up in a big pot. The flop came nine, seven, six. With a nine and a ten in his hand, Doyle had the top pair and needed an eight to make a straight. Treetop, with a nine and a seven, had two pair and moved in on him. When an eight came on the river, the tallest of the Texans said *sayonara*.

Now it was down to Puggy and me and my old buddy from Texas. I'm always at my best against a small field—that's why I like playing head-up so much—and I felt like it was my tournament to win. At that point a friend came up to me and said, "Say, Slim, a man just laid me $8,000 to $5,000 that you don't win it."

"The odds are getting a little better anyway," I said.

"The oddsmaker says you're probably the best player left in there, but you're still on the short end of the chips."

"Well, my God, boy, I'm really pulling for you to win it," I told him.

"You better be, damn it—you got half of it." And before I got a chance to say anything, he walked off.

We continued play, and Pug had almost $40,000 in chips, while Doyle was down to about $20,000, just a little less than me. We broke for an awards banquet, which is the only formal recess of the tournament. I normally liked to joke around with the crowd and the press, but this time I was mentally exhausted and decided to go to my room to catch my breath and regain my focus for the final push.

When I made it down to the banquet, I heard that Doyle and Pug were looking for me, and I went and joined them in a private booth in the Sombrero Room. Doyle said that something he ate didn't agree with his stomach and was worried that if he kept playing, he'd be running out of both ends. I didn't know whether it was a put-on or not, but even though it was against the rules of the freeze-out structure, Doyle convinced Puggy and me to let him cash in his chips, take $20,000, and go home and try to get better. I was just as happy to have that pug-nosed bugger to myself, and when we got back to play, the Greek made the announcement that Doyle had to forfeit due to an illness.

To this day I'm not sure what really happened. Remember, at that time playing poker was still looked upon as a profession for lowlifes by most folks in America, and Doyle had a real religious family back in Texas. Also, a lot of times over the years, when I got to running my mouth, Doyle used to repeat one of Nick the Greek's favorite lines: "Fame is usually followed by a jail sentence." So whether it was something he ate, his family, or just wanting to keep a low profile, Doyle was out of the tournament, and Pug and I were back at the table competing for $60,000.

Pug had a sharp wit and not an overabundance of charm. He liked to needle just about anyone and always had something to say to us Texans. Of course, he was outnumbered, but he liked jiving us cowboys. "If it wasn't for Tennessee," Pug said, "there wouldn't be no Texas. You're lucky to be here in the first place."

"If there wasn't no Tennessee, there wouldn't be no Texas, huh?" I said. "Well, if you folks could suck like you could blow, we wouldn't need to be shipping no oil there."

That got a good laugh, but by now I wasn't in no laughing mood. I was ready to bust that cigar-chomping, flat-nosed sonofabitch. We counted down the chips, and he had $38,000 to my $22,000, with the ante now at $100 per hand. I liked to play to the crowd, and I was yakking with the hangers-on, which irked the hell out of Pug. When I wasn't talking to the rail, I was talking to Pug, trying to get inside his head.

"You better play 'em tight, you skinny sonofabitch," said Pug, "because I'm gonna break you before the night's over."

"Take your best shot, partner," I said. "I've been broke in bigger towns than Vegas and lost to better men than you."

I sensed that he was gonna start out playing conservative, so I started playing real fast, raising just about every hand, whether I had cards or not. I took pot after pot, and within an hour the chip count was even. We took a short break, and I went to water my horse, which, after about seventy cups of coffee that day, was much needed. I doused my hands and face in cold water and prepared myself to be a champion.

When we got back, I kept on raising just about every pot, and we got locked up in a hand where he bet $5,000 after the flop, and, with nothing, I raised him $12,000, just figuring that he was on a steal. I couldn't beat an egg, and when he counted out exactly $12,000 in chips, I tried to do like Nick the Greek and pretend I was sitting on an icicle. Puggy, of course, was watching my every move, trying to spot a tell, and I was thinking, I hope he don't call. Sure enough, he didn't and threw away the best hand.

At this point it was pretty obvious to everyone in the crowd what I had been doing. Don't get me wrong, there was no way that I would let anyone see my cards—certainly no one named Demetrius—but he was a pretty sharp guy, and he knew that most of my winning hands were bluffs. So the Greek leaned over and whispered something to Pug. And this is but another example of why I couldn't stand that fat old cat; he always had to be putting his nose where it didn't belong. Here he was supposed to be neutral, for crying out loud, and he was trying to help Pug beat me. I reckon that he still held a grudge from them golf bets, even though he knew damn well I hadn't done nothing wrong.

I made out the Greek telling Pug that I was taking his money without having a hand. I decided that the first time I made a good hand, I was going to sell it to him real high, playing it just like the bluffs I'd been taking him with all along. By now Pug had less than $10,000 in chips and knew he had to take a stand.

A few hands later, before the flop, Pug raised it $700, and I just called with a king of hearts and a jack of clubs in my hand. The flop came king, eight, eight of different suits, giving me two pair. If Pug had a king with either an ace or a queen, he'd have me beat, or if he had an eight in his hand, his trips would also have me beat. I didn't read him for either of those hands, and figured that I had a cinch.

Holding kings up, I decided that instead of making a sensible bet to suck him in, like $1,500 or $2,000, I'd move in on him. Ordinarily you wouldn't sell that hand nearly that high, but because I'd been running all them bluffs, I knew he was fixing to call me the first time he got anything. Pug didn't stall long: With $8,900 left, he called my bet and went all-in for the first time.

Since there was no more betting, we turned our hands over, and Pug had a pair of sixes. Just like the hand when Doyle had a pair of aces against Johnny, there were only two cards left in the deck for Pug to beat me. But, shoot, I wasn't counting my money yet; I'd seen better hands drowned at the river. The turn card was a deuce, and I was one card from busting Puggy and taking the crown from Johnny Moss.

The dealer turned the last card—and there was no Tennessee miracle. It was the eight of diamonds. Now I had made eights full of kings, and everyone was looking at the 1972 World Series of Poker champion!

When Thackrey came to interview me, I pushed my Stetson up and said, "I'm looking for a game, any game at all, as long as it's for real money. Seems like a fella should be able to get a game in a town like this. But I swear I can't find a thing to occupy my time!"

"Goddamn it, Slim," he screamed, "you just won sixty thousand dollars in the World Series of Poker!"

"But that was *then*, and this is *now*. Fella like me, he's kind of like a doctor or a lawyer. You know, pretty near the only stock in trade he's got is his time."

After I'd done a million more interviews, everyone wanted to go celebrate, but I was so worn out I could barely stand up. I went back to my room, called my family, and lay in bed forever without getting to sleep.

Don't feel too bad for old Pug. The next year it got down to him, Treetop, and Johnny Moss, and Pug's ace-seven beat Moss's king-ten to make him the 1973 World Series of Poker champion. After Pug won it, he bought himself a bus and traveled around the country taking bets on anything from golf to pool to cards. On the side of his bus were painted the words PUGGY PEARSON: I'LL PLAY ANY MAN, FROM ANY LAND, ANY GAME HE CAN NAME, FOR ANY AMOUNT HE CAN COUNT. Underneath that, in very fine print, he added, "Provided I like it."

In 1974 Johnny Moss won it again, and in 1975 my buddy Sailor took the title. In '76 and '77 Doyle, whose family had now gotten used to the fact that he was a professional poker player, was the first player to win it back-to-back. In 1978 Bobby Baldwin, a sharp cat from Tulsa, Oklahoma, who is now a big-shot executive at Bellagio, was the champ, followed in 1979 by Hal Fowler from Norwalk, California, the first nonprofessional player to win. Then, in 1980, and again in 1981, the youse guys finally got one as Stuey Ungar—a 125-pound kid backed by the New York mob—became the youngest champ in history.

After a four-year drought for us Texans, Treetop won the title in 1982. After being down to a single chip, Treetop won the tournament and inspired the phrase "a chip and a chair," which poker players use all the time to this day when they get low in chips in a tournament. Mr. Strauss didn't exactly ride off into the sunset. At age fifty-eight, while playing in a game of no-limit Texas Hold'em at the Bicycle Casino in Los Angeles, Treetop made a big bet and then had a heart attack and died right there at the table. The players at the table looked at his cards, and it turned out that old Treetop had run a big bluff. As sad as I was to see him go, at least he went out in the same fearless manner in which he'd lived his life.

On another sad note, on Christmas Day in 1989, Benny Binion died of heart failure. In my eyes, Benny was either the gentlest bad man or the baddest gentleman who ever lived.

If he were alive today, Benny would be thrilled to know that in 2002, thirty years after 8 players competed for $80,000, 631 players from all over the world played for more than $6 million in prize money. The only unfortunate part was that a youse guy won it, as Robert Varkonyi from Brooklyn took home the $2 million. My friend Gabe Kaplan (the actor who played Mr. Kotter in that TV program *Welcome Back, Kotter*) held the mike instead of Jimmy the Greek, and another Benny, Benny's grandson Benny Binion Behnen, was the master of ceremonies. ESPN covered the tournament, and just about every major newspaper and television station in the world was there too. All this just fifty-one years after a man called Nick the Greek walked into the Horseshoe and said he was looking to play some high-stakes poker.

As for me, I thought winning the World Series was the culmination of twenty-five years of playing poker. Little did I know that I was just getting started.

My good buddy Brent Musburger and me, after I helped him do commentary for the World Series of Poker and before he got sucker-punched by Jimmy the Greek. Later, I was Brent's guest for the Super Bowl between the Cowboys and the Broncos at the Superdome in New Orleans. *(Las Vegas News Bureau)*

9

Celebrity Has Its Perks

Fame is a powerful aphrodisiac." That's what that writer Graham Greene said, and, neighbor, he got that one right. Some people say that success will change a man, but it didn't change me one bit. I'll tell you what did change, though: *everything around me*. With the deal of the eight of diamonds, people went from looking at me as a back-alley, no-good gambler to a world champion. It got to the point where every time I traveled in the state of Texas or to Arkansas, it was news that a "world champion" was in town. And I'm not gonna lie to you, the attention suited me just fine.

Another person who it suited was Benny Binion. "Slim," Benny said, always the marketer, "you're the only sonofabitch that can get this up out of the dirt." Johnny Moss was sixty-five and had the type of personality that was well suited to a poker game but not much else. Pug was always an abrasive sort; Doyle was still a bit of a recluse; Sailor had a criminal record; and if there was one thing everyone knew I could do, it was run my mouth. Just as Benny had done, several other casino owners asked me to help change the image of poker, and I became sort of a touring ambassador for the sport.

Before 1972 poker players were stereotyped as a bunch of backroom bums, people of low character and low morals, who sat around a smoke-filled room waiting for some sucker to show up so they could cheat him out of his money. But with all the legitimate attention that Thackrey and his boys in the press gave the World Series, people started to see poker players for what they were—mostly just ordinary guys with a heckuva lot of talent. Benny's son Jack described professional poker players as "mental athletes."

For the same reasons that Brent Musburger later had me on his telecast, my style agreed with the American people. I don't know whether they were laughing *at* me or laughing *with* me, but they were laughing, and that's all that mattered. I didn't give much thought to what I was saying, but everybody seemed to get a hoot from what came out of my mouth.

The publicity was more than this country cowboy ever could have dreamed of. A story ran in *Parade* magazine, which was in practically every Sunday newspaper in the country, about my victory in the World Series. Then, the TV folks came after me, and I went on *Ralph Story's AM* —which was kind of like *Good Morning America*. Then I went to San Francisco and Seattle for a bunch of TV appearances, before coming back to Los Angeles to do Bud Furillo's radio show. The program was such a success that after that one time in the studio, it didn't matter where I was, Bud would call me and have me on the show from anywhere.

Before long, word got out to Freddie De Cordova, the producer of *The Tonight Show*, that I would be an interesting person to have as a guest. So they booked me, and Johnny and I got along like ham and eggs. In fact, Johnny liked having me on *The Tonight Show* so much that every time Bob Hope came on, Johnny invited me so Mr. Hope wouldn't make him so darn nervous. Remember, Bob and I went back to 1948, from the times we both toured Europe entertaining the troops.

I appeared on *The Tonight Show* eleven times, and the time I was on with Joey Bishop as host, I was there to plug Hoyle playing cards. But when he was asking me questions, Bishop wouldn't bring it up. Then, during one of the breaks, I cursed that Rat Pack sonofabitch up and down. Freddie D. came running over to us and said, "Something wrong, Slim?"

"Yeah," I said. "You need to tell this sonofabitch that he needs to ask me about Hoyle playing cards."

"Once we get back from break, Joey," Freddie said, "the first thing you're to ask him is about Hoyle playing cards. Got it?"

So we sat back down, and Joey said, "Oh, Slim, tell me more about these Hoyle playing cards." And that was that.

I did other television shows like *60 Minutes*, *Good Morning America*, and *The Tomorrow Show* with Tom Snyder. I even went on the game shows *To Tell the Truth*, *What's My Line?* and *I've Got a Secret*.

After a while these shows became kinda routine, but I kept making appearances, because I knew it'd be good for Benny and the World Series of Poker, and, as it turned out, it was even better for old Slim. I started getting paid to do television commercials, and over the years I've pitched anything from oil companies to saddle companies to boot companies.

Steve Badger, a poker writer, said, "Amarillo Slim Preston is the most famous professional poker player to ever play the game. No other person living or dead has ever brought more attention to the game of poker, or to himself."

I know damn well that's both a compliment and a put-down all in one, but playful boasting has always been my style, and these newsmen seemed to like my stories. And get this: The feature product in the Neiman Marcus catalog—not long after I won the World Series—was, as a gift for "people who had everything," poker lessons from Amarillo Slim, for $50,000! Couldn'ta been worth seven cents, but four people paid for it;

they got ten lessons of an hour each, and most of what they wanted to do was just yak, really.

Remember I talked about how much resistance the Binion family put up when Benny wanted to add a poker room in 1970? Before then, with the exception of the Horseshoe, the Golden Nugget, and the Dunes, there wasn't hardly a casino in the world that had a poker room. Any bean counter could tell you that it just didn't make financial sense. But with all the coverage of the World Series, it wasn't long before just about every casino in the whole world had a poker room. And even though they don't make a tenth of the money that slots make, they helped bring people into a casino, and, if you can believe this, many casino owners claimed it made a place more civilized and attracted a higher-level clientele. Well, I'll be damned!

EVEL KNIEVEL, BIRTHDAYS, AND A HALL OF FAME BASKETBALL COACH

Another advantage of all this celebrity was that, rather than me having to look for propositions, people sought me out. It became like a badge of honor to gamble with Amarillo Slim, and that suited me just fine. Most people who approached me to gamble *expected* to lose—and rarely did I disappoint them.

In 1973 I was invited to be the guest speaker at the NFL banquet in Dallas. The banquet happened to be held around the same time Evel Knievel was attempting to break the record for the longest motorcycle jump at Green Valley Raceway in Dallas. In front of a live audience and broadcast by ABC's *Wide World of Sports*, Evel cleared thirteen Mack trucks on his Harley and became a national celebrity.

Born in 1938 as Robert Craig Knievel in Butte, Montana, he owned several Honda dealerships in Washington State in the sixties and ran a promotion that a person would get a hundred dollars off a car if he could beat Evel in arm wrestling. He was arrested for kidnapping his future wife, Linda, as well as for stealing hubcaps. While in jail, Mr. Knievel was in a cell with a gangster named Awful Knofeel, and the prison guard joked that he had Awful Knofeel and "Evil" Knievel the hubcap thief in the same cell. Robert adopted the nickname, and then later, to pacify some of his religious fans, he had his name legally changed to "Evel." See what I mean about the importance of a gambler having a good nickname. No one would have ever remembered anyone named Robert Knievel, Rudolph Wanderone, Alvin Thomas, Nick Dandalos—or Thomas Preston.

I made a lot of bets with Evel Knievel. A man who gambled with his life every time he hopped on a motorcycle was more than willing to gamble away some of his hard-earned money. First off let me just say that I liked him and admired what he did. He had more pain tolerance than any sonofabitch I've seen in my life. He was so tough, you could take his hand, hold it under a blowtorch, and he'd just sit there and look at you and never bat an eye. But Evel loved risk so much that he was an easy mark for a gambler. One day he told me that he could beat any PGA golf pro as long as they were playing for $100,000. Sometimes I think Evel actually believed what he said, even though on his best day he shot ninety-two.

That type of thinking made Evel easy pickings on the golf course, and I once bet him that I could beat him at golf using a carpenter's hammer. He used regular clubs, and the only club I could use was that carpenter's hammer—the kind you drive nails with. We played from the same tees, using the same rules, except he gave me a stroke a hole. I'd drop down on my knees most of the time and swing away. I practiced almost every day for three months, and, with all the money Evel was making (including proceeds from the $300 million in products named after him), we bet enough money that beating him was certainly worthwhile.

After the NFL banquet in Dallas, it got to where there were about thirty people in the room, including Evel, and I made a statement that I'd bet any amount of money that at least two of them had the same birthday. Everybody in that building bet me except Pete Rozelle, the NFL commissioner at the time, and Lamar Hunt, the former owner of the Dallas Texans and now the owner of the Kansas City Chiefs. Evel, of course, made the largest wager.

So we went around, checked everybody's license, and, sure enough, two people had the same birthday. Everybody gave me his money without any fuss, except Evel, who, thinking he'd been had, threw his on the floor.

"Nobody does that to me," I said. "Pick up that goddamn money like a man and hand it to me." We sounded like a couple of guys named Doyle and Sailor, but I meant it, and he wouldn't do it. But being more concerned with my wallet than my ego, I cooled off a little, and said, "Now, Robert, I can see you're dissatisfied with what just happened. If you want to do it again, we'll go to a bowling alley or a movie theater or a police station or anywhere you can go and get thirty people together. You choose where we go."

Of course, we had everybody's attention by this point, and some man from the peanut gallery said, "Why don't you call thirty taxicabs and don't ask 'em nothing. They've got an ID thing up over the visor with their license number, and it says when they were born."

"That suits me," Evel said. "How about you, cowboy?"

It sure did, so I pulled the old Texas rules on him and made him double his bet, while that man got on the phone to call the taxicab company. By the time we walked outside, they had thirty cabs lined up in front of that hotel. We went to each car, asked to see their licenses, and wrote down all their birthdays on a yellow legal pad. I gave all of the cabbies twenty dollars for their time, and they drove off when we had recorded their information. These drivers were going nuts in that line; they couldn't imagine what the hell was going on.

As it turned out, I paid off the last eight drivers and didn't even bother to look at their licenses. The twenty-second driver had the same birthday as the second, and Evel all but beat the poor driver to pieces.

Mama would have been proud to know that I learned about this bet in math class at Peabody Academy. In fact, it might have been the only thing I learned there besides how to play snooker. It's simple statistics; if you choose twenty-three people at random, it's even money that two will have the same birthday. When you poll thirty people, the odds go up to 70 percent. The only proof I need is that of the dozens of times I've made that bet, I never have lost. The best one was when I made the bet with Ira, my friend from New York, before he walked into a diner. Wouldn't you know it, right when we walked in, there was a set of identical twins sitting right at the counter.

After we got done with the cab drivers, one of the league owners approached me about a famous basketball coach he knew who claimed to shoot free throws better than anybody in the country and wasn't shy about wagering on it. I always had pretty good aim—which not only helped in pool and shooting a gun but also allowed me to shoot a basketball real well.

There are rumors that I shot free throws with Rick Barry, but there's not much to those. Barry may have been the best free-throw shooter in NBA history—he shot "granny" style, taking the ball and throwing it underhanded to the hoop—but in gambling circles the best free-throw shooter was a coach, not a player, and he will remain anonymous to protect the innocent. All I can tell you is that he's now in the Basketball Hall of Fame and that he coached at a college west of the Mississippi. As has always been my custom, I went to find this champion so I could go make a sucker out of him. It turned out that I didn't have to go too far.

I met up with the coach at his college, and we made a wager for a pretty good-size figure. There was no handicap or nothing, but I told him that I got to bring the ball. He agreed, and then I heard him say to one of his friends, "That's all right. He probably just wants to let a little bit of air out of it or something."

I set up this bet just like I had done the Ping-Pong bet with the skillet and later with those Coke bottles. I knew that I had no chance to beat him shooting free throws with a regular ball. It didn't matter how much air was in it; this man had a basketball in his hand every day of his life, and he knew how to put it through a basket. That's why I told him that I would furnish the *ball*, not the *basket*ball. I also told him that I'd like to wait two weeks so word would spread to the hustlers out there who were now lining up to fleece me.

Two weeks later I arrived at the same gym, and you could barely stand in that place. The coach got to warming up, and I excused myself to go out to my truck to grab the ball that I wanted to use. As I was walking out, I saw this coach sinking one after another—I don't think that the ball even hit the rim in a dozen straight shots. Even Rick Barry wouldn't have had a prayer against this cat. So I went to the truck, and when I came back into the gym, I did my best Joe Namath Super Bowl III impersonation and threw that *football* to the coach!

He didn't think much of it when he caught it. Then I said, "Do you wanna shoot first, or shall I?"

Well, his eyes just about jumped out of his head when it dawned on him that the ball I had furnished was brown and had strings on it. Before he could say one word, I said, "I didn't say nothing about no *basketball*."

CATCHING A SORE THROAT AT THE AUTHORS' CONVENTION

It seemed like every time I went on a TV or radio show after I won the World Series, the host would ask me the same question: "Why don't you have a book to promote?" Here I had never even been to college and just months before was looked upon as a menace to society, and now I was being told that people wanted to read what I had to say.

I hooked up with an author named Bill Cox and a publisher called Grosset & Dunlap, and in 1973 my first and only other book, *Play Poker to Win*, was published. It wasn't nothing more than a few stories from the World Series and some basic strategies on poker, but it managed to sell real well.

The first place they wanted me to go to promote the book was Los Angeles, to what they called an authors' convention. There were twenty-nine authors and me out there, putting on a dog and pony show for all these booksellers.

It killed me to know there was poker action in the nearby town of Gardena while I had to hobnob with them cultured folks. They had booths set up in groups of three: I was in the center one, which seemed like a prime location. On my right was Clair Huffaker, who had written *The Cowboy and the Cossack*, and on my left was that cat Richard Bach with his *Jonathan Livingston Seagull*. I called it "The Goddamn Birds," which he didn't think was as funny as I did. I never did think them inspirational types had much of a sense of humor.

We were autographing books, and because I had gotten a lot of notoriety after the World Series, I was attracting almost as much attention as them famous authors. Then I winked at my PR guy, Mr. Finklestein, jumped out from behind my booth, and said to these people, "For *Christ's sake*, why don't you get out of this line and get over there and get you something fit to read? I wouldn't give a bar of soap for this book; you think I'd piss off my money for something like this?"

That scared Harold Roth, the big dog for Grosset & Dunlap—but Finklestein, who knew a thing or two about psychology himself, said, "You just leave him alone, Harold. He knows exactly what he's doing." And, sure enough, after I said that, you couldn't get near my line with all the people pushing and shoving to check out my book. That's what's called "reverse psychology." It's a simple fact that the less you brag on something, the more it will sell.

It turned out that Norman Mailer, the author of *Marilyn*, had the same publisher I did, and old Roth from Grosset & Dunlap threw him a birthday party. Finklestein suggested that I attend, and I wound up really having fun with that bunch. One of the authors in attendance was Linda Lovelace, who had written a book called *Inside Linda Lovelace* about her experience in the film *Deep Throat*. It was a *bad* book—I believe that the industry she was in rhymed with "corn"—and it wasn't exactly something I wanted my kids reading. I did my best to steer clear of this wild woman—who started her book off with the famous line "I live for sex"—but as much as I tried to avoid her, that got her chasing me more. It was that old reverse psychology again. Finally she cornered me and said, "Are you ducking me? Do you dislike me?"

"No, ma'am," I said. "I don't even know you. In fact, I like what you can do." She seemed pleased by this, and I seem to recall an inference that she might give me a free demonstration of her abilities. I wanted no part of that and said to her, "I haven't read your book about the *sore* throat, but I'm sure it's entertaining, and I'll certainly get me a copy of it."

Well, everybody got a kick out of it, except Ms. Lovelace of course.

YOU'RE LOOKING AT ONE COWBOY
WHO *WILL* TAKE A BRIBE

On January 1, 1939, at age nineteen, Matt Helreich, a dirt-poor kid from Philadelphia, of average height, average looks, and with no automobile, made an interesting New Year's resolution. He told his buddy Mel that if movie star Betty Grable ever were to come within ninety miles of Philadelphia, he was gonna go meet her. That summer Mel saw in the paper that Grable, who was twenty-two at the time, was opening at the Steel Pier in Atlantic City, New Jersey, for a guy named Eddie "Rochester" Anderson, who was one of Jack Benny's regulars. Since Atlantic City is only sixty miles from Philly, Helreich was looking forward to keeping his promise.

On August 16, 1939, Helreich hopped on a bus to see Grable, whose beautiful legs were later insured for $1 million by Lloyds of London. After she performed, the sign ABSOLUTELY NO ADMITTANCE wasn't gonna stop Matt from going backstage, and, just like it was nothing, the two got to talking. Betty told him that she would be performing at the Earle Theatre in Philadelphia in two weeks and asked him to be her guest backstage. In less than a year, they were engaged. Now, you want to talk about *cojones*—Matt was my kinda guy.

I was lucky that when I hired a firm named Mahoney Wasserman to help me with PR, Matt happened to be the guy who was in charge of my affairs. Finklestein might have been the best book PR man in the business, but when it came to entertainment, Matt was second to none. To this day I consider Matt—who still lives in West Hollywood and knows just about every celebrity in town—a close friend.

After the authors' convention, he got me a gig as a celebrity judge for the *Mrs*. America contest—not *Miss* America—at the Las Vegas Hilton. The other judges were Richard Dawson, who hosted the hit TV show *Family Feud*, and Jim Mahoney, the president of Matt's PR firm. They made a big production out of welcoming these ladies, and my friend Barron Hilton, who owned the joint, said, "Let's let Slim welcome the ladies to Las Vegas and the Hilton."

These women walked out onto the stage, and it looked like recess in heaven—all the little angels were there. Man, they were beautiful. So with all of us judges standing there, I went into a little rigmarole about what they could look forward to in this swell contest. Then, at the end of my little stump speech, I said, "I cannot speak for the *ability*, the *honesty*, or the *integrity* of any of these other judges, but you're looking at one skinny cowboy who *will* take a bribe."

I want to tell you that auditorium broke up. The press just loved it, and the laughter went on forever. And I hadn't been up in my suite but a few minutes when I got a couple of calls. Naturally, I had to disappoint some of these fine young ladies—they *all* couldn't win, you know.

WHAT I *REALLY* LIKED ABOUT THE SOUTH

One celebrity that Matt introduced me to who had more money than brains was a singer named Phil Harris. Harris was married to movie star Alice Faye and was best known for singing "That's What I Like About the South." You know that song: *Won't you come with me to Alabamie and let's go see my dear old Mamie, she's frying eggs and boiling hammies and that's what I like about the South.*

Harris performed at the Desert Inn, which had one of the nicest golf courses in Nevada, making it a popular destination of mine. I was at the DI one day, which is what everybody called it, and Phil Harris told me he wanted to play some gin. Knowing he had a reputation for gambling, the folks at the hotel kept a pretty close watch on Harris. When I couldn't convince him to play down at the Horseshoe, we went to the clubhouse at the DI—way in the back, where I didn't think anybody could find us. I got

Harris stuck pretty good, and the next thing I knew, I felt somebody tap me on the shoulder. Without even turning around, I said, "Man, get away from me. I'm busy."

I didn't know who it was, but he tapped me a little harder this time. Without turning around again, I said, "Take a hike." I thought it was one of my friends and didn't pay it no mind.

The tapping got a little harder, and I turned around and looked, and there was a guy who looked like Man Mountain Dean standing there. This guy was as big as Dallas, and he said, "Slim, one of the bosses wants to talk to you."

This wasn't a man I was gonna argue with, so I took about a ten-step walk, and the boss was standing there at the corner, and he said, "How we doing, partner?"

"Partner, your ass," I said. "I haven't got no partner, and I don't need one."

"Listen, cowboy, we pay that man thousands of dollars a week to entertain here. And if anybody's gonna rob him, it's gonna be us, *partner*."

They overpaid Harris because everything he made he lost at shooting craps before he left anyway, and if he was gonna lose it gambling, they wanted to make sure it stayed with them. So I got to thinking about it and figured my choices were to quit playing and make *no* money or continue fleecing this man and make *some* money. It turned out that the owners of the DI weren't the only ones who got a piece of Harris's paycheck.

♠ ♣ ♦ ♥

After I won the World Series, my life was never the same. It opened up doors and allowed me to travel and meet exciting new people. Above all, it led to even more lucrative gambling opportunities. The one thing I had on most of these celebrities was control of my ego. I found that most millionaires, especially famous ones, had so much confidence in themselves that they'd make bad bets. I, on the other hand, continued to treat gambling as my profession. But as it was, in November 1972, just six months after I won the World Series, I let hubris stand in the way of reason and made a bet that had the potential to take everything away.

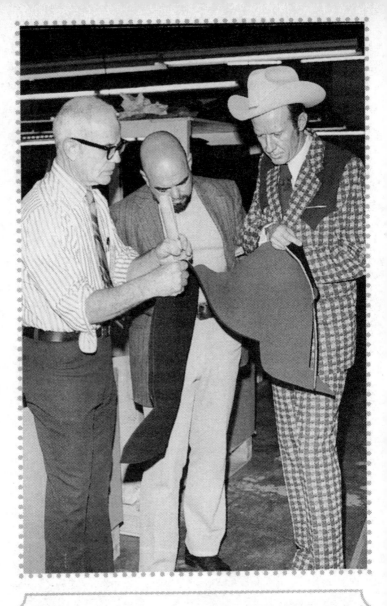

Here I am getting fitted for a wet suit in 1972, with the general manager of Jacques Cousteau's company and Ted Thackrey (middle), before my near-death on the River of No Return. *(Courtesy of the author)*

10

The River of No Return

In 1972, I was on the joyride of my life. I was forty-three going on twenty-three, had three beautiful kids, a wonderful marriage, and every live one in America coming out of the woodwork to gamble with me and throw away his money. I was at the height of my profession and it seemed like I had nothing to prove. Life could not have been better.

At that time—and still to this day—I had a standing offer that as long as a person would post $25,000, I'd fly anywhere in the world to gamble with him. One man who took me up on this challenge was none other than the Amazing Kreskin, a man who claimed to have ESP, and had one of the most popular acts in Vegas.

In August 1972, I went out to the Stardust in Las Vegas to play the Amazing Kreskin in gin and test my own special brand of ESP: *Every*

Sucker Pays. About ten days earlier, I had taken my son Tod, who was only eight at the time, to Idaho for a fun little trip down the Snake River. While we were floating down the river, the raft got a tear in it and collapsed—and when it started to sink, we had to swim out. It wasn't nothing—there weren't any rapids, and we couldn't have swam more than thirty or forty feet to get out of the river. The Las Vegas papers ended up getting ahold of our little mishap, and everyone was talking about how my son and I had capsized in a raft and had nearly died trying to swim out of the river. The power of the media . . . it really is something, isn't it?

While I was playing Kreskin, Jimmy the Greek—Mr. Big *I* and Little *You*—came up to me in the middle of a hand and said, "Slim, if you were trying to kill yourself, why didn't you take a gun?"

"What the hell are you talking about, Demetrius?" I asked.

"Well, it looks like you were some kind of a daredevil or something, trying to drown yourself in that Snake River."

"Wasn't nothing to it," I said, which I didn't think there was. I had been rafting hundreds of times in my life, and sometimes you have to swim. Eventually I found out that the Greek and two other people that I had beaten pretty good over the years—Bill Boyd and Puggy Pearson—had gone out and made calls to some authorities about white-water rafting. Evidently these experts told the Greek that there was another river in the primitive area of northern Idaho, called the River of No Return, that a guy could really be taking a chance on. "That's for people who have a death wish," one of the authorities told him. "Sure, some folks have made it, but there's been a lot of people killed on it, too."

"Could a guy do it in the winter?" the Greek asked. The so-called experts said it would be impossible, because the water level would be down and there would be jagged ice and sharp rocks that would just cut a guy to pieces if he moved his raft the wrong way.

Armed with all that knowledge, the Greek approached me at the Stardust with revenge, money, and my death on his mind—or at least some combination of those three. "Well, Slim," he said, "I guess you think you could go down the River of No Return?"

"And carry you piggyback, Demetrius," I said.

"I guess you think you can do it in the winter, too?"

Well, here I was trying to win a damn bet off this charlatan, and I wasn't paying the Greek no mind. So, to get rid of him, I said, "Hell, I could do that standin' on one foot. I could probably just skate down it."

"Well, are you arguing about it?"

Remember, I really didn't like this fat cat, so I said, "Well, I guess I am."

Now, all my life I've always said that if there's anything worth arguing about, I'll either bet on it or shut up. So when I said I was arguing about it, the Greek pounced on it and said, "Post your money, cowboy."

I didn't give much thought to the fact that I was fixing to bet on going down a river that I didn't know nothing about, and in the wintertime no less. Well, none of that seemed to bother me, and I told him that after I beat this "amazing" cat playing gin, I'd post my money.

After the match, the Greek and I went to the cage and posted the bet—$25,000 apiece that I couldn't float down a twenty-nine-mile stretch of the middle fork of the Salmon River, called the River of No Return, in winter. After the trouble I had with the Greek wanting to off his bets in the past, I wasn't for a minute gonna take him at his word, and Johnny Drew, the card-room manager at the Stardust, arranged for us to keep our money with the casino. We wrote down all sorts of rules, but the one stipulation that I insisted on, and had to really push for, was that I was allowed to bring one man with me, and I already had a guy in mind. I later made a side bet of $6,000 with the Greek, since I knew that the original $25,000 was probably put up by Boyd and Puggy, and I wanted some of the Greek's money.

Now that I'd made this bet, I figured I should do a little research. Right away I made the same phone calls that the Greek had made to find some experts to tell me what I needed to know. I called the Idaho Fish and Game Commission first, and they said that the river was treacherous. Then I asked 'em about floating down the river in winter, and their reply was, "That would be impossible. You might as well go down the river in a coffin instead of a raft."

They told me that in the winter the water is choked with ice floes that sometimes form floating bridges that a raft can be forced under by the current. U.S. Army Captain Reuben Bernard, operating out of Fort Boise, had chased Indians there in 1892 and described the passage as the "impassable gorge." And just that past spring, three men had died on the same stretch of water—and they didn't have floating ice with sharp, cutting edges to contend with. None of this was good news.

The middle fork of the Salmon River wasn't called the River of No Return for no reason. I'd never heard of the damn thing before, but once I started doing my own homework, I'd learned that Otto Preminger made a movie about it in 1954 called—what else?—*River of No Return*, starring Robert Mitchum and Marilyn Monroe. But what the hell, they just went through that white water in a big old raft like it was no big deal.

Seeking a second opinion, I called the forestry service, and they told me the same thing the Idaho Fish and Game Commission had said—ain't no man going down that river in the winter and coming out alive. Now it dawned on me that I'd made a bet that I couldn't win without killing myself. So I discussed it with some of my close friends—and, even Doyle, who'd never back down from a bet in his life, said, "Well, shit, Slim, ain't no bet worth your life. Give it up. You've lost bigger figures than thirty-one thousand before."

"Do what?" I screamed. "I'd rather wet in my britches than have that Greek sonofabitch carry any of my money." Now, I told you that I had promised myself earlier that I would never, *ever* give that man the satisfaction of taking a penny from me. If it had been anybody else in the world but the Greek, I'd a let it go and done the honorable thing and just paid off the bet. Heck, I would even have admitted that I was stupid for taking the bet in the first place. But I don't think I could have lived with myself if I forked over thirty-one grand to the Greek—at least not without *trying* to win first.

Well, Doyle, who probably knew me better than I knew myself, was smart enough to know that there was only one man in the world who could talk me out of what would surely amount to suicide. That man, of course, was Benny Binion. One day Benny, who feared nothing and no one, came up to me at the Horseshoe and said, "Hell, Slim, give it up. Let's have some fun instead. Going down that river's only gonna get you killed. This ain't no good for you."

I knew he was right, but, like I said before, I'm human and I'm a gambler—and I'm the first to admit that I let my own damn hubris get in the way of common sense. All I could say was, "Benny, you know how I feel about you. You're a great friend, and I always respect what you have to say. But let me tell you something: There ain't no way in hell I'm gonna let that motherfucker Jimmy the Greek carry none of my money."

And while it might not have been the dumbest thing I ever *said*, I can tell you now—at age seventy-four—no question about it, it was the dumbest thing that I ever *did*.

JERE AND JACQUES (BUT NOT LLOYD)—MY PARTNERS IN CRIME

For years I had gone hunting and fishing with a guy named Jere Chapman, who lives in Boise, Idaho. Jere likes to say that we're "shirttail relations," because my darling wife, Helen, is the sister of one of his uncles. I still haven't figured that one out myself, but the fact that he thought I was kinfolk wasn't a bad thing. Jere had gone down the River of No Return twice in the summer. It wasn't no picnic for him either—on one of the trips, he had trouble and had to walk fifty-one miles just to get the hell out of there. Jere isn't but five-seven and is built like an ordinary guy, but he was raised up in the woods of Idaho and knows his way around nature like George Strait knows his way around a guitar. And if he hadn't been such a great outdoorsman, he mighta still been down there searching for traces of civilization.

I called Jere and asked him if he wanted to accompany me on my little winter vacation down the River of No Return.

"What?" he asked. "No one can go down that river in winter."

You're probably wondering why I didn't call him in the first place when I started doing my research, and that was just the very reason. I was afraid that if I had, I might have chickened out, but by now I was committed.

"Well, I've got to, Jere. I made a bet."

"What did you bet?"

"I bet thirty-one thousand that I could go down the River of No Return, and I'm allowed to take one man with me. I want you to be that man."

"Well, if you're going, then I guess I'm going, too. Blood is thicker than water—ain't that how the saying goes?"

Talk about a friend. But then his brain got the better part of his heart, and the thirty-eight-year-old said, "My God, Austin, I got a family." Other than my wife, he was one of the few people who called me Austin.

"I'll get us some life insurance," I said. "And that way, if we do have trouble, then your family's taken care of." I guess that satisfied him, because once we got off the phone, we started preparing for our journey. The first thing I did was call a representative out of San Francisco for Lloyds of London and told him I was seeking an insurance policy on a man going down a river in Idaho.

"That's kind of unusual," the insurance man said.

"Isn't that what you all do?" I asked. "Insure unusual things?"

Well, I knew the answer was yes. They insured Betty Grable's legs and her trumpet player husband Harry James's lips. A lot of people in Hollywood have insurance against a facial cut or some such nonsense. That's what Lloyds of London *does*, for crying out loud.

So he called me back, told me that he had other business in Idaho, and agreed to meet with me. Before our meeting, he had done some homework, and when I asked him about the policy, he looked at me and said, "Sir, you've got no chance."

So what do you think I said back? "Well, hell, then, I'll bet you, too!" Now my ass was red, you understand? Everybody was so damn sure that it couldn't be done. Naturally, being Square John Businessman, he didn't want to bet me. But I still had a promise to keep to Jere, and I went ahead and made some arrangements with my attorney in Amarillo that if something happened to us, Jere's family would be taken care of. Jere didn't need to see no paperwork; my word was all he needed to hear.

While all this was going on, I saw a show on television about a diving suit made by Jacques Cousteau, whose company was out in Santa Ana, California. For you young'uns out there, Jacques Cousteau was that famous Frenchman who made all them great underwater TV shows. His program, *The Undersea World of Jacques Cousteau*, was a hit TV series for nearly seven years. I figured that if there was one man on this green earth who knew a little something about water, it was him, right?

So I called Jacques with my request about a special wet suit, and he said, "I think I can keep you from freezing to death if you can find a way out of there. I can make you a wet suit that will keep you alive for up to about fifteen minutes in that water—no longer."

"Okay," I said. "Then what do I do? Just put some life jackets on over it?"

He asked me how much I weighed, which was about 170 pounds at that time. "Good," he said. "I'll build a hundred and eight pounds of buoyancy into the wet suit, but you'll have to come get fitted for it." In other words, rather than my having to wear life jackets, he was gonna build the wet suit with the Styrofoam-type stuff that would make it float. I guess he realized I needed to be as mobile as possible while maneuvering around the rocks and ice on that river.

I asked Jere to come with me so he could get fitted, too, but he said he already had a good wet suit. So I flew to Los Angeles, rented a car, and drove down to the headquarters of the U.S. Divers Company in Santa Ana, which is about an hour south in Orange County. I was greeted by the general manager, who made me a wet suit that was burnt orange with an outline of the state of Texas in blue on the back. The wet suit had been tested for thirty-three degrees below zero and would float a man weighing up to 255 pounds.

Now, the wet suit would keep me alive in that water if there was some trouble—that was the guarantee—for up to fifteen minutes. But who was gonna come get me during that fifteen minutes?

My friend Joe Batson, the one who had introduced me to LBJ, had an old helicopter that he'd used for his advertising agency. I asked him if he would come up to Idaho with me and Jere and just hover over us while we went down that river—in case something funny happened.

"Lord, yes," he said. "Boy, that'd be a good project for me—and we'll film it, too."

"Well, I don't care nothing about that," I said. "I just want to make sure I get out of there alive."

As Saturday, November 19, was approaching, we made all of our preparations—or at least we thought we had. And in case you're wondering about the date—November 19 might not technically be considered "winter," but let me tell you that for all intents and purposes it was the dead of winter in Idaho on that river about that time. About a few days before we were set to go down the river, I remembered that everyone said the jagged ice would cut the raft. So I started making some more calls but couldn't find anybody to make me a raft that they could guarantee wouldn't get cut up. Finally I got a hold of an outifit in Seattle, Washington, called Puget Sound Sand & Gravel and got them to design a special raft. In fact, I had them make two of 'em, with five separate compartments each. The way the raft was constructed, even if as many as four of the compartments got cut and burst, we would still be able to float. All of our gear was in rubber boxes that could float, too. In the boxes we had food, and I also put some first-aid stuff and extra water mittens and hand warmers in there.

We had two rafts because Joe Batson had intended to make a documentary about the trip. Bill Rhew and Fred Potter of Amarillo filmed us from the other raft, which was being guided by three river runners that Jere had recommended. Of course, if any of them had to help us, I would automatically lose the bet. So I made it perfectly clear that they were *not* to help us out—under any circumstances. I wanted to win this bet, and if I couldn't win it, then at least I was going to die trying.

Since the primitive area had no roads, and motorized vehicles were prohibited by the National Forest Service, getting there required three airplanes and one helicopter. We were to launch from the Flying B, a famous lodge on a dude ranch at the head of the Salmon River that was owned by Bill Harrah. A big group of reporters came, and that old genius Thackrey, of course, was right in the middle of it. Joe Batson was coordinating all the media, and before we left, the whole group was in my room at the Flying B—Jere, some other friends, the press, and photographers. The Greek and his cronies were in Vegas, but they had sent one of their own men from one of the Las Vegas papers to make sure there wasn't any skullduggery going on.

Then the phone rang, and it was a minister in Florida who said that his entire congregation would be praying for me. Of course, I was more interested in playing than praying, but after word spread about all the preparations I had made, I couldn't get any more action. I said to the press corps, "I can't get anybody else to bet against me. I was kinda hoping to get the stakes up to fifty thousand dollars before we started."

Jere had estimated that the trip would take five to nine days, since we planned to do some elk and deer hunting along the way. "We have no set schedule," Jere said. "We'll probably run into more ice than I've ever encountered before. The temperature has been down to about five degrees already."

My family, of course, stayed back home in Amarillo—they were all scared to death. In fact, they begged me not to do it, but I was too damn selfish to listen. My daughter, Becky, who was thirteen at the time, cried when she saw some of the pictures that were taken of the journey. According to Helen, Becky would wake up every day, look at the paper, and say, "Look where my daddy is. He's not gonna make it." Just thinking about it now, it makes me want to cry for getting that sweet little girl so upset. If there's one thing in my life that I regret, it was putting my family through the torture of waiting out this bet. I can say this now, but all I cared about back then was saving face and showing Demetrius that he should never have messed with old Slim.

TAKEOFF FROM THE FLYING B

Before we got going, one of the photographers who was there from Sweden to cover the event asked me, "Mr. Slim, can I hitch a ride on your helicopter this evening and go down through there, just to check it out?"

"Sure," I said. "Have a ball."

So we let him go down there on the helicopter, and when he got back, he looked like he damn near saw a ghost.

"Let me tell you something," he said. "I am catching the first flight back to Boise!"

Now, here was a guy who wouldn't even *fly* down through there in a helicopter. It looked that treacherous. Granted, I had gone down there a couple of times myself on the helicopter to scout out what the hell I was getting myself into, and even I could see that it wasn't no place to be—believe me.

On Saturday at 2:00 P.M., in the most primitive area of Idaho, the wind-chill temperature was forty-two below zero. Before we took off, my last words to the press were, "I don't want to be looking to play no billiards with any of these boulders."

The first three days of what was to be a twenty-nine-mile float down-river were fairly routine. Jere sat in the back of the raft and called the shots, and the guys on the other raft took pictures and shot film. Then, at night, we'd camp out, build a fire, cook up some food, and relax. It almost felt like more of a vacation than a life-threatening adventure.

At the end of every day, Batson would lower a bucket from his helicopter, which we filled with messages and film. That way Batson could give the media—who were covering this from all over the world—an update along with a quote from me. I'd write on a little notepad, "Today was sort of like drawing to an inside straight," which Batson could then send off to the media.

When we got up on Tuesday, we knew that the honeymoon would be coming to an end. We were approaching the Haystack Rapid, where the river ran straight into a solid rock wall that we'd have to veer away from. We could hear the roar of the water crashing for a long ways—I still hear that sound in my dreams sometimes, a loud, crashing roar, like the sound of a lion who's been stuck with a hot poker. Jere and I weren't but two feet away from each other, and we couldn't hear the other talk.

We found a place where we could get out of the raft so we could walk around the bend. We tied the raft and walked along the edge of the river, and we could see these rocks sticking out from the water, covered with ice. We figured if we could get past this one rock and then row just as hard as we could—I mean real hard and fast—it wouldn't slam us into that wall. We were afraid that if we got slammed into that wall, we might get pinned against it.

We might have been crazy, but at least we had a plan, right? So we got back into the raft, and I was in front, on my knees, with an oar in my hands. Our plan seemed like a good one, because when we got to that rock that we could see stickin' up, I started rowing just as hard as I could, and we missed it by a few feet. But what we didn't see was another rock, even sharper than the first, just under the surface of the water.

Thwack!

We struck it so hard that the inflated side of the raft just collapsed, and my knees took most of the shock as we came to a sudden stop. Well, it hurt me real good; it busted my knee, and a sharp pain coursed through my entire body. When the raft hit that rock, we were forced against it and had no chance to get around it. We were up shit's creek without a paddle.

We were stuck on this jagged rock, with the current crashing all around us, and Jere said to me, "Austin, *some*body's got to get into this water and get us off here." I may have been a little bit in shock, but I knew that "*some*body" didn't mean him. Now, I'm a skinny sonofagun, but, being that I didn't have much of a choice, we tied a rope around my waist and an extra rope around my chest as I got ready to take a dive.

"Now, you're not gonna get but one chance," Jere said, and didn't I know it. "You're gonna go under the raft and try to raise it; all you got to do is raise it maybe a foot or so, and it will go over this submerged rock."

Was I scared?

Shit no, I didn't have time to be scared. I knew I could either sit there and die or take my chances getting out of that sonofabitch. So I went under the water and the raft, and I knew I had one shot, and *up I came*. I was pushing on the bottom of that raft, and of course by now my weight wasn't on it, so it raised up just enough, and, with Jere paddling, the raft took off like a shot from a cannon.

The current slung me like a yo-yo, and I just flew across there. Since I was tied to the side of the raft with a rope, I was getting dragged around, and my legs were hitting rocks and ice, and, by golly, did it hurt!

I hadn't given much thought as to how I would get back *in* the raft, and I ended up getting the sort of ride that is usually associated with har-pooning whales out of a lifeboat. By that time, thankfully, the water had gotten deeper. Once we passed the wall, I wasn't hitting ice or rocks anymore—I could focus on just trying to breathe—but I still had to find a way to get into that raft. I finally managed to get up near the front of the raft, and I said to Jere, "Can you get me back in?"

"I got to, Austin, or else you're gonna freeze or drown to death!"

So, with all his might, he found a way to pull me into the raft. Had it not been for Jere and Mr. Cousteau, I would have been dead by then—and that's the truth. Now we had to find a place to stop, and, as soon as we could, we got out and set up camp. We took off our wet suits and gutted up some wood and built a fire. About twelve minutes later, my knee got about the size of my hat.

I took out some hand warmers from those boxes, put one on each hand, and started rubbing my knee to give it some heat. Finally the swelling went down a little, and we put that wet suit back on me, and I said, "Now we'll just let that knee bust if it has to; whatever it's gonna do, I ain't gonna take that wet suit off no more. That's the end of taking it off, because if my knee swells again, I can't get it back in there."

Our plans of hunting along the way were put to rest after that accident, and now I wasn't all that interested in taking our time. Wednesday morning it was ten degrees, and we had to take an ax and chop the raft out of the ice and push it into the main stream. The middle of the river was mostly slush. Lucky for us, the worst was behind us, and on Wednesday afternoon, November 22, 1972, we made it to the campground at the northern end of the River of No Return. It seemed like every TV station, newspaper, and photographer in the world was there to greet us, and the first thing I said was, "You can tell the fellas in Las Vegas to count that money kinda slow, because all I want right now is a nice hot bath and an airplane ride home to Amarillo."

Thackrey noticed how awful my hands looked, and I said to the crowd, "These calluses sure didn't come from shufflin' cards, neighbor." Among the press corps, there was also a representative from a company—I believe it was Boise Cascade—and they offered Jere and me $25,000 if we'd float another twenty-five miles down the river to a resort that they owned down there. By then the river was calm, but I was ready to go home and celebrate Thanksgiving with my family in Amarillo. I couldn't remember any Turkey Day when I had more to be thankful for. Before long, Batson's helicopter had dropped into the mile-deep gorge to pick us up and fly us back to Boise.

When we arrived in Boise—I never will forget this—my hotel suite had a great big heart-shaped bathtub, and they had set bottles of champagne all over the rail, and everybody said for me to get into the tub. I don't drink, but I had a good time popping them bottles and spraying 'em all over them reporters. Then I put 'em all in shock—I took off my wet suit and got into this big heart-shaped bathtub stark naked. It wasn't a good thing to do, because sooner or later there were a bunch of lady reporters and photographers who had come into my room. Fortunately, there was this bubble-bath lotion that covered me up and made me presentable to the press for my interviews. There was some celebration that night in Idaho.

Now, here's one thing that I do know: I wouldn't do it again any way unless one of my grandbabies was stuck down there. But I would not do it again for all the money in the world—even if old Demetrius had bet me to do it again. Of course, he never did hold a penny of my money, and as bad as I talk about him, I did say a prayer for him when he died in 1998 from heart failure.

After the bet I read some articles in *Time* and *Reader's Digest*, and every one of them said that the Idaho Travel and Tourism Bureau was concerned that my little stunt would cause an influx of fools to start trying to go down the River of No Return in the winter. Well, I didn't have nothing to say about that, because I knew I was a damn fool for having done it myself. But do you know how many people have gone up there and tried it since then?

None.

You've heard me talk about not playing results, and just because everything turned out swell, it doesn't mean that I made the right decision in the first place. It's like playing a bad hand, like a deuce and a four of different suits, in Hold'em, only for the flop to come ace, trey, five and make you a wheel. Just because you won, it doesn't mean you should be playing cards like deuce-four offsuit.

In other words, I made a bad decision, even though the result was okay. But it could just as easily have not come out okay. Forget the $31,000 that I won from the Greek, Pug, and Boyd, I didn't make nothing on that bet. Between the wet suit and the raft and all that stuff, it cost me an arm and nine hundred legs to get down the river. But out of pure stubbornness—you might use that word "hubris" again—I did it anyway. Call it whatever you want, because it was just damn foolish any way you slice it.

One thing that did please me to no end was all the mail I received before and after the trip. I got three or four big bags of mail every day with letters and cards from all over the world, wishing me luck and saying how they hoped I made it and that they were praying for me. And, by golly, it helped.

Besides a busted-up knee and a finger that I almost lost, I came out of the River of No Return in one piece. It was the first bet I'd ever made where I threw in my own personal life to sweeten the pot. And it would be the last one, too. I made a vow that from that day forward I'd do my gambling with just plain old currency. Batson and his boys never did make that documentary, but compared to what was about to come, an itty-bitty documentary didn't seem like such a big deal.

Presenting the winner's loot to Mr. "Spit and Pull It" himself, Bob Stupak, at the Super Bowl of Poker. *(Courtesy of the author)*

Spit and Pull It—Leading Men and the Super Bowl of Poker

When a football team wins a Super Bowl, its city throws a parade, the team goes to the White House, the star player writes a book, and, if the team doesn't repeat as champions, it's not long before they're getting booed by their fans. I figured it wouldn't be much different for me. After the River of No Return, my celebrity status had really grown, but I thought that if I didn't win the World Series of Poker again in 1973, my honeymoon with the public would be over.

Well, as you know, I let the whole state of Texas down when a pug-nosed sonofagun from Tennessee took the title from me in '73. But to give you an idea how it affected me, in the *Houston Chronicle* on May 21, 1973, after they congratulated Puggy on his victory, the article said:

We are saddened, however, by the blow to colorful language and image which Pearson's triumph represents. Having a champion poker player nicknamed "Puggy Wuggy," as Pearson is, in no way can be as delightful as having one called "Amarillo Slim," the beautifully descriptive nickname carried by last year's champion, Thomas Preston.

So not only was the press still behind me, but more and more opportunities came my way. The biggest one came when award-winning director Robert Altman asked me to be in his movie *California Split*, starring George Segal and Elliott Gould. I couldn't believe it, old Slim hamming it up for the camera in a film about two hustlers—and I got to play myself! My big scene was shot at the Mapes casino in downtown Reno. George Segal's character, Bill Denny, joined me in a game of California Lowball, and during a break in the action, I went up to the bar, pulled out a wad of about $40,000 from inside my suit-coat pocket, and said to the bartender, "In the second race down at Santa Anita, there's a horse running I need to make a little bet on—Ol' Blue out of chute number two. Give me four hundred to win on the second horse in the second race."

The movie came out in 1974, and the supporting cast included Ann Prentiss, Gwen Welles, and Bert Remsen, who played the cross-dressing Helen Brown. This Internet site called IMDB.com says that "*California Split* endures as one of the most probing examinations of the soul and psyche of the abnormal gambler ever filmed." If they're trying to say that it was a heckuva movie that gives a pretty good indication of what it's like to be a gambler, then I can't argue. For me it was just a lot of fun—and very profitable since George Segal and Elliott Gould loved to gamble. I seem to remember that Segal thought he knew a little something about math and made me a bet that eight numbers or more would fall on the outside row of the keno board. That bet was won before the board even lit up. Mr. Gould fancied himself a pretty good free-throw shooter, and I didn't need a football to show that he wasn't as good as he thought he was.

THE LEADING MEN OF NEVADA: WEBB, HUGHES, KERKORIAN, WYNN

By now you've seen how Las Vegas evolved from an itty-bitty town in 1946 to the gambling capital of the world and home of the ever-growing World Series of Poker. But just as Benny Binion made poker what it is today, four other men were largely responsible for changing Las Vegas from a frontier, one-horse town with a bunch of die-hard gamblers into a destination resort and the fastest-growing city in America.

Born in 1899 in Fresno, California, Del Webb played minor-league baseball and might have made it to the big leagues had he not caught typhoid fever from an inmate during an exhibition game at San Quentin prison in 1927. And those ballplayers today think they have it tough! After giving up baseball, Webb became a contractor, got rich putting up buildings during World War II, and used some of his money to buy the New York Yankees and their farm clubs in January 1945 for $2.8 million. In 1964, after the Yankees won ten World Series titles while he was owner, he sold the club for $14 million. Even better for Webb, he had used Yankee tickets to get himself more construction contracts.

Webb claimed he didn't know who Bugsy Siegel was when he agreed to finish building the Flamingo hotel in 1946, but he found out in a hurry. Bugsy bragged that he had personally killed twelve people, and one time when he was real mad at some cat, Bugsy said, "I'm going to kill that SOB, too," and glared at Webb. Well, Webb must have looked like he'd seen a ghost, because when Bugsy saw the look on his face, he said, "Del, don't worry. We only kill each other."

In 1961, his company, Del Webb Corporation, became the first publicly held corporation to enter Nevada gaming after Webb bought the Sahara Hotel of Las Vegas, where the Beatles performed in 1964. This was a landmark moment, as it began the transformation of Las Vegas from a mob town to a Wall Street town. In 1964, Webb was voted *Time* magazine's Man of the Year, and also held the distinction as one of the few people that the eccentric and reclusive Howard Hughes would meet with face-to-face.

The DI, where I played Phil Harris in gin, was built in the fifties on the northern part of the Strip and was run by a mobster from Cleveland named Moe Dalitz—the man who brought Elvis Presley to Las Vegas. Toward the end of 1966, Howard Hughes rented the entire top floor of high-roller suites and the entire floor below it for ten days, with the stipulation that he get out by New Year's to accommodate Moe's big-spending clientele. When Hughes, who was addicted to opiates by then, refused to check out, Dalitz got hot on him.

Hughes had an ace in the hole, though: Teamsters Union president Jimmy Hoffa, who convinced Dalitz to leave it alone. But when Dalitz kept pestering Hughes to leave, old Howard just decided to buy the place for $13.25 million. Of course, a man who would do something like that could only be from one place, *Texas*, where he first got rich from his daddy's tool company. In 1925 Hughes moved to Hollywood and became known as a playboy and the film producer who discovered Jean Harlow and Jane Russell. On the side he dabbled in designing airplanes and breaking speed records flying them, and in 1938 he became a national hero with his famous 'round-the-world flight. When he sold his stock in TWA for more than $500 million, he bought four more hotels in Vegas—the Sands, the Castaways, the Silver Slipper, and the Frontier.

Hughes wanted to be the biggest of the big shots in Vegas and felt threatened when Kirk Kerkorian, a pretty shrewd businessman himself, started building the thirty-story International Hotel (now the Las Vegas Hilton) in early 1968, which at the time, with 1,512 rooms, was the largest hotel in the world. Just so he could have the *tallest* hotel in Las Vegas, Hughes paid $17.3 million for the Landmark, a lousy hotel/casino that had sat empty for the past five years. All Hughes cared about was that it was taller, by a peanut, than the International, which funnily enough, was the same hotel that Leon Crump couldn't hit that golf ball on top of. Hughes even bought the local CBS affiliate, KLAS-TV, from Hank Greenspun just so he could control which movies ran late into the night.

Steve Wynn, who I've already said is about the sharpest man not named Binion ever to come to Vegas, bought the Golden Nugget, which was right across from the Horseshoe, in 1973. In 1980, he built another Golden Nugget in Atlantic City, not long after gambling was legalized there, and paid $10 million for three years of Frank Sinatra's services. In 1986, Steve bought a big piece of land next to Caesar's Palace, sold the Golden Nugget in Atlantic City, and announced plans to build the Mirage, a hotel that would cost $630 million. To help pay for the place and the volcano that would erupt in front of the hotel every half hour, Steve went to Michael Milken and raised $565 million through junk bonds. When all the bean counters said the hotel would have to make $1 million a day just to pay off the debt, few folks gave Steve a chance.

Even though the popularity of poker took off after Benny created the World Series, hardly any new hotels were built in Las Vegas throughout the seventies and eighties. In fact, before the Mirage there hadn't been a major hotel built on the Strip since Kerkorian opened the MGM Grand (now Bally's) in 1973.

But talk about contagious. Even before the Mirage opened in November 1989, the company that owned Circus Circus started building a castle-like place on the southern part of the Strip with four thousand rooms, called the Excalibur. And then Kerkorian, who had sold the original MGM Grand, started construction on a hotel across the street from Excalibur with five thousand rooms that he would also name the MGM Grand. Are you seeing a pattern here with Las Vegas men and size? I wish old Siggy Freud were around to help explain this a little—and, shoot, we haven't even got to Bob Stupak!

I wish I could have taken action from all the naysayers about the Mirage, because, like I knew it would, the hotel was a huge success when it opened in November 1989. "Creation's okay," Wynn said when the Mirage opened, "but if God had money, he would have done this." It was only fitting that Benny was alive to see the opening of the Mirage, and when he died a month later, the torch had been passed from Benny Binion to Steve Wynn.

Not so much in tribute to Benny, but more because he was such a smart businessman, Steve built the biggest and nicest poker room in town at the Mirage. And while it doesn't bring in nearly the same revenue as them slot machines, it was no coincidence that the poker room was right next to the sports book. By attracting all the big poker players to the Mirage, Steve was able to get all their sports betting action as well.

In 1998 Steve built an even nicer place called the Bellagio. Like the Mirage, the Bellagio had three thousand rooms and was built on the property where the Dunes was before it got knocked down. This joint, where you can find Doyle, Chip Reese, and all the top poker professionals today, cost Steve only $1.6 billion. He also built a fancy place called the Beau Rivage on the Gulf Coast in Biloxi, Mississippi, and another three thousand-room joint next to the Mirage on the Strip, called Treasure Island. But when the stock of Steve's company fell from $18 in November 1998 to below $14 by August 1999, Kirk Kerkorian (net worth about $6 billion) bought out Steve's stock and renamed the merged company MGM MIRAGE. Bobby Baldwin, the 1978 World Series of Poker winner, who had been one of Steve's top guns at the Bellagio, stayed on as one of the top executives for MGM MIRAGE.

And talk about things going full circle. After Steve sold out, he bought Howard Hughes's old joint, the DI, tore it down, and is now building Le Rêve, which is supposed to open in 2005. The city of Las Vegas now has more than 120,000 hotel rooms and nine of the ten biggest hotels in the world. If Nick the Greek were to rise from his grave today, he wouldn't recognize the city that he visited in 1951 when he came west looking for action.

KENNY ROGERS, WILLIE NELSON, AND AN EXPENSIVE GAME OF DOMINOES

Even though I am fourteen years older than Steve Wynn, with my victory in the World Series in 1972 and Steve's purchase of the Golden Nugget in 1973, we both started making a name for ourselves in Las Vegas at the same time. And now that I had a book and a part in a movie, it was time to get involved with music.

I had played poker a few times with Kenny Rogers, who was born in 1938 in Houston, and we got to be pretty good buddies over the years.

One day in 1978, Kenny approached Steve and me about a song he was performing about gambling. Figuring that the best place to help him get a feel for the lyrics—which were written by Don Schlitz—would be in a card room, we sat down right in the poker room at the Golden Nugget and talked about "The Gambler." Steve and I played poker, and Kenny would watch us and ask us questions: "What's this about Hold'em?"

"Well, how does the song go?" I asked.

"The chorus starts with," Kenny said, breaking into song, "'You got to know when to hold 'em, know when to fold 'em.'"

"Well, that's the truth," I said. "But you also got to know when to quit."

So then Kenny sang the next line, "'Know when to walk away, know when to run.'"

Kenny just kept singing, and, gosh darn, I thought it was the greatest song I ever heard. And on December 23 of that year, Kenny hit the charts with "The Gambler," which was a number-one country hit, and two years later he starred in his own TV movie based on the smash-hit record. To this day Kenny and I are good friends, and he even takes my grandbaby Heather backstage whenever he has a concert in Houston.

With Benny running the show at the Horseshoe and Steve running the Golden Nugget across the street, whenever I was in Vegas, I left the fancy Strip for Demetrius and his cronies and spent most of my time in downtown Vegas, palling around with two of the most powerful men in Nevada. One time down at the Nugget, Steve asked me if I knew how to play dominoes.

"I know you already know the answer to that question, Mr. Wynn, but, yes, in fact, I'm a real good player."

"Willie won the national domino championship when he was nineteen years old," Steve said.

Well, I knew that Steve was onto something about getting me to play my friend from Ennis, Texas, Willie Nelson. So I just got right to the point: "Can't no fuckin' guitar picker beat me at anything." I said it like that for a reason.

Sure enough, Steve went straight over to Willie, who was in town, and told him what I'd said. Steve ended up betting me $50,000 and a new Jeep Renegade that I couldn't beat Willie in dominoes, and Willie ponied up another $300,000 on himself. A big bookmaker out of Ireland made Willie a 6-to-5 favorite, and I took some action with him, too.

Willie might have been a champion, and I hadn't exactly been spending my spare time playing dominoes, but, I figured if we played best out of seven games, as we did, skill would come through in the end. Don't worry, neighbor, it did, and I was happy to take money from two men who had more than they needed.

WORKING STIFF AND THE SUPER BOWL OF POKER

If there was one thing that I never did aspire to have in life, it was a job. The only thing was, I was never one to leave money on the table, and, after all those talk shows, I got approached by several outfits who wanted me as their spokesperson.

In 1978, when Jimmy Newman, one of the bosses of the Las Vegas Hilton, asked me to create a poker tournament for his casino, I thought it through and came up with the Super Bowl of Poker. Not only did it sound big, but folks would remember that it started right after the Super Bowl—when a lot of gamblers were in town to watch and bet on the big football game.

In 1979, right after the Pittsburgh Steelers beat the Dallas Cowboys, 35–31, in Super Bowl XIII, the first Super Bowl of Poker ran from January 25 to February 8 at the Las Vegas Hilton. It wasn't in competition with Benny's World Series, because his tournament was in May, and, with his support and blessing, the Super Bowl of Poker became a tremendous success. Even though it was a lot of fun and I made decent money, when the Hilton closed its card room before the second tournament even started in 1980, I would have been just as happy to give it up—especially because I didn't get to play, and playing is a heckuva lot more fun than hosting.

Then the Del Webb Corporation approached me about a job that seemed too good to refuse. Although Mr. Webb passed away in 1974, by 1978 the company was the largest gaming employer in Nevada with some seven thousand workers. I interviewed with Lynn Simon, the casino manager, and Tony Ashley, who wound up being the president. I also met

Larry Sanders, who was in charge of poker there and who became a real good friend.

The deal was that I would bring the Super Bowl of Poker to the Sahara Reno and keep it either there or at one of the other Del Webb properties, such as the High Sierra (later renamed the Sahara Tahoe), where the tournament later moved. The second part of the deal was that wherever I traveled, I would tell people *who* I worked for and speak highly of the Del Webb properties. They even gave me a card with my title listed as "International Director of Special Events." One of the funniest parts about my job was that they took out an insurance policy on me for $2 million. That way, if I called somebody a sonofabitch and couldn't prove it, the Del Webb Corporation would be protected against a lawsuit for slander, libel, or defamation of character. I told 'em I'd never in my life defamed a sonofabitch who didn't need it. And Tony Ashley said, "Yeah, Slim, but you decide who needs it and who don't, and that's not the way the law works." I sure got a kick out of that.

The highlight of my job with the Del Webb Corporation was the time I had brought some of my horses from my ranch in Amarillo to a cattle cutting we were holding at the High Sierra in Lake Tahoe. Somebody made me a bet that I wouldn't ride Rabbit, the turnback horse for the world's most famous ranch, King Ranch in south Texas, through the casino. Shoot, I even had my one-year-old grandbaby Heather on my lap while I was doing it. It wasn't harming nothing, but you know how them bosses get about liability and all, and before long I was getting an earful from one of the pit bosses. So, rather than argue, I just backed my colt up to one of the craps tables and said, "You want to find out how this here craps table got its name?"

He just kept yelling at me, so I said, "You want me to show you?"

That shut him up in a hurry! Now, I can do a lot of things, but I sure as hell can't make a skittish colt crap on demand. That sonofabitch pit boss wasn't about to see if I could, though, so he let me ride around for a while. This little stunt made me some good money, albeit on a different animal, while I was whooping it up at a posh casino in Marrakech, Morocco, a few years after—but more on that later.

The entire eight years or so that I was with the Del Webb Corporation, Caesars Palace had been wooing me, and finally their offer got too good to turn down. I kept the title of International Director of Special Events, and all I had to do was move the Super Bowl of Poker to Caesars and host three other events per year. Sure, running a tournament and being the International Director of Special Events was a job, but as far as I was concerned, I had the best damn job in Nevada. Shoot, I didn't even have to move there.

THE WHALES COMETH: STUPAK AND FLYNT

The more I traveled and the bigger my reputation became, the more offers I got to gamble. It was just like being the fastest gun in the West: Everybody wanted to test himself against me. Forget all the commercials and talk shows and that little job I had. What it really meant was that I got to gamble with a different caliber of person. Instead of playing a guy that had *$20,000*, I got to play a guy that had *$20 million*. These are the people who the casinos refer to as whales.

Bob Stupak and Larry Flynt were two men who came to my tournament, loved to play poker, and had plenty of money. And even though the two of them are disliked by a few folks, both are still friends, and I always got along with them just fine.

To say Bob Stupak is about the craziest sonofabitch that ever lived would be putting it mildly. Bob was born in Pittsburgh in 1942, where his daddy, Chester, ran floating craps games. As soon as Bob was old enough to gamble, he came to Las Vegas with big plans. Among his many jobs, Bob became a nightclub singer and cut several singles as "Bobby Star," served in the national guard, and started a thriving business in Nevada (and later Australia) selling two-for-one coupon books.

This man had to be the best promoter since P. T. Barnum. He bought the worst parcel of real estate in Vegas, in an area between downtown and the Strip called "Naked City," and on a Friday the thirteenth in July 1979, he opened a joint called Vegas World and turned it into a multimillion-dollar moneymaker. Taking a page from Benny's book, he plastered his motto, THE SKY'S THE LIMIT, across the building. Bob called himself the "Polish Maverick" and advertised the games in his casino as "easy to beat" because he was Polish and too stupid to know better. And people went for it!

The only thing Bob promoted better than his casino was himself. He ran for mayor in 1987, ran his daughter Nicole in 1991, and his son Nevada in 1999 for city council. While he lost all three races, he came much closer than anyone would have thought in each. He bet a million dollars on Super Bowl XXIII, a fact that got picked up by just about every newspaper in the country, and he won the bet when the Bengals covered the seven-point spread against the '49ers. He even created a board game called "Stupak" and challenged Donald Trump to a game for a million bucks.

Like some of Nevada's leading men who came before him, Bob was also obsessed with size, and in the mid-nineties he built the Stratosphere Hotel, along with a 1,149-foot tower, which was the fourth-tallest building in the United States at the time. Then he went and put a roller coaster on the roof! A lot of folks came up with some clever nicknames for this tower, but Bob always said the one he liked best was "Stupak's Shaft." Naturally, it went bankrupt and was later bought by takeover magnate Carl Icahn.

As I said, I always liked Bob and still consider him a good friend. He's always supported everything I've ever done in my life and is one of the most colorful characters that Las Vegas has ever known. To give you an idea of how far this man would go to get some publicity, he called me one time at my ranch in Clarendon and said, "Slim, do you have *People* magazine?"

"Hell no. Why?"

"How far are you from town?" he asked.

I told him about seventeen miles, and he said, "Well, the way you drive, it won't take long. Let me call you back in an hour, and you go get yourself a *People* magazine."

I hemmed and hawed about not wanting to drive thirty-four miles just to get a magazine, and Bob said, "Listen, there's something in there that you'll really like. I just gave a guy a million dollars to jump off the top of Vegas World."

"Do *what*, Bob?"

"I gave some guy a million dollars to jump off the top of Vegas World. Go pick up the magazine and see for yourself."

Vegas World was twenty-four stories high, and, as I said earlier, smack dab in the middle of all the sleazy nudie bars and run-down marriage parlors on the northern end of the Strip. Bob needed all the publicity he could scrounge up to get bodies inside his casino, and I guess he thought that if he could get someone to jump off the top of his hotel, then everyone and his Aunt Tillie would take notice.

But I still didn't believe him. Who in his right mind would jump off the top of a twenty-four-story hotel? Shoot, I might have been dumb enough to go down the River of No Return, but there was no way in hell you'd have got me to jump from the top of any hotel. I knew it had to be a publicity stunt, but when Bob wouldn't tell me the whole story, I hopped in my pickup, drove about a hundred miles an hour down into town to some rinky-dink supermarket there, and bought me a *People* magazine.

I jumped right back in my truck, zoomed back to my ranch in Clarendon, and there it was—a great big article just as Bob had said. There was a picture of a special aired-up mat that the guy was supposed to land on. One million dollars! Heck, I knew that Bob Stupak was one crazy sonofabitch, but I also knew that there had to be more to the story.

Not ten minutes later, the phone rang again. "Well," Bob said, "what do you think of that?"

I never pulled any punches with Bob, so I just said, "I think it's a lie."

"I knew you'd say that. You're doubtful of everything." Then he said, "What do you think *is* on the square, Slim?"

It was a damn good question.

"There's only two things left in the whole world on the square," I said.

"What's that?"

"Wrestling and Coca-Cola."

"*What?*"

"That's right," I said, "wrestling and Coca-Cola. But now I'm even a little dubious of Coca-Cola. They just took their product to China, where them folks don't know the difference between Coca-Cola and caramel-colored water, because they ain't never tasted Coke before. So them suits in Atlanta are probably watering down their product to improve their profits."

Bob laughed at that one, and after he pulled my leg a little longer, I had enough and said, "Let's cut out all the bullshit here. You didn't give this guy a million dollars—this is just a publicity thing."

"Nope," he said. "I'll take an oath that I gave him a million dollars."

"Okay, Bob," I said, "are you gonna tell me or not?"

"Slim, I already told you. I gave that man a million dollars to jump off the top of my hotel. Shoot, I charged him $975,000 just to land. That's prime real estate, you know."

Damn, that Stupak was one clever sonofagun. Wouldn't you know it, he got about $5 *billion* worth of publicity out of that stunt. And I just about laughed till I couldn't see.

A couple years later, Bob called me again and said, "You're one of the luckiest fools in the world, Slim. You've just made fifty thousand dollars, and you ain't even done a damned thing."

"Yeah, but what have I got to *do*?"

"I want you to sue me."

"Do *what*, Bob?"

"I'll give you fifty thousand dollars to sue me." And then Bob asked, "Do you remember when you broke me at the poker tournament in Dublin, Ireland?"

"It was no different than the usual," I said, "since it's a cinch I'm a better player than you."

"Do you remember what I said?"

Try as I might, I couldn't remember nothing about that game except for the fact that I took old Bob for everything he had on him that night.

"Surely you remember," he said, "the BBC came running up there to interview me just as I was walking off from the table, after you had just broke me, and I wasn't in too good of a mood for any kind of interview. And they said, 'Mr. Stupak, if you had to get broke, isn't it *great* that the world's most famous gambler broke you? You shouldn't feel too bad about getting broke by Amarillo Slim.'

"So I said to the interviewer, 'Let me tell you something about that Amarillo Slim. There are two things in Texas—steers and queers, and I have yet to see any horns on that country cowboy.'

"So my lawyer said that what I said about you was slander, and if you sued me, you'd win, because that quote was in all the tabloid magazines over there, and it was on BBC radio."

We talked about it a little, but there was no way I would do it. I believe that the law is something that should be handled between individuals, not attorneys—even when I had fifty thousand reasons to change my mind.

For all Bob Stupak's publicity stunts, people forget that not only is he a smart sonofagun, but he's also a heckuva poker player. In 1989 he won $139,500 for first place in the Kansas City Lowball tournament at the World Series of Poker and another $47,500 for first place in my Super Bowl of Poker Kansas City Lowball tournament. Whenever Bob and I got together at one of my tournaments, we'd play head-up Hold'em. "Come on, Slim," Bob said to me one time at the High Sierra, "I'll play you a ten-thousand-dollar freeze-out before the tournament gets started."

It didn't take me long to bust him, and Bob said, "Play another?"

So we played for $10,000 more, and I beat him again. Now I was ahead $20,000, and Bob said to me, "Slim, give me some money." And we always jived and kidded one another—I think that's why I like the crazy bastard—so I said, "Well, man, if you're a little short, go get you a ladder."

"Well, hell," he said, "I've got money on deposit."

I already knew he had money on deposit, but I wanted to razz him, so I said, "Nope, there's only one way we'll continue playing without you posting your money."

"How's that?" Bob asked.

"You spit and pull it."

"Do *what?*"

"You spit and pull it."

"What does that mean?"

I pointed to the twelve-carat diamond that Bob wore on his pinkie, and I said, "It means spit on your finger and pull old sparkles off."

"What, are you crazy, Slim? You think I'm gonna give you my diamond as collateral for ten thousand? You know what I got on deposit?"

Well, now I really wanted to razz him pretty good, so I said, "Bob, do you *really* wanna play?"

"Yes, Slim, you know I wanna play."

"Then spit and pull it."

So he finally went for it, and he made a big to-do out of spitting on his diamond. I pulled it off and set it on top of my stack of money. Then Bob must have drawn out on me and ended up winning the session. Well, that was all I needed to make it Texas rules, and when he beat me again, I was down $10,000 to him and didn't have his ring—or any money in front of me.

"Just a second," I said to Bob. "I'll be right back."

"What is it?"

"I'll go get some money."

"You ain't got no money?"

Now I was all heated, and Bob knew damn well that I had money on deposit. I told him that we should keep playing, and if I lost, I would just go over to the cage to get his money. Well, now Bob had *me* on the ropes, and he said, "Slim, you wanna play me some?"

"Yes, Bob," I said, "I sure as hell do."

"Then spit and pull it."

He pointed to my most prized piece of jewelry, a 7.5-carat diamond that I had bought in Pretoria, South Africa. I didn't find much humor in this, and I said, "Bob, I've owned that diamond for twenty-some-odd years, and I never have taken it off. I ain't taking it off for you."

"Slim, do you *really* wanna play me?" he asked.

"Goddamn right, I wanna play you."

"Then spit and pull it."

That was the only time I ever had my ring in hock, and I'll tell you that I didn't feel comfortable doing it—but that sonofabitch got my ass so red that I just had to show him up. So he made me take off my ring and play a

$20,000 freeze-out. My only consolation was that at least I had my other ring, which was gold and shaped like the state of Texas and had a diamond gem where Amarillo is and blue lapis boots at the bottom of it. It was entertaining for folks to see Slim on the ropes, but everything worked out in the end—especially since I never did have to go to the cage to get my ring out of hock.

Sadly, on March 31, 1995, Bob Stupak was in a major motorcycle accident that broke every bone in his face, put him in a coma, and nearly killed him. He pulled out of it like the warrior that he's always been, and I still wouldn't bet against him getting back in the casino business. But as much as Steve Wynn did to make Las Vegas a thriving city, it has also become so corporate that there may not be a place for a guy like Bob Stupak anymore. Even Bob himself said, "The days of those characters are gone. There's no more Jay Sarnos"—the colorful cat known as "Dream Weaver," who built Caesars Palace and Circus Circus—"there are no more me's around. It's all over."

As far as I'm concerned, Las Vegas could use a character like Bob. Then again there's always Larry Flynt. True, the poker club that Larry runs, called the Hustler, is in Los Angeles, not Las Vegas, but he's still a fixture in the gambling community. Between *Hustler* magazine and the movie *The People Versus Larry Flynt*, the man in the wheelchair has made himself a small fortune. His area of business isn't something I'm particularly fond of, but I will say that Larry is a stand-up guy. I'd make an agreement with him without a contract any day of the week and wouldn't question it one iota. And let me tell you, if the police came down there and put his nuts in a vise, he'd tell 'em to keep twisting. Now that's a pretty good recommendation.

Like Bob Stupak, Larry supported my tournaments and loved to play poker. Unlike Stupak, though, he wasn't much of a player. The first time I played him was at the Sahara Reno in 1980 during the Super Bowl of Poker. Just as the World Series of Poker has evolved into dozens of events beyond the $10,000 no-limit Texas Hold'em event, the Super Bowl had several different tournaments, including a $10,000 Kansas City Lowball event.

As you know, in a freeze-out tournament, once you run out of chips, you're eliminated. But because I didn't think Larry had much of a chance to win, when he busted out, I broke one of my own rules and let Larry buy $10,000 worth of chips. Word got around, but all the players had enough sense not to say anything. When Larry busted out again, I let him re-buy again for $10,000 more. Now I had added $20,000 to the prize pool from a guy who had no shot of winning. Well, this happened *thirteen* times, which amounted to a $130,000 bonus to the rest of the players. I don't need to tell you that Larry didn't win.

The next day we had a $2,500 buy-in no-limit Hold'em tournament, and we'd been playing only about fifteen minutes when Larry got broke. He called me over to his table and said, "Slim, I just got broke."

"No surprise to me," I said.

"What am I gonna do, Slim, can I re-buy like yesterday?"

"Well, Larry, I know the name of your magazine is *Hustler*, but this ain't a re-buy tournament."

"Yesterday wasn't either," he said, which was right, but because some of the players were different, I wanted to cover myself. I told him I'd be right back, and I went and got on the PA and said loud and clear and very distinct, "One of our leading players just lost his chips, and it's a miracle he lost 'em. I think that's the first loss he's ever had. He'd like to re-buy, but this is not a re-buy tournament. So if anybody in the room objects, no need to be embarrassed or intimidated or anything. Make a signal to me or wave or wink or just say something, and we'll settle the matter right now."

Well, everybody in the room knew what I was doing. I was just giving the eventual winner another $2,500 from Mr. Flynt, who had about as good a chance to win that tournament as a one-legged man did in an ass-kicking contest. And wouldn't you know it, just as I was about to collect Larry's $2,500, guess who stood up? Gabe Kaplan, old Mr. Kotter himself. "I object," he said, and everybody looked at him and called him every name in the world, because they knew that Larry would have lost that $2,500 faster than you could say Jack Robinson.

"Now I don't know what I'm gonna do," Larry said.

"Well, Larry," I told him, "if you wanna see if luck'll overcome sanity, you can play me some head-up."

"But you don't play limit, Slim," he said, which was true. I don't play limit. I mean, I will play limit if there's a fish on the line, but, like I said before, no-limit is really the only way poker was meant to be played. But I had a little plan for my good friend. "Larry," I said, "you're one hell of a poker player, right? Well, shit, you can play no-limit just as good as you can play limit, can't you?"

"But, Slim," he said, "you don't play seven-card stud either."

"I do if it's no-limit," I said. Even though Larry couldn't play Kansas City Lowball or Hold'em worth a lick, he could always play seven-card stud okay. And in his mind he played it better than anyone who ever lived not named Bill Boyd.

"So what do you think?" I said. "You think we got ourselves a game of no-limit seven-card stud?"

"Well," he said, "I never heard of you playing any seven-card stud. Now you're on my turf."

And that was Larry—thinking that he was gonna steal something from me. So I took Larry back in the corner, and he bought $50,000 worth of chips, and I bought $50,000. I'd never been much of a stud player, but since it was no-limit, I knew I'd have no trouble busting him. You've heard me say that poker is a *people* game, not a *card* game, and while I didn't know the intricacies of stud like I did Hold'em, Larrry was drawing real slim against me in any poker game—especially when I could move in on him. So we played, and I won all his money in about fifteen minutes. Then I pulled the old Texas rules on him, and before I was through with him, Larry couldn't wait to get back to his centerfolds.

♠ ♣ ♦ ♥

Las Vegas may have been settled by Brigham Young's followers in 1855 and officially made a city on May 15, 1905, but as far as it concerned me, it really didn't exist until Benny Binion arrived in 1946. From the early days of Benny, Bugsy Siegel, and Meyer Lansky, to Del Webb, Howard Hughes, and Kirk Kerkorian in the sixties, to Steve Wynn, Bob Stupak, and Larry Flynt, who are alive and well in the twenty-first century, I had the pleasure of being involved with some of Nevada's leading men over the course of almost sixty years. I had even the better fortune of gambling with some of Nevada's biggest whales. But whenever the whales became scarce in America, I would go anywhere in the world to find another one.

A fool trying to win a bet that he could ride a camel through the most beautiful casino in the world in Marrakech, Morocco. He won the bet, but almost got crushed by the camel doing it! *(Courtesy of* The Card Player *magazine)*

12

Very Seldom Do the Lambs Slaughter the Butcher—Getting Fat Overseas

I've played poker in just about every casino and private club in Europe, and Australia, and South America. I even had my own tournament in Sun City, South Africa, and when I won it, the headline in the Johannesburg paper the next day read: VERY SELDOM DO THE LAMBS SLAUGHTER THE BUTCHER. I was a regular at the Bayswater Casino in London, where I did some promotion for the Poker Million tournament. And when the BBC asked me to come to London to appear in some poker scenes they planned to film, I told them I wouldn't mind obliging them if they could bring some of the best players to London and make it akin to a world championship. When I asked how much the winner would receive, they said in the region of 10,000 pounds. So I told them, "Add a few *tons* to that figure and I will come on over." They did, and I went.

There's no doubt that poker is an international game, and while some of the places I traveled to had some unusual rules, I never had a problem finding a game when I left the friendly confines of the good old U.S. of A. I wasn't the first person to say that people are much more alike than they are different, and everywhere I went, I never had a problem finding someone who wanted to gamble.

MOSS AND I GO TO LONDON—NOT FOR THE FISH BUT FOR THE CHIPS

There was some high-stakes Hold'em being played in London in 1967—which I could handle on my own—but since I knew that the best way to hustle up a game of gin rummy was to have a partner, I took Johnny Moss over there with me.

Never afraid to take a chance with the places I gambled, I first took Johnny to a joint that was somewhere we probably should not have gone. It was off the beaten path, a place where they had a tendency to put the odds in their favor. But I just figured that Johnny and me were good enough to overcome it. If I'da quit every time I knew someone was cheating me, then I would have missed out on some great gambling opportunities over the years. Besides, there's something about beating a cheater that is particularly satisfying to me.

We sat down for a game of gin, and after we got beat a few hands, Johnny whispered to me, "Say, these people know my hand."

"Yeah," I said, "I can tell it," and I could tell for the simple reason that there weren't but five people in the world that could beat either of us in gin, and we sure as shit weren't looking at 'em.

"Well, we better pull up," Johnny said, which I thought was a little bit out of character for him. Remember, this was the cat who, when he found out Ti was cheating him on the golf course, was smart enough to strike back.

"No, no, no," I said. "Let's don't pull up. We gotta spank these cats now."

So I excused myself to go outside and bought an umbrella from the first stranger who walked by—and don't you just know that with it rain-ing every goddamn day over there that I had my pick of the litter to choose from if I'd wanted to. Then I went back inside and sat right back in my chair, opened this umbrella, held it over my and Johnny's heads, and, imitating those Brits a little, I said, "Deal the *bloody* cards. Now we're gonna play us some gin rummy."

By that time we had figured out that there must have been someone peeping through a hole in the ceiling or in the wall, looking through a tel-escope, and then relaying to our opponents what was in our hands. Well, if that was how they were gonna play, what were two smart Texans to do? Then out came the boss man, and, boy, he didn't like what I'd done. He started screaming and raising hell. "What in the bloody fucking world are you doing, Slim?"

"Well, sir," I said, "it *is* raining outside, isn't it?"

"Yes, but it's not raining in here!"

"Yeah, but I'm afraid it's gonna start raining, and I catch a cold real easy when it's damp. And if your doctors are as bad as your dentists, then I'd just as soon not get sick."

Now, I was trying to tell him we *knew* that somebody could see our hands, you understand? I never will forget it. Johnny got so goddamn mad, but, sure enough, the boss man couldn't hardly protest without really blowing his cover, and with that umbrella over us, we smoked them cats pretty good.

This was just another illustration of how a gambler has to under-stand human nature and how you've got to use your head instead of your ass. Someone else would have called them cheaters or raised Cain, but let me ask you something: How's that gonna help *you?* It's either gonna get you hurt or end your chance of fleecing a couple of suckers.

Gambling in London at that time, there was more to worry about than just a man hiding out in the ceiling. I didn't say nothing to Johnny, but after a few winning sessions, he took notice of the fact that we had us a companion in tow and he could just tell that this cat was connected. When Johnny finally asked me about him, I told him that this was just the cost of doing business to pay this man 30 percent of our action. As far as I was concerned, it was a small price for knowing that we'd be safe and that we could collect. I guess you could call it London's tariff on foreign gamblers.

"We don't have to stand for that," said Johnny, "'cause everybody knows nobody in England carries guns! Shit, not even them bobbies carry guns."

"Well, maybe this cat don't have a gun," I told him, "but I've heard from some folks who learned the hard way that he carries around this hatchet that he uses to pin your hands to the floor if you don't come through with the cut."

Johnny, an old-time Texas road gambler who was used to life in Texas, where his scattergun did the talking, wasn't hearing none of it. He decided that he'd go back to Texas because, to use his word, Texas wasn't *civilized*. Now, you might think that, by giving in to those guys, I'm just as guilty—like asking for a bribe and taking a bribe are one and the same— but that's how business got done over there, and it didn't bother me. So while Johnny couldn't bear to give up 30 percent, I stayed and turned my attention to poker. The Hold 'em over there was as soft as butter for me, since most of the Brits didn't have a heart as big as a pea. When one of 'em would come into a pot, I'd make a big raise, and he'd give it up like a little girl. My only challenge was finding a game where the stakes meant something to me.

INTRODUCING MR. MORE—AND PAYING THE PRICE

After I saw to it that Johnny made it to the airport, my friend Eric Steiner, owner of the Paradise Casino in downtown London, told me that they played for big stakes at a private club not far away called the Curzon House Club.

"Slim," he said, "you could probably get in it." You had to be invited, and Steiner's phone call did the trick.

"Etiquette" may be a highfalutin word for a poker player to use, but there are some dos and don'ts of conduct that are accepted more or less as standard behavior among poker players all over the world. I wasn't aware of it at that time, but I soon learned that in merry old England they really do play like gentlemen. As you know by now—and as Betty Carey learned—I talk an awful lot when I play, to try to pick up tells on my opponents. It's the most important part of my game, and I always knew that if I got laryngitis, I would lose my greatest asset—my gift of gab.

It was a foggy day in London town—not that I had any intention of going sightseeing or nothing—so I went to the Curzon to see what kind of stakes those gentlemen were playing for, and I saw that they had a real good game of no-limit Texas Hold'em going on. Naturally I plunked my skinny ass down to play. At about two o'clock in the morning, just when it was getting real good, a *big* pot came up, and I had one of them British cats locked up like a cold turkey. I mean, I could just smell what he was going to taste like when I cooked him. He made a big bet, and I had every intention of raising him, but I wanted to stall a little and sell him my hand a bit. Had he not gone back to the friendly confines of *un*civilized Texas, old Johnny Moss would have been proud.

The dealer said to me, "It is up to you, sir."

"Just hold on a minute there, partner," I said. "I think I got me a big pair down here in this hole, and I want to introduce that gentleman to Mr. More."

Well, now the guy who had made that bet, I think his name was Kenneth or something said, "Pardon me, mate?"

"*Mate!* Hell, where I come from, we only use that word for breeding horses."

"One more time, Yank?"

Now, I was just wanting to have some fun, so I told him, "I was just saying that I think it's about time that I introduced you to Mr. More. Ten thousand pounds *more*."

Just as I was pushing my chips into the pot, which was the equivalent of $26,000, Kenneth said, "Foul! Forfeit! You're out of the pot."

"What?" I asked. "What the hell are you talking about?"

"It's cheating, sir," the dealer said. This polished dude then proceeded to tell me that it was a "word-of-mouth" kind of cheating—that by talking about a big pair I may have in the hole, I'm "falsifying" my hand, and one does not falsify one's hand in London poker games, or some such nonsense.

"Whoa, whoa, whoa!" I said. "The man made a bet, and all I said was something to him when I raised, and you call that 'falsifying'? Where I come from, that's just called 'poker.'"

"Well, sir, here we call it 'cheating by word of mouth,'" he said.

"Fuck cheating by word of mouth, man," I said. "Now, what do you plan to do about it?"

"Disqualify your hand and award that gentleman the pot," he said.

Well, I was on *fire!* This was a stickup without a gun, so I said, "There's gonna be the goddamnedest squabble you ever saw before he's gonna take my pot—especially without showing his hand."

"No, sir," he said, "in the Curzon House Club"—and this rule goes throughout most of Great Britain—"there are only three things you can say when it is your turn to act: 'Call,' 'Pass,' or 'Raise'—no more, no less. What you did is try to induce a person to either call or not call, which is an automatic forfeit."

Well, I was sorer than the queen after a fox hunt, but I realized that all the hell raising in the world wasn't gonna do me no good, so I accepted the ruling and tried my damnedest to keep my mouth shut. And, boy, was it hard on me. I wanted to talk to them folks, because when I get 'em speaking, they betray themselves and tell me what their hand is. But after losing that big pot—you didn't need to tell me but once—that put an end to my talking, at least during a poker game in England. Anyone who knew me would not have recognized old Silent Slim during the remainder of *that* game.

The next day, at the Paradise Casino, some of the other Yanks who were over there came up to me and said, "Slim, how are you making out playing that *mum* poker?"

"Do what?" I said.

"It's called mum poker," one of the guys said, "because you can't say nothing."

I learned the hard way that if you open your mouth at the wrong time in one of these English poker games, somebody will put his foot in it!

BECOMING AN HONORARY SHEIKH AND RIDING A CAMEL IN MOROCCO

According to legend, the El Mamounia Hotel was opened in a magical garden in the heart of Marrakech, Morocco, in the 1920s. People like Rita Hayworth, Erich von Stroheim, and even Winston Churchill would go there to vacation.

Sometime in the mid-eighties, King Hassan II, who owned the joint and just about everything else in Morocco, spent $70 million to fix it up. When I went there in 1989, it was the most beautiful place I ever saw. This hotel had six gourmet restaurants, Persian rugs everywhere, Carrara-marble interiors, and mosaics that I'da given a herd of cattle to have in my house. That author boy Holden, who I think had followed me there, wrote in his book *Big Deal*, "The suites suggest what Caesars Palace might be like if the world had been scoured for the highest-quality marbles, gold, and silver available, all of which had been flown in with no regard for expense." Well said, partner!

I went to Casino El Mamounia to play in the first European poker championship. Now, I wasn't up on current events—shoot, I only read the newspaper to get the point spreads on the ball games—but I found out when I got there that, because of some political mumbo jumbo, very few players had come to play. The Ayatollah Khomeini got hot on an author named Salman Rushdie, who had written a book called *The Satanic Verses*. Well, I wasn't about to let that bother me, and I set out to find a way to make me some money.

On a walk through town one day, I had the misfortune of stepping in some camel droppings, and when I got back to the casino to play poker, some of the folks complained about the smell. "Hell, that ornery critter's left me his calling card!" I said. What else can a man say if he's tracking around camel shit, right?

Now, I'm used to those types of smells down on my ranch, but these folks didn't find it very funny. Larry Sanders, who moved over to Caesars from the Del Webb Corporation just as I had, overheard all this and started telling everybody about that time I backed my horse up to the craps table at the High Sierra in Lake Tahoe. Then it came up that a camel had never been seen inside the casino, and I immediately took that as a challenge. Since Larry knew my reputation as a proposition bettor, I could only talk him into betting me $1,000 that I couldn't parade a camel through one of the world's fanciest hotels. But it wasn't about the money, see. Now I had me a challenge—and old Slim never backed down from a challenge. I played poker all night, and as soon as it got light outside, I set about trying to find me the right animal.

I'd never been on a camel in my life, but surely if I could ride a horse, I could find some way to tie me on a camel. When I finally found me one, and paid his owner a couple of bucks to rent him out, I wasn't scared of him at all. Truth be told, I felt like I was stealing something from Mr. Sanders, because there really wasn't much to getting that camel *into* the casino. But when I got ready to ride *through* the casino, that's when the trouble started.

It might have looked like *I* was riding that camel through the casino, but let me tell you, that humped beast was really riding *me*. Let's just say that we were going where *he* wanted to go, and I was holding on for dear life. Heck, I was drawing stone-cold dead at getting this camel out of there, and since I had no reason to keep a poker face, everyone knew from the looks of me that I was in trouble.

So the casino manager came over and said, "Slim, that sonofabitch is gonna go berserk in about a minute, and he'll wreck this joint if you don't get him the hell out of here."

"I reckon he will," I said, " 'cause there ain't a goddamned thing I can do about it!"

I told him he better figure out some way to get this camel out of here without me going through a plate-glass window and getting killed on the spot. Then, just as I felt like I was really about to lose it, one of the poker dealers there came up to me and said, "Mr. Slim, I know how to get him out."

I managed to reach in my pocket to hand him a hundred-dollar bill, and I said, "Well, get to it, neighbor."

He said it would take about three minutes, and sure enough, he came back inside of two with a little female camel—and, boy, was she a sight to behold. So naturally my camel stuck his nose right to that girl's privates and just followed her out the door. Talk about the ride of a lifetime!

Word of this stunt spread to all the newspapers, and the king named me an honorary sheikh of Marrakech, Morocco. He had the whole uniform tailor-made, with a tassel-like thing on the fez, a yeropa, and them pointed-ass shoes with the back end out of 'em. Boy, was I flattered.

The next day I was playing a guy head-up Hold'em, and all of a sudden I felt something funny kinda brushing up behind me. Because we were playing for such high stakes, we had the area set off by velvet ropes, and it was known that spectators were not welcome. So I turned around, and there was this elegant woman dressed to the nines sitting there.

I asked for a five-minute recess, and I walked right over to the card-room manager and said, "Say, I don't know who the lady is sitting behind me, but she's gotta go. We're playing for serious money. And while she's a hell of a looker, I sure as hell don't want her a-looking over my shoulder."

"She can sit wherever she wants to," he said, without as much as flinching.

Well, that got me hot, so I said, "Man, I'll tell you one place she *can't* sit. She can't sit behind me anymore."

Before I really laid into him, he told me that this woman was the king's sister, and I changed my tune on the fly. "Well, then tell her to get up a little closer," I said. "Maybe she'll help me!"

So I went back to playing, with her sitting behind me, not saying a word, and when I finally broke this guy, she said, "Mr. Slim, I'm Salma. I belong to this country, and I've always admired you. I know you don't drink, but if you'd care to have a cup of coffee, it would be my pleasure for you to join me."

Well, that suited me just fine, and we went over to one of the fancy bars in this joint and started having a nice chat. Then I got to thinking about her intentions. If she liked me, I thought, then she might not let me leave. And if she didn't like me then she might have me beheaded. Well, ain't this a bitch, I thought. So we talked for a couple of hours, and, boy, I think that was the longest I ever went without cursing in my life. She even told me that I was a perfect gentleman before I walked back over to the poker room. Then, two days later, she called me and said, "My brother's giving us the jet today. We're going shopping—to Casablanca."

Salma and I, along with four bodyguards and two pilots, took the king's plane for a day of shopping in Casablanca. We went to the world's largest market, where they had thousands of camels tied up there and everyone went in and traded their goods. Let's just say it wasn't your everyday Texas swap meet. Salma didn't act like she was on much of a budget, and when the day was through, she had given me a couple of Persian rugs, an old-time pistol, and what I called a *vayse*.

"No," she said, "that costs too much money. It's a *vaaahhze*."

"Pardon me," was all I could say, and when I look at the vase now, along with the Waterford crystal vase that the casino gave me—which was engraved GOLDEN OASIS POKER TOURNAMENT MARRAKECH 1989—it brings back one of my best memories of traveling overseas.

Boy, I love America, but with experiences like those, I never did mind traveling. Anything I could do to help the economy of Texas by importing some foreign money was always a pleasure. But as many good times as I had overseas, I still haven't told you about the time that I went to South America—and almost didn't make it back.

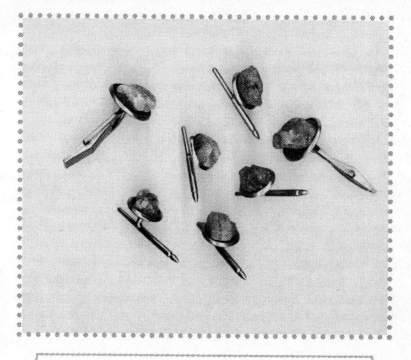

Do you like these emeralds? These are raw, uncut, unpolished emeralds, but neighbor, you wouldn't want to have gone through what I did to get 'em.

Willie and me with a gas-operated Beretta automatic shotgun, a gift from Steve Wynn, the sharpest casino executive not named Binion ever to come to Las Vegas. *(Courtesy of the author)*

13

A Rattlesnake, an Alligator, Pablo Escobar, and Another Trip to Idaho When I Almost Didn't Return

They say a cat has nine lives, but if that were the case with me, I'd be dead three times over by now. Between being wired up in Georgia, getting hijacked in Texas more times than I care to remember, and floating down the River of No Return in the dead of winter, it's a miracle I'm still alive.

If you're not familiar with how things work on a ranch, I can tell you that if you want to hunt a certain animal, all you gotta do is put out enough of the right type of food, and, don't worry, those animals will come after it. On my ranch in Clarendon, I had one laborer, Francisco, and his whole job was to keep the quail feeders full.

One day in 1978, I walked up to one of the quail feeders, pulled the lid off, and stuck my hand down there to stir the grain. I didn't think nothing of it—which was my first mistake—and sure enough, a rattlesnake was lying in there and bit me right on the top of my hand (I still have the scars to prove it). I don't blame him; I guess I was disturbing his business.

When you get bit by a snake, you're supposed to either split it—cut a slit between the two fang bites and let it bleed—or let a person suck the venom out. Well, I didn't relish the idea of Francisco using a knife to cut my hand, and he wasn't too interested in sucking the venom out. So instead he cut off a piece of Piggin string, which is a little rope that you tie to a calf, put it around my arm, and took some fencing pliers and made a tourniquet and twisted it up. The snake was still buzzing, so Francisco got a stick and lifted him out of there, smashed his head with a rock, and killed him. We knew we were gonna come back and cut the rattlers off, so Francisco hung him over a plum thicket.

We got in my truck, and Francisco was driving like a bat out of hell to Clarendon Hospital. Then my whole arm and hand started turning blue and purple. By that point some of the venom had gone to my heart, and, boy, did it hurt. So he twisted the tourniquet up some more, and I said, "No matter what I say—my arm can just fall off—don't let me take that tourniquet off. Even if I pass out, don't you take it off."

Of course, he was scared to death, but we made it to the hospital, and they started giving me them antivenin shots. Lucky for me, we made it in time, and there wasn't much damage done. All I had on was one of them gowns with the whole south end out of it, and once I started feeling better, I was ready to go home. When the nurse came by, I told her I was fixing to go and would need my clothes.

"That's what we thought you'd say," the nurse said. "I'm not getting your clothes, and I'm gonna go get the orderly."

So she went out the door one way, and I went out the other, barefooted and bare-assed in that little gown. The nurses were screaming and hollering after me, and I got Francisco and we hopped in my pickup and just took off. Well, when we got to Amarillo, my driveway was full of ambulances and police cars—everybody in town, it seemed.

"What the hell's the matter?" I said to one of the cops.

"We just thought you weren't gonna make it home, and if you did, you were gonna die when you got here."

I told him I was all right, but the cop said, "Mr. Slim, you gotta get in the ambulance. We're taking you back to the hospital."

"You're gonna be taking me against my will," I said. "Now, if you all are prepared for a lawsuit, you should know that there's not a goddamn thing wrong with me and I'm not in any danger."

I'm not one for lawsuits, but he didn't know that, and I figured it was a pretty good bluff to get me off the hook. So he asked the nurse, who was right there as well, what would happen if I didn't get those shots.

"He'll die," she said.

"We consider that danger," the cop said.

"What's to keep me from getting them shots here at my house?"

So then everybody started looking at one another, and I said to the nurse, "Have you ever had a five-hundred-dollar bill before? I know you've had five hundred dollars, but have you ever had a five-hundred-dollar *bill?*"

"No sir."

"How would you like one?"

"I'd love it."

"If it suits you, get off duty and stay here and give me my shots for the next sixteen hours."

Now, there wasn't a thing the police could do about that. She stayed, I got my shots, and there wasn't nothing to it. And the best part about it was that when I went back to my ranch, I skinned the snake and sent it to Jonas Brothers in Seattle with a note to make me something unusual. I assumed I'd get a belt or a billfold, but instead they made me a hatband with the head of the snake attached to the front and the rattlers on the side. I put it on my best Stetson, so the sonofabitch that nearly killed me sits right on top of my head now! But, as I said, what I faced later in South America made getting bit by a rattlesnake seem like a paper cut.

PABLO ESCOBAR LIKED MY BUTTONS

Back in the early nineties, when I was working for Caesars, Lynn Simon, my old boss from the Del Webb Corporation, bought the Casino de Caribe in Cartagena, Colombia. Lynn was a good friend and a very capable man in management. He had uncovered four of the biggest swindles that ever occurred in the gaming industry, and while that didn't make him real popular with a lot of the sharps, it made him real popular with casino owners.

Lynn decided to use me in a promotion at their casino—to tell you the truth, it was to help attract some of the big drug lords to come to Cartagena to play at the Casino de Caribe. I'm not saying it was the right thing to do, to participate with all them bad dudes there, but Lynn had asked me if I would help out, and since I knew them fellas had deep pockets, I obliged. To be honest, I was a little surprised how many of these guys knew me. I'm not sure how, and I don't really want to know—because if there's one thing in this life that I can't stand, it's drugs—but some of these guys were actually excited to be playing against old Slim.

I had no intention of going down there to get shot up, so the first thing I did when I hit the casino was to get all the head honchos together so we could declare Cartagena the new Switzerland. The truce was on. Every leader and every boss in every district agreed not to kidnap nobody, not to kill nobody, and not to raise any hell for ten days—just in time for me to get my skinny butt on that plane back to peaceful Amarillo.

It looked like the truce was going to last, 'cause everybody was acting like they were going to abide. Then, about the third day, I walked out onto the porch of the casino, and one of the bad dudes had a sawed-off shotgun and shot one of the ladies who was standing there less than three feet from me. Man, I can still remember the last time her heart beat before blood squirted out the top of her head and got all over my suit and boots. And I thought, Ain't this a bitch? All hell's about to break loose, because there's about forty of them bad dudes running around there, and every one of them has a machine gun.

I don't know why this man shot the woman—I think they must have had some kind of an argument—but I sure as hell didn't ask him. I found out later she was the girlfriend of Johava, one of the drug lords from the Cali cartel. The run-in was with a drug boss from the Medellín cartel, which was led by one of the most feared men in the world, Pablo Escobar. With the tension between these two groups, I should have known something worse was bound to happen, and I should have gotten on the next plane back to Texas.

But, shoot, I stuck around—maybe because part of me always liked danger, or more likely because I had never seen men with more money and less brains than these drug lords. It was like Jimmy Chagra awaiting trial in Vegas all over again. I was gonna be there for seven more days, so I did what I always do in bad situations—make the best of it, play some poker, and get real friendly with all the bosses. That old expression, "Stay close to your friends and even closer to your enemies," was at the forefront of my mind. I went ahead and played poker with some of 'em, and I didn't feel any immediate threat from them, 'cause I was on the square. They thought I was all right, and I sure as hell didn't do anything to dissuade them from that notion, you understand?

So then, about three nights after the shooting, when I really started to think everything would be okay, I went back to my suite at the Cartagena Hilton. The Casino de Caribe didn't have a hotel, and the Hilton was a beautiful place right on the beach down there. I had security with me, but somebody came down on my security pretty hard and pretty quick, and that didn't do me any good at all. All of a sudden, I was robbed of everything—including my two prized rings—taken against my will, and thrown in the back end of a helicopter.

My first thought was that these guys were gonna do what they'd always done, which was fly over the jungle and throw poor fellas like me out. I figured that I better learn how to fly in a hurry, or else it was going to be the tail end of me. You see, down in Colombia you're either a user, a seller, an informant, or a DEA agent. There is no in-between, and since I wasn't an obvious user or buyer, naturally they thought I was working for the feds.

It didn't take me long to figure out that I had been taken on by the boss of all bosses, Pablo Escobar. As far as I was concerned, he was the most notorious of all of 'em, and he struck fear in everybody's heart that saw him. I guess mine, too, although I hate to admit it, because a guy like me ain't supposed to be scared of nobody.

Pablo Escobar had been nothing but a car thief and a small-time gangster in Medellín when he quickly got as much cocaine as he could get his hands on and sold it even faster, becoming a billionaire. If you've seen the movie *Blow*, you'll know that George Jung—the character played by Johnny Depp—was the biggest distributor in the United States, and he got a lot of his goods from Escobar. In his desire for wealth and political power, Escobar even went so far as to run for polit-cal office and earned a seat in Congress. He built loyalty through charity, constructed two hundred homes for the poor folks, sponsored soccer teams, and commissioned artists to paint murals. For more than a de-cade, he and his army of killers from Medellín were at war with the Colombian and American governments. Let me put it to you this way, neighbor: I wasn't in real good hands, no matter how charitable Mr. Escobar appeared to be.

It was just my luck that these guys all had radios and liked to broad-cast news of their latest victim. Those drug cartels had a pretty good net-work of communication, and Escobar's henchmen started describing me over the radio. This had to be some kind of miracle because a Colombian guy that I knew pretty well from Las Vegas picked up on the fact that the person they were describing was *me*. This man was one of the bosses from Barranquilla, a port town on the coastline, who liked to gamble at Caesars and who I'd gotten to know on one of his many trips to Las Vegas. He got on his radio and said that I was Amarillo Slim and that I was an employee of Caesars Palace. So one of Escobar's henchmen said, "Describe him."

He described me pretty well, but these guys weren't buying it for a second. At that point all I was thinking about was what was the best way to try to land when I hit the ground. Then this boss said, "Does he have a map of Texas on his finger?"

They looked down at my hand and said, "No, he doesn't."

Well, I just knew I was a goner. But then I managed to explain to this cat that he *had* my ring of Texas in his possession after he had robbed me, and when he found it in his pocket, he finally started to believe it *was* me. So this boss told them that I was all right, that I wasn't a stool pigeon, that I wasn't a dope dealer, and that I wasn't looking to buy any drugs or sell any drugs or turn anybody in that was. I was just there to gamble, as a guest of the Casino de Caribe.

They finally gave in, but rather than taking me back to the casino, they decided to take me to the house of none other than the main man himself, Pablo Escobar. "House" wouldn't be exactly the best way to describe it—"mansion" would be more like it—and what I remember most was that he had twelve Mercedes limousines in his garage, which would have made one hell of a house for 99 percent of the people in that poor country. After Pablo showed me around, he decided that he wanted to give me a little tour, so he took me up for a ride in the same helicopter that I was kidnapped in.

Up there all I could think about was getting a chance to push Escobar out of that damn helicopter. If there was any way that I could've flown that thing myself, I'da tried it, too. While we were flying around, Escobar pointed out a great big cathedral-type thing, a real nice church that he had built. Escobar spoke English, and he said to me, "See that chapel, Slim? That's the one I built for the poor people."

Then they lowered the helicopter to get a real close look at a zoo Escobar had built for—as he called them—the *people*. He said it cost $8,000 a day to maintain that zoo. I wanted to say, "Tough shit," but I showed more restraint than I ever had in my life and decided just to make conversation with him.

"Señor Escobar," I said, "you know you caught a little heat in the American press when you killed that editor and publisher of the Bogotá newspaper." Then he said something about that guy being killed in the exact spot as the attorney general, and he offered to show me where. He talked about killing these men like it was *nothing*—and here I was in a helicopter with him!

He was going on and on about all he had done for the poor folks down there, and I could only listen and try to keep my big mouth shut. If there's one thing I can't stand, it's a hypocrite, but I tried to be appreciative of the fact that nothing bad had happened to me, even though I was bleeding internally at the thought of having to humor this drug dealer and cold-blooded killer.

So he just kept going on and on about all these charitable things—I suppose Siggy would have said something about a guilty conscience—and what a good guy he was. I wanted to say, "Don't piss on my shoes and tell me it's raining! You're a drug lord, Mr. Escobar, plain and simple, and not only have you destroyed your own country, but you've damn near destroyed mine."

Then, out of nowhere, he said to me, "I really like your buttons." I wear uncirculated one-dollar gold coins on my dress shirts for buttons. So I said to myself, There's a man who's got everything, and he likes my buttons. By then I think Escobar had told me just about everything there was to tell about his charitable activities, and he was even nice enough to drop me off where he had gotten me in the first place, in Cartagena. I even got all my belongings back, with the exception of my Texas ring—which was no small loss.

I told Lynn that it had been a real pleasure and got on the next plane that I could back to the States. Well, it wasn't long after that that Lynn was told by some folks who you don't say no to that he'd be best off if he took his show out of Colombia. So I guess it was out of appreciation to Pablo for not killing me—or maybe because I didn't know when I might run into him again—that I sent him a matching set of my buttons. Uncirculated one-dollar gold pieces are expensive, but I heeded that advice about staying closer to my enemies and paid for 'em without a second thought.

About six or seven weeks later, I was back in the States and lying up in my suite at Caesars, when the phone rang. I picked it up, and the guy on the other end of the line said, "*Sleem*, this is so-and-so." I recognized his Colombian accent (it was one of Escobar's lieutenants), and then he said, "I've got something for you."

"I've got something for you, too," I said. "You're in America now!"

"No, no, no!" he said. "Pablo has sent you something. It's some buttons. I'll bring them up to your room."

"Oh, no you don't. Don't you dare come up here."

We agreed to meet right in the casino, under the big ship that sticks out by the disco there. I called management, and they set me up with some plainclothes security guards, and we were ready for any surprises. I believe if that man had sneezed, he'da got unlucky. But as it turned out, it was all on the square, and Escobar really had made me a set of buttons. All those drug lords down there, they own emerald mines, and Escobar had made me a set of raw, uncut, unpolished emeralds about three or four carats apiece. Now, would you think that a guy like that would have emerald buttons made for me? I can't imagine what they're worth.

Then, in 1993, I picked up the newspaper in Las Vegas one day and saw that Escobar had gotten unlucky—he was shot while hanging out the window of an apartment house—and met his demise at age forty-four. I can truthfully say I felt no sadness whatsoever for that happening.

I still have them emeralds, though. They're the prettiest gems you ever saw on a white shirt. I'm not proud of where they came from, but I'm proud of the buttons and thankful to be alive to wear 'em—that's for damn sure.

WHATEVER YOU DO, DON'T FEED HERMAN THE ALLIGATOR

Not too long after I got back in one piece from Colombia, I told myself that I would be a little bit more careful when I traveled. One day when I was just sitting home in Amarillo, I got a call from Dewey Tomko, my old buddy in Haines City, Florida, not too far from Orlando.

Dewey was a top poker player who took home $1.1 million for second place in the 2001 World Series of Poker. When he said that he was playing in a real good poker game in Haines City, I said, "Well, it's a goddamned shame you all don't have any good players down there. If you had any, I'd come down and play 'em head-up."

"Okay, Slim," he said. "Hold on just a minute, will you?"

Dewey put his hand over the receiver and mumbled something I couldn't really make out, and then he came back on and said, "What's the least you'll play for?"

"Twenty-five thousand has always been my minimum, Dewey. I got to make the trip worth my while."

"Okay, Slim, twenty-five ain't no problem. We've got a guy here that will play you head-up."

Sailor always had a thing for Florida, so he agreed to go with me. Five of Dewey's buddies put up five thousand apiece, and they took out their best player to face me. Well, I went down there and beat the guy on the square in no time at all. But I'd just traveled more than a thousand miles, and I figured I might as well hang around awhile. Then Dewey said, "Let's go to the golf course. I'd like a shot at that fifty thousand dollars in your hip pocket."

Dewey was too sharp to make me a proposition that he couldn't win, but Sailor was able to hustle up a game with a favorable handicap, and we all went down there together. Right after the eighteenth hole, I said, "Sailor, let's act like tourists! Let's go to Tampa and go to Busch Gardens. And let's go down to Orlando and go to Disney World, and let's go to a few of them places, Cypress Gardens and all, and just have a good time. I've already had a good gambling trip, and it's time to have some fun."

So Sailor and I hit the road, and it wasn't long before we found this town where they had the world's biggest alligator farm. It was kind of a tourist trap, but we said that we wanted to act like a bunch of tourist fools, and this seemed like a good place to start. When we got in, there was a pit about ten feet deep and fifty feet wide and a beat-up old sign that said DON'T FEED HERMAN.

Well, old Herman was the boss alligator. He was about twice as long as me, and he was lying down there asleep, with about four other prehistoric monsters down there with him. "Look at that sleepy sonofabitch," I said. "If I was in there with him, I'd kick him right in the ass."

That got Sailor's ears all perked up, so he said, "Yeah, *in there* with him? He's asleep right now, Slim. Shit, you wouldn't go over that fence and get down there with them."

"I'll bet a thousand dollars I will."

"Listen," Sailor said, "if you go down there—and you got to walk over old Herman—I'll bet you a thousand dollars. A thousand dollars says you won't do it."

I couldn't pass up a bet from Sailor; especially since I knew this one was a cinch. So I lowered myself over the side of that fence and into the alligator pit—it was concrete down in there—and I just dropped in on those creatures. Herman was sound asleep—them alligators don't even move in the afternoon after they've already eaten.

I was tiptoeing; naturally, I didn't wanna take any chance of waking them ornery critters. Just about the time I got to straddle that critter, Sailor had a stick in his hands, no more than about a foot and a half long and kinda skinny. He threw it—I swear to God, he couldn't have done it again in a million years—and he hit old Herman dead center right between the eyes, and Herman went, "Wooooow!" He jerked his whole body up out of its slumber and knocked my feet out from under me. Sailor swore I did a complete flip when that gator hit me.

I hit the ground and I looked to get out of Dodge right quick. But as I got on my feet, old Herman turned around and started to come right at me. Sailor, who was just then realizing what the hell he'd just done, screamed, "God, Slim, please jump for it!"

I was gonna try to jump, and they were gonna try to catch my hands and pull me up over the fence. By then everybody in the gator park could hear us screaming and hollering over there, and they knew somebody was in the pit with Herman.

And I was glad they knew, because when I jumped, I caught the edge of the fence, and Sailor and some other tourist grabbed my wrists and held on for dear life. But I was still dangling there, see, so I said, "Goddamn, get ahold of my belt." They did, and they managed to pull me up out of that pit just as old Herman was trying to rear up and take a pound of flesh out of my ass.

Boy, when I got out of there, I could've killed Sailor. I guess it served me right, though. I never should have put my life on the line for a bet—not a bet that small anyway.

DIFFERENT KIND OF CHICKEN FIGHT

Between Herman the alligator and getting wired up in Georgia, the southeastern part of the United States wasn't too good to me. I wish I had thought of that when I got invited to Florida on account of the chicken fights. I never did like watching two chickens go at it. I mean, how fun is it to see two chickens kill each other? There's not much sport to it, just a lot of blood.

A buddy of mine named Johnny Tyler, who is now deceased, never saw it that way, though. He loved them chickens so much that he followed them all over the world. Over the years I'd been to the chicken fights with him in Hot Springs, Arkansas, and the Philippines. I reckon Johnny liked them so much because people bet big on these events, and Johnny booked all the action. I wouldn't go so far as to say that it's like betting horses, because it doesn't come close, but I guess if there's any skill in picking the winners, it's knowing who the owners are and trying to get a feel for the chickens' dispositions before the fight. Let me put it to you this way: Timid isn't exactly the trait you're looking for in a winner.

When Johnny called me and invited me down to Florida, just outside of Fort Lauderdale, he said it would be real good for me. He had a Quonset barn—a big old circular corrugated metal thing—where they brought the chickens to fight, and after the fights were over, Johnny had eight twenty-one games and two craps tables set up. He didn't like having to be there every minute, so he brought me down there to help him run the show.

We had plenty of security—good security, we thought—but they must have been a little lax in their responsibilities. The first introduction to our new guests was the sound of some Thompsons across the ceiling: *brrrrrr, brrrrrr, brrrrrr.* Five people were spraying that ceiling with machine-gun fire, and on that tin roof it made a lot of noise.

That *does* get your attention, you understand? After they stopped shooting, the good, loud word was, "Everybody lay down on the floor, facing the wall, facedown."

Me, I was just like everybody else. I got as low as I could and hid right against the wall. They had on masks and used code names. One of 'em came by, and my pant leg was up a little 'cause I was stretched out on the floor, and he saw my name on my boots. This guy hollered, "Hey, hey, I think I got Amarillo Slim lying over here on the floor."

"You're kidding," another guy, who I made to be the boss, said.

"Nah, I think that's who it is."

"Well, get that motherfucker up from there and see if it's him," the boss shouted.

So this small-time stickup man, on orders from his boss, said, "Get up from there, man." I didn't move at first, and then he kicked me in my leg real hard and screamed, "I said get up from there!"

Seeing as it didn't look like I had many options, I stood up. The guy looked me over a little and said, "Yeah, it's Slim, all right."

"Ah, Slim," the boss said. "We're busy as hell, so go and get yourself some coffee and take it easy till we get through here. We don't want you lying on them dirty floors like them other suckers. So just relax till we're through."

They went about their business and when they got ready to leave, after they had collected everyone's money, the boss said to me, "Slim, you have a good day. We've had a real good one. And come back to Florida and visit us."

Mind you, I didn't know who this man was, but there wasn't no way in the world he was leaving *without* robbing me. "Say, you're not leaving," I said. "You've got to rob me."

"There ain't no chance I'm gonna do that."

"What do you think's gonna happen to me if you don't rob me?" I said.

"Oh," he said, "shit, it'll look bad, won't it?"

"It sticks out like a sore fuckin' thumb," I said. "Like I'm in on it with you, you understand? How you all are gonna come and rob eighty people and not rob me, too?"

"Ah," he said, "okay." So they took my watch, my diamond, my studs and cuff links, and my money, and they left. Shoot, I didn't need eighty pissed-off Floridians thinking I was in cahoots with those bastards so I took my lumps just like everyone else and chose not to trade on my name.

About ten days later, after I got back home to Texas, I was down at my ranch in Clarendon. The phone rang, and the guy on the other end of the line, said, "This is a friend of yours."

"Yeah, well, what can I do for you, friend?" I said.

"There ain't nothing you can do for me, but I'm fixin' to do something for you. Can you see your mailbox?"

"Not from where I am now."

"Well, can you move your phone?"

"No," I said, "but I'll go over there to the door and look out if you give me a little time."

So I walked over to the window, came back to the phone, and told him I could see the mailbox. He said, "Don't go up there now. After you see a vehicle stop at the mailbox, don't you even go up there for a good half an hour. In fact, make it forty-five minutes for sure."

"This who I think it is?" I asked.

"Well, if you think this is some chicken fighter who always wins." In other words, he wasn't gonna lose. He didn't bet on the chickens; he just robbed everyone who did. So I walked up to my mailbox about an hour later, and sure enough, there was my watch, my diamond, my studs and cuff links, and all my money. Now, ain't that something? Whether it was out of respect or fear don't matter much, but let me tell you, neighbor, let's just say he did the right thing.

FOUR THINGS THAT SAVED MY LIFE

I suppose you could call it a reunion of sorts when, just about two months shy of the thirty-year anniversary of our trip down the River of No Return, I met up with Jere Chapman for a hunting and fishing trip in Idaho. It was Labor Day weekend 2002, and we were more in the mood for hunting than rafting and decided to go to this primitive area of northern Idaho in the Bitterroot Wilderness of the Sawtooth Range.

My nephew Johnny Byler and I hauled a trailer from Amarillo with three of my horses, including a pretty little yellow thing named Butterscotch. We met up with Jere, Jere's son Lance, and my coauthor, Greg

Dinkin. After spending the first night in Caldwell, Idaho, where we got a good night's sleep in a motel, we headed out into rougher pastures. We loaded up a mule in the morning, which we would use to carry our food and supplies in the mountains, and drove up to the Sawtooth Lodge.

Jere's son Lance and Greg are both about thirty, but they couldn't be any more different. Greg is a city boy from Washington, D.C., who thinks danger means holding the nut flush in a no-limit Hold'em game and having the board pair on the river. Lance, on the other hand, was raised in Idaho and ever since he was a pup, Jere had taught him to live off the land. He wasn't more than 160 pounds or so, but he was strong as an ox and the type of outdoorsman that you'd want by your side in a pinch.

The second day of our trip, we sorta got the lay of the land, took a little practice ride on the horses, and had a real nice supper in that lodge. The next morning Lance, Johnny, and I checked out of the lodge and headed up toward this high lake, while Jere took Greg fishing before Greg went back to the airport in Boise. Try as I might, I couldn't get Greg to stay up there with us more than two days, especially after he'd fallen plumb off one of my horses the day before! It turned out that his little accident would be the least of our troubles.

Early the next morning, the four of us set out on a weeklong camping trip with plans to eventually make it over to the lake up there. I think it was about eighty-five miles from where we were originally staying, and this was on a trail that hadn't been opened in about thirty years. The rangers had made us a concession that if we'd help open up the trail, they'd let us take in guns, a four-wheeler, and some power saws. Whenever you open a trail, it's one of them known things among outdoorsmen that you do your best to make the trail easier to pass for the next guy.

If you're wondering what would inspire a seventy-three-year-old man to blaze a dangerous trail in a remote part of Idaho—without any money on the line, no less—I guess you don't understand me too well, partner. The only thing I love as much as gambling is the outdoors, and when you add a little challenge to a journey and put my skinny ass on a horse, there ain't a thing in the world that makes me happier.

The reason they let us take guns was that they had introduced wolves back into the wilderness up there. There were two packs of wolves that inhabited the trail and this big lake, and they had also turned two grizzlies loose that they had transplanted from Yellowstone National Park. So I said to the rangers, "I sure as hell ain't coming face-to-face with no wolf or grizzly bear if I'm not packing some heat. If it's me or the bear, god-damn, I'm going to be eating bear stew for a month!"

Then I asked them, "Now, why in the hell did you introduce two packs of wolves and two grizzly bears into the wilderness anyway? We spent all of our lives trying to kill them creatures, and now you're openly stocking 'em? All they're gonna do is put you and the citizens up here in an uproar."

They told me that the conservation movement was alive and well, and they were doing their best to reestablish the animals' natural habitat. That's why they allowed us to take guns. They also let us take saws to cut down trees and branches that were blocking the trail. On what was to be the first day of our journey through this trail, Jere and Johnny stayed down at the camp and readied our packs and our camping gear for the rest of the trip. The weather was beautiful in early September—sunny during the day, with temperatures in the sixties, but at night the tempera-ture dropped below freezing, and Jere was making sure that we'd be pre-pared.

Lance and I set about trying to open that trail up to the head of that lake. Lance rode a four-wheeler and carried the saws, and I rode my yel-low horse, Butterscotch. By then I'd had Butterscotch for five years. I bought him as a two-year-old in Deanville, Texas, from the Cook County barn. I've always been a sucker for a good-looking horse of an unusual color. Butterscotch came from a breed of buckskins, but he wasn't a buckskin, he was more of a cream-colored colt, and I just thought he was about the prettiest thing I'd ever seen. He was 1,280 pounds, and for the past five years I was about as close to that horse as I was to my own kids. And that's not a knock on my kids, you understand.

Butterscotch was a little skittish all day, 'cause he didn't like it when that saw would go off. *Rrrrrrrr!*—it made all that noise, and it scared him half to death. We must have cut thirty trees and logs from the middle of the trail where you could get through there. As we progressed up this trail, all of a sudden we came to a heavily wooded area with a creek running through it, and Lance said, "By God, Slim, we can't cross here."

"Well, I think I can," I said.

"No, hell no! You'd be crazy to even try to cross it with a horse, and I'm definitely not crossing it with this four-wheeler."

"So what do you propose?" I asked him.

"Let's drop down below it until we can find a place where we can cross this creek."

So we went down the trail about thirty or forty yards, and we found a place where we had felled three trees and moved some big boulders out of the creek. Lance had a come-along (a steel cable that you attach to an object to help pull the four-wheeler), and he pulled that four-wheeler across the creek. I didn't have any trouble riding my horse across the creek where we were. So we went around and cut some more logs; we even moved some more rocks.

When Butterscotch was walking, he was stepping in holes that were deep from the rocks we had moved. And he wasn't the kind of horse that should have been in that terrain either. So Lance said, "It looks like it's getting pretty tough on Butterscotch."

"Yeah," I said, "this is not the kind of animal that needs to be going across these rocks. I'm going to go back down off of here. Either we'll find a new trail or a new way to get up there or I'm not going."

"If it's all right with you, Slim, I'll go ahead up here and mark with a yellow flag the exit as to where the trail cuts off of this rockslide." We were doing our best to help the forestry service so that anyone else who used the trail wouldn't have any trouble finding it.

"Well, certainly," I said. "I'm going to keep going down the trail."

"Okay, I'll probably catch up," Lance said. "You're not in a hurry, are you?"

"No, we'll ride back to camp, eat supper, and stay all night, and we'll bring the packhorses and mule and everything tomorrow, and we'll try to get on up there."

So after I got back to the trail, I got to the creek, maybe twelve feet deep, that was flowing. Then I saw an area off the trail where I thought, if I could get to it, I could climb it with my horse. I have a pacemaker, but it's not something I really think about. I guess I always had too much damn heart for my own good, and, foolishly, I decided to cross.

Now, keep in mind that there was nobody in the world who knew where I was. I had no business being in there, and because I had now veered off the trail, Lance would have no way of finding me if something were to go wrong. It was a calculated risk, but one I'd taken hundreds of times in my life, and I didn't give it much thought. Old Butterscotch was getting used to the terrain, and he didn't spook or nothing as we started to go over that creek.

By now it was about five o'clock, and the sun was on its way down. The other side of the creek, where we were trying to get to, was much higher than where we started, so not only did Butterscotch have to get through the water, but he had to walk uphill.

Then I saw it coming. I mean, I just knew what was about to happen, and I tried to get off him, but before I could jump, Butterscotch started falling backward, and I fell off the rear end of him. Just as my back hit the ground, the horse—more than half a ton of him—fell square on my chest.

When I came to, I was partially in the water. One of my legs was hanging over a log, and it was in the water, from the knee on down. I didn't even bother trying to move because I didn't need an X ray to tell me that every rib on me was broken. But that's when all them years of near-death experiences came in handy. Somehow I had the presence of mind to know that there wasn't anybody who was gonna look for me in there, and, since I was off the trail, there wasn't any way that Lance would be able to find me. By now it was down to about thirty degrees, and I could see that if I wasn't rescued, I was gonna freeze to death that night. I had no chance *not* to freeze; I didn't even have a match with me. And of course I couldn't scream, because my ribs were broken and my chest was crushed.

This was the first time that I really felt like it was curtains for old Slim. Every little old dirty trick I'd ever done in my life flashed before me—and yet all the good things that ever happened to me in my life flashed before me, too. Because I couldn't get any air to my lungs, the only thing I could think about was whether I would die from suffocating, freezing, or from them wolves that were sure to find me before long.

Somehow I managed to crawl maybe thirty or forty yards—later I'll get into how I was able to do that. What I was trying to do was get back to the trail, because I knew that Lance would have to see me if I was lying there. I just laid myself sideways in the middle of that trail, and then I passed out. Butterscotch had run off by now, but, knowing that I had broken his fall, I figured that if I died, at least he might make it.

Sure enough—I don't know how long it was—I heard the four-wheeler coming. Lance found me, helped me onto the vehicle, and tried to get down the trail where we could get some help. We were going off this mountain on this four-wheeler, and we were doing maybe four miles an hour most of the time, and every bump the vehicle hit, the pain just seared through my body. I was sitting behind him on that four-wheeler, and it's not even meant for two people—much less a seventy-three-year-old man with a pacemaker and a collapsed chest.

Because of all the logs and rocks, I had to keep getting off so he could take that come-along out and pull the four-wheeler across. I think I got off it five times, and every time I got off it, I'd pass out. Since it was very painful to even move—the most pain I've ever experienced in my whole life—he'd have to pick me up each time and get me back on that thing. I wasn't particularly thankful right then, but I can tell you that if there was only one person in the world I'd have wanted there, it would have been Lance. Thirty years earlier his dad would have been my guy, and while Jere had helped me win a nice little bet on the River of No Return, Lance was now helping me in a fight for my life.

We got pretty far down the trail. We were still a little ways off, but I was in real bad shape, just moaning and groaning every inch of the way. So Lance said, "Slim, partner, it's obvious to me you're not gonna make it."

Well, that was not very good news for me to hear. "What?" I muttered. "What the hell are you talking about?"

"Slim," he said, "I gotta go get some help for us. I'm gonna lay you down over here out to the edge of the trail, and I'm gonna cut some boughs off the trees and cover you up." That was in case he was late getting back to me, so that I wouldn't freeze to death. It was now dark, and he was also trying to conceal me from them predators we knew were up there.

We hadn't seen any of them, but we knew they were there. Now, if those wolves or bears had found me, I would have had two chances—Slim and none, and Slim wasn't in real good shape. For one thing, I didn't even have a toothpick. For another, what difference would it have made if I had ninety machine guns? I couldn't have used any of 'em on account of the sheer pain I was in.

Lance took off, and when he got back to camp, he called 911 on Johnny's cellular phone—it was a miracle that he was able to get a signal. I was slipping in and out of consciousness, but I didn't think an ambulance would even be able to get to me, since there weren't any roads up there for an ambulance. So when Johnny, Jere, and Lance finally got there, they decided that it would be best to get me out themselves. They helped me into the cab of the pickup—don't ask me how—and drove me to a little town, and I sat in the cab of this truck until an ambulance showed up.

About ten minutes later, the ambulance came, and the EMTs tried to examine me, but I couldn't hardly stand it, and they figured it would be best not to move me. They also made the decision—and it turned out to be a good one—that the closest hospital wouldn't be worth a damn for me, because they didn't have an intensive-care unit, and it was obvious that I needed a little bit more than an emergency room.

They called Life Star, a helicopter service that's all over the country. Here I was, thirty years after I had gone down the River of No Return, which was *supposed* to have killed me, and what started as a fun little vacation was *about* to kill me. I waited for what seemed like an eternity for the helicopter to show up. While I waited, the first thing they did was put me on a stretcher, put one of those collars on me, and bound me so I couldn't move. I'd seen enough football games to know that the only time they put them collars on is when they think you might be paralyzed. I couldn't wiggle my toes, and I couldn't look three feet either way, and I figured that only being paralyzed would be a *good* outcome at this point.

Finally Life Star showed up, and the EMTs put me on a helicopter to go to Boise, Idaho, to a famous trauma center called Saint Alphonsus. Once I got on the helicopter, I didn't think I was gonna die, and I just kept telling myself that I'd been in worse spots before. The only problem was that I had a tough time believing my own lie.

When I arrived, the doctors went to work on me, and I somehow came through. Then, after their very, very thorough X rays and examination, I put them in shock when I wouldn't take any painkillers. And this neurosurgeon said, "You will tomorrow."

"Nah, shoot," I said. "I don't take no pain pills. Why would I need them tomorrow?"

He said that they were gonna put me through a CAT scan and give me an MRI. Well, it's a good thing I didn't bet him, because he was right about my not turning down those painkillers. I'd never experienced more piercing pain in my life.

Meanwhile I had sent word to Johnny, and he went back to our temporary camp and told everybody that I put out a $5,000 reward for Butterscotch. Some rancher came up to Johnny—and, boy, I'm glad I wasn't there—and said, "You can tell that old man he saved his five thousand. My son owns the ranch at the bottom of that trail, and he heard the wolves eat his horse last night." When Johnny called me at the hospital from his cell phone, that didn't do much to ease the pain.

Johnny's son had flown up from Texas to take the mule back to Caldwell and make the two-day drive back to Texas with my other two horses. They left in the middle of the night, and just as they started on the road, their headlights hit some eyes. Johnny flipped his lights up on bright, and— wouldn't you know it—there was Butterscotch. According to Johnny, he looked like he'd been through a sausage grinder. He had teeth marks all over his legs, around his flanks, and on his throat and neck. Sure enough, the wolves had gotten to him, but they never did get him down. When they found him, he still had my saddle on him, but everything else was gone—

the bridle and the halter and everything else. It was a cinch he had gone through a fight for his life just like his old man. Johnny put him in the trailer with my other two horses, and he's alive and well on my ranch in Amarillo.

When I finally started to feel a little better, the trauma surgeon, who was as nice as he was competent, said, "Well, now, let me tell you something: *Four things saved your life.*"

He said that the first thing was that if the horse had fallen just five inches farther to the left, it would have killed me immediately. That saddle horn would have hit me right in the heart and gone plumb through me. If it hadn't, it would have knocked my pacemaker completely out.

The second thing the doctor said was that it was a certainty that the horse rolled to his right. I got to thinking about it, and it was the truth. If Butterscotch had rolled to his left, he'da rolled over my chest and just crushed me. I couldn't have stood 1,280 pounds on my chest, especially with a saddle horn going across there.

So I think that was somebody's doing. It's a cinch that somebody was looking after me. I said, "All right now, man, I'm enjoying this a little bit. What was the third thing?"

He told me that the tests showed that I'd gone into shock. I asked how that saved me, and he said, "People can do *supernatural* things in shock that they can't do otherwise. There've been cases where a guy has walked a quarter of a mile with a broken leg. There are people who have had their necks broken that have walked to get help. I know you couldn't even move, but you crawled out of that hole, which should have been impossible under normal circumstances. You crawled down that path to lay sideways in that trail. If you hadn't crawled far enough for that man to see you, you would have had no chance to live."

He was right. I would have frozen to death that night, or been dessert for them wolves. Then the doctor was complimentary of the rescue crew, and so was I, so much so that when I later got a helicopter bill for $11,000, I couldn't have been happier to pay it.

The fourth thing that saved me was that Lance finally took me off that four-wheeler. This one rib was moving toward my lung, and it missed by about a sixteenth of an inch. There's a good chance it would have punctured my lung to the point where it would have been fatal.

I'm very appreciative of that hospital; the doctors that I had did wonders for me. Even after I got back to Amarillo, I didn't leave my house for more than a month, aside from going to the hospital. So I feel like one more time somebody looked after me. To say it was a miracle wouldn't begin to do justice to exactly how lucky I was.

Receiving four gold commemorative coins from Jack Binion for my induction into the Poker Hall of Fame at Binion's Horseshoe. *(Courtesy of the author)*

14

The Last Hand

I'm kinda like the guy who gets a big box of horse shit from some joker for his birthday, and when he opens it up, he's happy as hell and starts digging in all that horse dung—looking for the horse. That's always been my way of looking at life, and let me tell you, neighbor, it's been a good one.

Writing this book has taken me back to memories of growing up in Texas all the way to nearly dying in Idaho. In between it's been mostly stories about gambling, which I suppose is what most folks find the most interesting. But as much as I like to keep family matters within the family, I do feel like it's important to say that, of all the great times I've had over the years, none of it would have meant a damn thing without my wife, Helen, my three kids, Bunky, Becky, and Tod, and my seven grandbabies.

My family is the most precious thing I have. For my wife and me, our lives revolve around them grandbabies and our children. The only financial goal I've ever had was to see to it that all seven grandbabies had enough money for as much education as they wanted and a little bit of a stake to get started in life, which I've been able to do.

Folks have a hard time believing that when I was at home, I was just your average, everyday father in Amarillo. I coached Little League baseball and football and drove my fair share of car pools, especially for all my kids' golf tournaments. In fact, one of my best memories wasn't the 1972 World Series of Poker but the 1959 World Series of Little League between the Pleasant Valley Prairie Dogs and the Avondale Cyclones. My son Bunky played first base for the Cyclones, and yours truly was the manager.

Before the game I promised all my players that if we won the World Series, I'd take them all waterskiing up at Lugert Lake near Altus, Oklahoma. When we got beat, let me tell you, the tears did flow. Finally I just couldn't stand it, so I said, "All right, I'm taking you anyway. We've had a good season and everything. We're all going waterskiing."

So we planned a trip, and when my players showed up to go, every one of 'em brought a little brother or a little sister or two brothers and a sister and some of their cousins and anybody else who ever wanted to go. I took twenty-some-odd people to Lugert Lodge and put 'em up and fed 'em for four days. It was around the Fourth of July, and I'd bought a bunch of firecrackers, which were illegal on lake property. We didn't pay that no mind, though, and when we set 'em off, we damn near set the side of the mountain on fire. We took off running, and by the time the police came by, we acted like we didn't know nothing about nothing. So we all had us a good secret: We'd done a no-no and didn't get caught.

Shoot, I enjoyed coaching. I also coached Becky's T-ball team, and she was a heckuva player. I gloated over all my kids' accomplishments. When they'd get a pretty trophy or accolades for winning a golf tournament, it would really make me proud. Both Bunky and Tod were MVPs of their high-school golf teams and went on to earn golf scholarships to college. I'm even more proud that my kids got their education—all three graduated from college. A big reason for that was Helen, who was about the best mother a kid could ever wish for.

I discouraged my children from gambling. I told 'em that it was a pretty tough go and not many survive it—which is true. You've heard me talk about how I feel that making my living as a gambler was an honorable profession, and while that's the truth, I'd hardly say that I'm pro-gambling. It's a hard way to make an easy living. If someone wanted to follow in my footsteps and be a gambler, I'd tell 'em that they'd be better off getting a driver's license and start driving a dump truck. I've seen thousands try to give the gambling life a go, and fewer than I can count on both hands have succeeded.

MY LIFE TODAY

I'm the same as always and still active on my ranches. I've got a herd of registered Brangus cattle, a herd of registered Tiger Stripes, and the finest-looking herd of horned-Hereford cattle there's ever been. I've also got about a dozen horses. On a typical day, I'll do things like carrying sixty-pound blocks of salt to all three of the windmills on my ranch and feeding the cattle three hundred pounds of cottonseed cubes to keep 'em big.

I still go hunting quite a bit. I'll go white-wing-dove hunting in Mexico in September, pheasant hunting in South Dakota on the second weekend of October, and quail hunting in Texas from November to February. When I get a hankering for something a little bigger, I'll go to Alaska and Canada for big game.

I go to most of the major sporting events: the Masters golf tournament, the Super Bowl, the National Rodeo Finals in Las Vegas in December, and most of the championship fights all over the country. I'm also a regular at the biggest poker tournaments in the country, and whenever I'm in Vegas, I'll stop by and see all my old friends. Doyle still plays poker just about every day at the Bellagio, and you won't hear many people argue when I say he's the best poker player that ever lived. Go join him up there—I know he'd be glad to have you. It's a pretty cheap game, too; all you need is about $100,000 to buy in. I still play poker, but mainly at the big tournaments like the World Series of Poker at Binion's Horseshoe in May, the New England Poker Classic at Foxwoods in November, and anytime I can get to Europe for a major tournament.

My various businesses occupy a lot of my time and every one of 'em is in partnership with my family. We built a golf course in Amarillo, which Bunky and Helen look after. Before we make investments, we discuss them among ourselves. We've got such a good reputation in business that Pat Hickman and Gary Wells from the First State Bank of Amarillo like to joke that we built their new branch with all the interest we've paid over the years.

Within the family we own four Pizza Planets, two Swensen's, and three Smoothie King franchises, which Tod runs down in Fort Worth, where he lives with his wife and four girls (Hayley, Hannah, Molly, and Caroline) and one boy, Jack. Becky lives in Houston with her husband, and her daughter, Heather, attends Sam Houston University. Bunky and my grandbaby Austin live right at the end of my block in Amarillo.

I stressed to every one of my kids to go into business for themselves. My logic was, if you worked for the other man and you wanted to go fishing, if he *let* you, you could. But if you owned the place and you wanted to, you *went*. If you work for the other man, you've got to be making him money, or he wouldn't be employing you in the first place. Because of that philosophy, I'm proud to say that all my children have been in business for themselves.

PUTTING MY KNOWLEDGE OF U.S. PRESIDENTS TO USE

Unlike pool, poker, and booking sports, proposition betting never was an everyday thing for me. Proposition bets are just one of those things that come up from time to time, and I'm always prepared when they do. My reputation has helped me, because now people come looking for me with propositions of their own, and I can just sit back and pick and choose the ones I want.

The 2000 presidential election reminded me a little bit of the 1972 World Series of Poker, since it featured a lanky Texan against a pretender who claimed to be from Tennessee but really wasn't. In the summer of 2000, a banker friend of mine from Albuquerque called and asked me if I wanted to make a big bet on the election. He knew of a prominent Democrat who was looking to put down some money on Al Gore at even money. I'd be the dirtiest sonofabitch in the world if I said who he was. I think he deserves some courtesy and respect because of what he is and who he is—and I don't think his party or his peers would appreciate this getting out, but the man wanted some action, so I was more than happy to oblige. I'm never one to let politics get in the way of gambling.

The first person I called was David Sklansky, another one of them Ivy League math whizzes who is an expert on statistics and has written a bunch of books on poker theory. David told me that the most accurate polls showed that Gore had 54 percent to George W. Bush's 46 percent. I called back my friend and said I'd be interested in betting on Bush if I could get 6 to 5, but when he said that his associate was looking for even money, I told him I wasn't interested and didn't give it any more thought.

Then the polls began to turn, and the minute I saw them turning, I called Sklansky again. He said the trend looked good, and it got to the point where Mr. Bush was a slight favorite. That's when I called my banker pal back, told him I wanted to bet, and booked a flight to Albuquerque to post my money. I didn't know this politician from a grape, and I wasn't gonna bet with anyone over the telephone—not out of respect for Bobby Kennedy and his Wire Act but because I wasn't interested in taking a stranger's word for being good for the money, especially a politician's!

The bet was in excess of half a million dollars, and I had a couple of other folks who wanted some money on Bush that contributed to that figure. So I packed the money in a satchel and flew with two guards to Albuquerque, to this bank that will remain anonymous. With the exception of the prominent Democratic politician, I knew just about everybody in the room, including a buddy of mine from another bank in Albuquerque—a gentleman by the name of "Banker Sam."

We got to talking about the bet, and when Sam pointed to my satchel, I said, "Yeah, I brought it with me." Then I said to the president of the bank, "Where should we put this—with your bank, sir?"

"Pardon me?" he said.

"Well," I said, "I've got this satchel here completely full of money. We need to put it somewhere."

That's when the man I was betting with spoke up and said, "Oh, Mr. Slim, we all know you. We're not concerned about you. You don't need to put up."

Well, it wasn't *me* who I was concerned about. I was real sure about me. But you think I was gonna let some sonofabitch bet me that much money and not post it? What was I gonna do if he said to get lost? What was I gonna do if he said he'll pay me $3,000 a year for the rest of his life?

But here is where my style of hustling—the polar opposite of Minnesota Fats or Titanic Thompson's—really helped me. I knew that if I made it seem like I was doubting this man's intentions, he'd get his britches all knotted up, so I had to find a way to word things that would get him to post his money and feel like he wasn't being questioned.

"Let me tell you, sir," I said as I put my hand on my heart, "I'm an old man, and between this pacemaker and my thirst for risk, I'll be lucky to be alive by the inauguration. And if I was to die, the last thing I'd want was to go to my grave with an unpaid debt."

Now, everybody in the room—including him—knew what I was saying, but because of the way I said it, not only did I come off looking like a gentleman, but I put this man in a position where he couldn't possibly object. "I guess we need to post this," he said. And sure enough, it didn't take but one phone call for his cash to appear at the bank.

I think you're familiar with how this went down. It reminded me a little of the "Dewey Beats Truman" election, and I had all but written that money off. After Herman the alligator and the chicken fights, it seemed like the state of Florida was gonna find a way to fleece me again. But, just my luck, the Florida governor hailed from Texas, and he made sure them votes in Palm Beach County were counted just right. Whoever said presidential history was boring?

HALL OF FAMER

I may be seventy-four, but the over-under on the number of years I have to live is twenty, and if you're interested in betting the under, I'm taking that action. I don't think of myself as old, and I sure as hell ain't sentimental, but if there's one thing—besides my grandbabies—that gets me choked up a little, it's the Halls of Fame that have chosen to induct me as a member.

In 1992, I was inducted into the Poker Hall of Fame at Binion's Horseshoe. It pleased me to be recognized among the best poker players, including Johnny Moss, Doyle Brunson, and Puggy Pearson. It was a fine presentation, and a bunch of my peers made some nice long stump speeches and told lies about what a good sonofabitch I was. It was a great feeling to be in the Hall of Fame for playing poker, because, even more so than playing pool, that was the endeavor I had devoted the most time to.

In February 1999, the Tropicana Hotel and Casino decided to create a permanent museum of gamblers, which they called the Legends of Nevada. Hank Greenspun said to me, "Slim, you'll be very pleased to know that there was an eighteen-member committee that made these nominations, and your selection was unanimous."

The fact that I was included with folks who were pioneers and leaders in the gaming industry made me feel pretty good. Everyone thought it was unusual, because I'd never been a casino owner and I'd never been a resident of Nevada. I got all dressed up, and they had a big screen—about as big as Boulder Dam—come on at both ends of the showroom with my picture on it. Then, a senator from Washington lied and told everyone what a good sonofagun I was. Then the governor of Nevada said I was as fine a man as ever put powder in a safe. And then they played my song, which goes a little something like this:

Do you dare make a bet with Amarillo Slim?
You play his game with one condition for him.
From Ping-Pong to golf or baskets in the gym.
Do you dare make a bet with Amarillo Slim?
Hell, the devil don't bet with Amarillo Slim.

The whole room stood in recognition, and that made a country sonofagun feel good. Written by John Lutz Ritter, that song is still played at the World Series of Poker every year and it never fails to put a smile on my face.

CASHING IN YOUR CHIPS

Gambling is a reflection of life. A man's true character comes out when he's sitting at the poker table—his strengths and his weaknesses, his good traits and his faults. Whenever money is involved, you see the worst in people. When you put a bunch of competitive folks around a table in a game where short-term luck plays a big factor, you'll find out what a person is made of.

The first thing a professional gambler has to do is make friends with himself. If you think you've done something awful, then go own up to it. Give yourself an order to make sure you don't do anything like that again. And, damn it, forget the whole thing. Then, get rid of any excuses you may already have in stock. Making peace with yourself is the first thing a winner must do—at gambling or anything else in life.

Remember what I said about being able to shear a sheep many a time but only being able to skin it once. It sounds corny, and it is corny, but it works. Be good to people—treat them nice and they'll want to gamble with you again.

Take care of yourself, neighbor, and please don't do no arguing. Because, like I've always said, if there's anything worth arguing about, either bet on it or shut up.

Recommended Reading

Big Deal, Anthony Holden
The Biggest Game in Town, Al Alvarez
Caro's Book of Tells, Mike Caro
Doyle Brunson's Super/System, Doyle Brunson
Fast Company, John Bradshaw
Finished Lines, Frank R. Scatoni
The Man with the $100,000 Breasts, Michael Konik
The Poker MBA, Greg Dinkin
Poker Nation, Andy Bellin
Positively Fifth Street, Jim McManus
Real Poker: The Cooke Collection, Roy Cooke and John Bond
Shut Up and Deal, Jesse May
The Unsinkable Titanic Thompson, Carlton Stowers

My grandbabies on the diving board at the pool behind my house in Amarillo. From left to right: Hannah, Molly, Caroline, Heather, Jack, Hayley, and Austin. *(Courtesy of the author)*

Acknowledgments

I first want to thank my lovely wife, Helen Elizabeth, for putting up with me for more than fifty-three years. I'd like to remind my three kids, Bunky, Becky, and Tod, and my seven grandbabies how much I love them. I also must give thanks to the head of the Baptist people: Winfred Moore.

My agents from Venture Literary (www.ventureliterary.com), Greg Dinkin and Frank Scatoni, did a great job negotiating my contract and were fantastic to work with, especially since they understood that quick pay makes for lasting friendships. And Greg, who doubled as my co-author, made the process of writing this book a lot of fun.

I also want to thank my two former partners, Sailor Roberts and Doyle Brunson, for thirty years of great friendship (and for having enough integrity to stick to an agreement and not gamble with one another). I also want to thank Matt Helreich, who has been a friend and a contributor to my well-being over the years.

All the folks at HarperCollins were great hosts when I visited New York, and as far as youse guys are concerned, Mauro DiPreta and Dawn DiCenso were all right with me.

Lastly, thanks to all the great gambling bosses for making Las Vegas what it is today. Benny Binion, Yale Cohen, Steve Wynn, Bobby Baldwin, Lyle Berman, Bob Stupak, Lynn Simon, and Syd Wyman are just some of the great men I want to acknowledge for their contributions to gaming.

When I told my friend Bryan that I was writing a book with Amarillo Slim, he said, "Wow, that would be like a baseball fan getting a chance to write a book with Babe Ruth." Nice analogy, Bryan, but it doesn't even come close. Not that hanging around with the Babe wouldn't have been interesting, but what good would it have done for me to learn how to hit a high fastball? With Slim, not only was I in perpetual laughter, but I received an education in human nature that was priceless.

I first met Slim at Binion's Horseshoe, at the World Series of Poker in 2002, when I was promoting my second book, *The Poker MBA*. Slim seemed to like the fact that I had written a book that related poker to business and compared him to Bill Gates. Why not? They both revolutionized their respective industries.

After chatting with Slim for ten minutes, he invited me to join him for dinner, just like it was nothing. For all his celebrity, he had not one ounce of pretense, and his demeanor was every bit the simple country cowboy that he likes to portray. I guess the only thing that was unusual about our meal is that when I asked him how much a "peanut" was on the under for the Celtics game we were watching, he casually told me it was $8,700.

I later traveled with Slim to Idaho but left the day before he nearly died. It really hit me what a shame it would have been for Slim's life not to have been captured, and I felt even more fortunate to be getting the opportunity to work with one of the most colorful characters this country has ever known.

I made a few trips to Amarillo and got to be a part of his daily routine—from rounding up his cattle for their semen testing to playing poker with the locals at the Seventh Street Lodge to waking up on a Saturday morning and watching Slim stroll into the Toot 'N Totem in his bathrobe and slippers to grab a newspaper. But what I really enjoyed was just getting a chance to see his mind work—and I never stopped being amazed. And between the Texas hospitality and the home cooking that Mrs. Preston so graciously provided, it was hard to get me to leave.

I consider Slim to be the world's leading authority on human nature. Here's a man who, simply by understanding basic human psychology, was able to travel all over the world, achieve celebrity status, and live life by his own rules. He's no Babe Ruth—no, that would hardly do Amarillo Slim justice.

The only thing more helpful in writing this book than spending time with Slim were the Internet newsgroups United Poker Forum and RGP (Rec.Gambling.Poker). If I had a question or a gap in research to fill, all I had to do was post a question there, and the responses came flooding in. Matt Matros, Ashley Adams, Victor Royer, Randy Refeld, Jim Muehlhausen, Bill Burton, Bill Murphy, Max Shapiro, Vince Burgio, Perry Friedman, Steve Badger, Harry Baldwin, I. Nelson Rose, George Fisher, and Chuck Ferry all contributed to research. Jesse May, Andy Bellin, Katy Lederer, Jim McManus, Mike Sexton, Andy Glazer, and Nolan Dalla, all great poker writers, were incredibly generous. And Bob Stupak, Doyle Brunson, and Puggy Pearson were gracious with their time when I interviewed them.

Larry Grossman, who hosts a radio show in Las Vegas called *You Can Bet on It*, is one of the great voices in gambling and was a tremendous help in gathering photos. Howard Schwartz, who runs the greatest bookstore in the world, called the Gambler's Book Shop, was a great help in tracking down rare books and little-known nuggets of information. I also want to thank Jeff Shulman and Steve Radulovich at *Card Player* magazine for being flexible with my column and always supporting my books. Jon Furay, my buddy from New York, used his great film sensibilities to help shape the structure of the manuscript.

My friends Jimbo Patterson, Jeremy London, Brett Silver, Mike Kelly, Marc Bruno, and Michelle Charles, as always, were great sounding boards throughout the writing process. Mr. L.A. himself, Dr. Darren Carpizo, was an inspiration for embodying the principles of W.M.I. My friend Bryan Blanken, who has taught me more about human nature than even Slim, is the greatest friend a person could ask for. My dad, a great poker player in his own right, offered his fantastic, albeit anal, editing that really improved the book. My Shuggiesis and my brother, Andy, whose perspective on life never ceases to amaze me, managed to keep me balanced. I also want to thank my beautiful and brilliant godkids, Logan and The*adorable*, just for being themselves and never failing to put a smile on my face.

The whole crew at HarperCollins, from our editor, Mauro DiPreta, to our marketing manager, Dawn DiCenso, were phenomenal to work with and gave Slim's life story the attention it deserved. Dave Brown was as tenacious as Slim on the publicity front. I also want to thank George Bick, Mike Spradlin, and Brian McSharry for their enthusiastic sales efforts.

To say that Frank Scatoni, my business partner in our agency, Venture Literary, was like a second editor for this book wouldn't be fair. He was much more like a third author, who tore up the first two drafts and gave me all the right guidance in telling Slim's story. But for this book, the biggest thank-you of all goes to my mom, Erlaine from Baltimore, who forced me to take typing in high school—and warned me to be leery of men with names like Amarillo Slim.

About the Authors

THOMAS AUSTIN "AMARILLO SLIM" PRESTON is the winner of the 1972 World Series of Poker and the author of *Play Poker to Win*. He has appeared on *The Tonight Show* eleven times and made international headlines when he rafted down the River of No Return in Idaho. He is married and has three children and seven grandbabies. Amarillo, Texas, of course, is the only place he calls home. Visit www.thepokermba.com/amarilloslim to learn more.

GREG DINKIN is the author of *The Poker MBA* and *The Finance Doctor* and a columnist for *Card Player* magazine. He is the cofounder of Venture Literary, where he works with writers to find publishers for their books and studios for their screenplays. Greg splits his time between Las Vegas and southern California and can be found online at www.thepokermba.com and www.ventureliterary.com.